WORKING WITH YOUNG CHILDREN IN MUSEUMS

Working with Young Children in Museums makes a major contribution to the small body of extant research on young children in museums, galleries and heritage sites.

Bridging theory and practice, the book introduces theoretical concepts in a clear and concise manner, whilst also providing inspirational insights into everyday programming in museums. Structured around three key themes, this volume seeks to diverge from the dominant socio-cultural learning models that are generally employed in the museum learning literature. It introduces a body of theories that have variously been called new materialist, spatial, posthuman and Deleuzian, theories which enable a focus on the body, movement and place and which have not yet been widely shared or developed with the museum sector or explicitly connected to practice. This book outlines these theories in an accessible way, explaining their usefulness for conceptualising young children in museums and connecting them to practical examples of programming in a range of locations via a series of contributed case studies.

Connecting theory to practice for readers in a way that emphasises possibility, *Working with Young Children in Museums* should be essential reading for museum practitioners working in a range of institutions around the world. It should be of equal interest to researchers and students engaged in the study of museum learning, early childhood education and children's experiences in museums.

Abigail Hackett is a Research Fellow at the Education and Social Research Institute, Manchester Metropolitan University.

Rachel Holmes leads the Children and Childhood Research Group in the Education and Social Research Institute at Manchester Metropolitan University.

Christina MacRae is a Research Fellow at Manchester Metropolitan University.

GLOBAL PERSPECTIVES ON CHILDREN IN MUSEUMS

Series Editor: Sharon E. Shaffer

Museums have long been known as educational institutions, but throughout history museum audiences have traditionally been defined in a very narrow way. Researchers, educators, and other innovative thinkers with a passion for children and learning have worked tirelessly over the last couple of decades to change the perception of learning in the early years, and in many ways, have played a vital role in establishing a new path for museums as places for young visitors. Museums now recognize that they offer unique experiences to nurture a child's growth and inspire learning with young children now welcomed into a broad range of institutions, yet there is still a minimal amount of research and documentation of theory and practice related to this growing field. *Global Perspectives on Children in Museums* addresses this oversight by helping to build a strong understanding of children's development and their capacity as museum visitors.

Including contributions from practitioners, researchers, and academics, the series will present literature that represents diverse cultures and experiences. As a result, *Global Perspectives on Children in Museums* will help to build on knowledge of the early years and develop greater understanding of young children's school age counterparts. The series will also inspire and empower educators and museum professionals in their work with children and encourage them to advance knowledge through sharing of research, theory, and practice with a focus on early learners and children prior to adolescence.

Titles in the series:

Working with Young Children in Museums
Weaving Theory and Practice
Edited by Abigail Hackett, Rachel Holmes and Christina MacRae

For more information about the series please visit https://www.routledge.com/Global-Perspectives-on-Children-in-Museums/book-series/GPOCIM

WORKING WITH YOUNG CHILDREN IN MUSEUMS

Weaving Theory and Practice

Edited by Abigail Hackett, Rachel Holmes and Christina MacRae

Routledge
Taylor & Francis Group
LONDON AND NEW YORK

First published 2020
by Routledge
2 Park Square, Milton Park, Abingdon, Oxon OX14 4RN

and by Routledge
52 Vanderbilt Avenue, New York, NY 10017

Routledge is an imprint of the Taylor & Francis Group, an informa business

British Library Cataloguing-in-Publication Data
A catalogue record for this book is available from the British Library

Library of Congress Cataloging-in-Publication Data
Names: Hackett, Abigail, 1980- editor. | Holmes, Rachel (Rachel D.), editor. | MacRae, Christina, editor.
Title: Working with Young Children in Museums : Weaving theory and practice / edited by Abigail Hackett, Rachel Holmes and Christina MacRae.
Description: London ; New York, NY : Routledge/Taylor & Francis Group, 2020. | Includes bibliographical references and index.
Identifiers: LCCN 2019041905 | ISBN 9781138352964 (hardback) | ISBN 9781138353008 (paperback) | ISBN 9780429434457 (ebook) | ISBN 9780429785047 (adobe pdf) | ISBN 9780429785023 (mobi) | ISBN 9780429785030 (epub)
Subjects: LCSH: Museums–Educational aspects. | Museums and children.
Classification: LCC AM7 .W67 2020 | DDC 069.07–dc23
LC record available at https://lccn.loc.gov/2019041905

ISBN: 978-1-138-35296-4 (hbk)
ISBN: 978-1-138-35300-8 (pbk)
ISBN: 978-0-429-43445-7 (ebk)

Typeset in Bembo
by Swales & Willis, Exeter, Devon, UK

CONTENTS

FIGURES AND TABLE

Figures

Table

CONTRIBUTORS

Elaine Bates, as the Early Years Coordinator at Manchester Museum, she has developed programmes and resources for young children and their families in partnership with local early years settings, creative practitioners and parents. She is also a governor at a local nursery school and children's centre. She recently led on the redevelopment of Nature Discovery, a natural history gallery for Under 5s which was underpinned by research with young children and their families and documented as part of a Masters in Education (Early Years) which she undertook at the Centre for Research in Early Childhood.

Danielle Carter is a museum educator, researcher, writer and editor based in Amsterdam, the Netherlands. She researches effective and innovative museum education, with a recent focus on play, narrative and young children. She has presented at several international conferences, has published articles on arts and museum education and maintains a monthly blog on contemporary theory and practice in cultural, arts and museum education.

Elizabeth Clayton is a freelance play artist and early years specialist. Until recently she ran and developed family groups, museum interpretation and training at Craftplay (-2004–2018), the specialist early years project at Bilston Craft Gallery, Wolverhampton UK. Working with local families has led to an intricate understanding of parents and children in a museum and creative play environment. She has a particular fascination with sensory play engagement, creating "supportive museum spaces" and establishing meaningful dialogues between museums and their audiences. Alongside this is a passion for co-production, art-making and creative reflection that runs through all of her work.

Lucy Cooke completed a BA(Hons) in English Literature and a PGCE specialising in the lower primary age range (both at York St John University) and has worked in teaching and related roles within schools and childcare settings prior to joining the heritage sector. She has been in post as Under 5s Learning Co-ordinator at the East Riding of Yorkshire Museums Service since 2016. Her role has recently expanded and now includes broader work on audience development in learning and health and wellbeing contexts, as well as continued provision and advocacy for under 5s and families.

Joanne Drum is Education Officer at the National Gallery of Ireland, where she began working in 2006. Joanne manages programming for children and families, as well as many adult and lifelong learning strands. She established and continues to manage the Gallery's early years programme and is involved with offsite community-based projects for this age group. As part of the Lifelong Learning strand, Joanne plans and coordinates lectures, talks and workshops. In 2018, Joanne curated the exhibition *Circus250: Art of the Show*, incorporating programming for diverse audiences and accessible labelling and display.

Roxanne Finn has experience and scholarship that spans early childhood and primary education with a focus on inclusivity. She is interested in diverse ways to practice education across temporal, spatial and relational boundaries. Her research applies ecological psychology to analyse learning and data.

Abigail Hackett is a Research Fellow at the Education and Social Research Institute, Manchester Metropolitan University. Her research focusses on the role of place, materiality and the body in young children's lives in numerous contexts including museums. Her original doctoral research looked at the meaning making of young children in museums and she currently holds a British Academy Postdoctoral Fellowship entitled "The emergence of literacy in very young children: place and materiality in a more-than-human world."

Esther Hallberg is the Access and Family Learning Officer for Hull Museums and Ferens Art Gallery based at Heritage Learning. Coming from a more general museum and heritage education background, Esther developed a specialism in creating bespoke spaces and sessions for under 5s as the Under 5s Project Developer at Hull Museums from 2015–2018, funded through the Arts Council as part of the Humber Museums Partnership. During this time she project-managed the creation of the Explore Art gallery for Under 5s and the establishment of regular Under 5s programming such as Transport Tots, Gallery Expedition and Mini Masterpieces.

Lucy Hill is the inaugural John Coolahan Early Years Artist in Residence at The Ark Children's Cultural Centre, Dublin. A visual artist, educator and researcher, she has exhibited nationally and internationally and has won several awards and public art commissions. Since 2003 she has designed and delivered numerous Early Years visual art projects and exhibitions and has been an "aterlierista" with Woodland Park preschool for ten years. Lucy is currently a Government of Ireland Postgraduate Scholar working on an Early-Years-focused PhD.

Katharine Hoare works as a School and Young Audiences Education Manager at the British Museum. She has previously taught in primary and secondary schools. Before joining the British Museum she worked as an advisor for the London Fire Brigade supporting their fire safety education programme. Katharine has a background in history and archaeology and a passion for experimenting with new ways for everybody to engage in creative heritage learning.

Rachel Holmes leads the Children and Childhood Research Group in the Education and Social Research Institute at Manchester Metropolitan University. Her research activities appreciate the complexity of the contemporary worlds that young children, families and communities occupy. The work she engages with includes the development of theoretically-driven intellectual, as well as diverse empirical, research and evaluation projects. She is committed to promoting research innovation and the creation of new critical knowledge by developing creative, arts-informed methodologies, engaging with challenging theoretical landscapes and being mindful of the complex ethical implications in the work she does with colleagues.

Lisa Howarth has had a passion for museums since she was a child. After studying Ancient History and Archaeology and with a MA in Museum Studies, Lisa started her career in archaeology. She soon realised her true passion was for learning and audience engagement and she became the Learning Manager at North Lincolnshire Museum Service in 2009. During this role she led the Arts-Council-funded "Under fives" project on behalf of the Humber Museum Partnership and then became strategic lead for Heritage and Museums in North Lincolnshire. She is now Heritage and Arts Manager for Rotherham Metropolitan Borough Council.

Kate Kelland began her career as an archaeologist working for Wessex Archaeology and then moved into museum education. She has worked at the British Museum for over ten years as well as freelancing at many other London museums and heritage sites. Kate works primarily with younger visitors and family audiences as an Education Manager in the Schools and Young Audiences Team.

Molly L. Kelton is faculty at Washington State University's College of Education. Her research investigates integrated STEAM learning in out-of-school time and across formal and informal environments, spanning K-12 classrooms, museums, maker spaces and after-school clubs. She has contributed to the research and design of several major mathematics exhibitions in the United States. Across diverse settings, Dr Kelton examines the roles of physical movement, embodied experience and place in processes of thinking and learning. Her broader mission is to contribute to more humane, creative and expansive places for both human and non-human flourishing.

Christina MacRae is a Research Fellow at Manchester Metropolitan University whose research interests lie in the Early Years and, in particular, in the way that sense, affect and movement express a bodily relationship with the world. Her research has focussed on young children's learning in classroom contexts as well as in museums and galleries. She has been an Early Years teacher in inner-city nursery schools, most recently in Bradford. Alongside her teaching, she has an interest in art-making and she has also worked as an artist in collaborative projects with young children in schools.

Katy McCall has worked as the Family Learning Manager at Manchester Art Gallery (MAG) since February 2017, where she tests out ways to make galleries and museums accessible and creative spaces for everyone. Working in partnership with other agencies from the NHS, Sure Start and MMU, Katy is interested in re-imagining what a gallery setting can offer families. A key element of her work is around raising awareness and facilitating debate around the importance of creative and playful experiences for child development. Additionally, she is keen to discuss how, in times of austerity and desperate inequality, we might achievably work collaboratively with other public services to offer resident families a creative sanctuary in the city centre.

Ricardo Nemirovsky is professor at the Manchester Metropolitan University in Manchester, UK. He has directed educational projects in Argentina, Mexico, the USA and currently in Europe. He is conducting research and theory development on the interplay between embodied cognition, affects and mathematics learning. Part of his work focusses on the synergy between art and mathematics. He has been working with several science and art museums in mathematics-oriented projects that combine research, development and museum staff professional development. In addition to research papers, he has co-authored curricular units and has designed multiple devices for students' use.

Kate Noble is a creative practitioner and researcher with extensive experience designing and leading learning programmes with children and young people in museums and galleries. Kate oversees the schools and teachers programme at The Fitzwilliam Museum and leads a teacher training programme encouraging creative teaching approaches using collections. She holds a PhD in the Development of Visual Literacy in Young Children and a BEd in Art and Early Years Education. Kate has led learning research projects on behalf of the University of Cambridge Museums and The National Gallery, including the Nursery in Residence, Practical Evaluation and UCM Digital Makers.

Aisling O'Gorman has worked extensively as an arts facilitator and project director in a wide variety of community and educational contexts with children, young people and adults since 2003. She began working at The Ark Children's Cultural Centre, Dublin, in 2011 and is currently Creative Arts Manager, in which role she leads the multidisciplinary arts programme commissioning, developing and curating work specifically for children aged 2 to 12.

Kate Pahl is the author, with Jennifer Rowsell, of *Artifactual Literacies: Every Object Tells a Story* (Teachers College Press, 2010). She is a literacy researcher as well as having an interest in the arts. Her work has involved co-produced projects with children and communities, focussing on artistic methodologies for social cohesion. Her current projects include working with street-connected and refugee young people in Uganda, Kenya, and the Democratic Republic of Congo to investigate ways in which policy makers can listen to their voices using arts methodologies and "Feeling Odd in the World of Education," which explores with young people about how they feel within school. Both projects are funded by the Arts and Humanities Research Council, UK.

Louisa Penfold is a curator who works with young children in art museums. She is currently doing her PhD in the School of Education at the University of Nottingham in partnership with Tate and The Whitworth Art Gallery in the United Kingdom. Louisa has also worked as a children's curator at the Ipswich Art Gallery (Australia) and as a research fellow on Serpentine Galleries' *Changing Play* programme.

Louise Gwenneth Phillips is an Associate Professor in Education at James Cook University, Singapore. Her career spans theatre in education, early childhood education, storytelling, environmental education, children's rights and citizenship research and arts-based research methodologies. She is particularly interested in story as theory and method, decolonizing methodologies, sensation and place. See http://louptales.education.

Barbara Piscitelli (barbarap@bigpond.net.au) has an academic background in early childhood education and creative arts. She specializes in audience research and programme development for children in cultural spaces. Bright and Shiny was developed, delivered and researched by the Ipswich Art Gallery in 2008. The project team included Michael Beckmann (Director), Bonnie Smith Melrose (Children's Program Officer), Anne Marlay (Group Leader), Ngaio Parr (Gallery Trainee) and Barbara Piscitelli (Researcher).

Jennifer Rowsell is Professor of Literacies and Social Innovation at University of Bristol's School of Education in the United Kingdom. Her research interests include multimodal, makerspace and arts-based research with young people; digital literacies research; digital divide work; and applying posthumanist and affect approaches to literacy research. Dr Rowsell has worked and conducted research in Australia, Canada, the United Kingdom and the United States. She has written, co-written and co-edited 25 books on a range of topics from handbooks on literacy studies to multimodality to Bourdieusian approaches to ethnographic fieldwork. She is a co-editor of the *Routledge Expanding Literacies in Education* book series with Cynthia Lewis (University of California – Santa Cruz) and she is the Department Editor of Digital Literacies for *The Reading Teacher.* Her most recent co-authored book with Dr Kate Pahl (Manchester Metropolitan University) is entitled *Living Literacies: Rethinking literacy research and practice through the everyday* (MIT Press).

Jack Shuttleworth is passionate about cultural access. He has worked in the Theatre in Education movement, including in the Belgrade TiE Company where he developed a fascination for pedagogy outside the classroom. At part of the Herbert Art Gallery's Inclusion Team, he curated installations for under 5s and developed an agenda for Early Years access. At Craftplay he was inspired by the way regular groups provided a wonderful opportunity to examine and develop practice. With an excellent core practice, it was possible to experiment and receive honest feedback from well-informed children and carers, creating a crucible of reflection and improvement.

Victoria Smith qualified as a primary school teacher in 2011. She has taught in nursery settings in both the public and private sector as an Early Years Practitioner and nursery class teacher. Her passion for museums and early learning led to her joining the Museum of London in 2015 as the Early Years Programme Coordinator. She has since gone on to become the Early Years Programme Manager and is responsible for the museum's programming for under-fives and their families, including: weekly baby and toddler sessions, a two-day weekend Toddler Takeover and an outreach programme delivering projects within the museum's local community.

Alex Thorp is an educator and curator who has been working in the field of arts education for over 12 years. As Education Curator at the Serpentine Galleries, she leads on collaborative programmes and projects with children and young people. These include *Youth Forum*, a programme connecting young people with artists to make changes in their communities and *Changing Play* which brings together artists, children, families and educators to critically reconsider Early Years education and care. From 2007–2014 she worked at Manchester Art Gallery where she initiated projects such as *The Clore Art Studio*, a children's space, and *Open Doors*, a programme for children on the autism spectrum.

Lucy Turner is the Early Years Coordinator at the Whitworth, Manchester. Lucy has worked at the Whitworth since 2012 and in that time she has built up an extensive programme of activity for under 5s and their parents/carers. Previously Lucy has worked at BALTIC Centre for Contemporary Art, Gateshead, and the Laing Art Gallery, Newcastle. Lucy studied Fine Art: Sculpture & Environmental Art at Glasgow School of Art and has an MA in Fine Art from Manchester School of Art.

Nicola Wallis is an experienced Museum Educator currently working at the Fitzwilliam Museum. She leads on the Early Years programme which aims to establish authentic connections between young children and great artworks. After completing teacher training in 2002 Nicola worked as a Primary and Nursery teacher and undertook post-graduate study in both Museum Studies and Early Childhood. She has a keen interest in the use of rigorous, ethically-generated research data to inform and develop pedagogical practice in museum work with young children, which she is developing as a member of the RSA Evidence Champions network.

Helen Whitty works as a writer and consultant to museums and related industries. Previously she crafted public programmes, authored museum publications, consulted on exhibitions and conceived and curated collection-based exhibitions for the Museum of Applied Arts and Sciences in Sydney. Awarded a doctorate from the University of Technology Sydney (UTS) in 2017, the research looked into the relationships between families, literacies and collections. Helen continues her connections with the university sector as a UTS Visiting Fellow (Faculty of Arts and Social Sciences).

FOREWORD

Over the past 40 years, there has been significant growth in interest in the ways in which children and their families inhabit public spaces, particularly museums, galleries and libraries. In 1979, during the International Year of the Child, UNESCO published a themed edition of *Museum*, featuring children and museums around the world. The Australian contributor claimed that "children and museums have always gone hand in hand, though not always willingly" (Hodge, 1979: 160). In remarking about the potential of museums to connect with children, Hodge issued a quiet challenge to the sector to become better at harnessing the great potential of the museum to engage with children's ideas, interests and activities.

When we first started doing systematic research on young children's engagements with museums in the 1990s, a review of the literature showed that there was a moderate amount of research relating to education programmes for school-aged children, but little understanding of the ways in which young children, aged four to six, experienced their visits to museums – either as a student or a member of a family group. In collaboration with a group of museums (natural history, social history, art and science), we began to explore young children's learning and aimed to establish policies and practices which could strengthen the potential for young children's learning in museums by: documenting the characteristics of young children in museums; identifying social interactions which promote young children's learning in museums; analysing relevant museum policies; and developing strategies for building strong links between museums, schools and families (Piscitelli et al., 1999). Over five years, we explored children's learning and engagement and discovered that children and museums could, in fact, develop very willing relationships.

Today, for the most part, young children are a valued part of museum culture and feature in many research and evaluation projects. This book features several important contemporary perspectives and approaches to researching children's engagements in museums, and offers fresh theoretical views for understanding how children engage in public places. The theoretical discussion is placed alongside essays and case studies that document the rich and dynamic nature of children's entangled, emplaced and embodied knowledge as well as their cognitive, sensory and aesthetic experiences.

This book takes us into new territory and makes us think about how best to explore, engage and enjoy young children's encounters with objects, ideas and people in the museum. The case studies give us a good look at children in UK and beyond, where museums have developed and sustained innovative programmes and a research culture to explore children's engagements in museums. In the next 40 years it will be interesting to see how young children experience museums in diverse countries and cultural contexts, especially since there has been a boom in museums in China, South America and throughout Asia and the Middle East. I look forward to reading new studies which draw upon the inspiration of this book and which help us to understand more about the magical and diverse world of children and culture.

Dr Barbara Piscitelli AM
Brisbane, Australia

References

Hodge, John (1979). 'Museums and children in Australia', *Museum*, 31 (3), 160–163.

Piscitelli, Barbara, McArdle, Felicity A., & Weier, Katrina L. (1999). *Beyond "look and learn": Investigating, implementing and evaluating interactive learning strategies for young children in museums*. Queensland University of Technology, Australia.

1

INTRODUCTION

Abigail Hackett, Rachel Holmes and Christina MacRae

> Imagine a young child enters a museum. Perhaps they are 2 years old, or five and a half years, or 10 months. Maybe they come with their family, or a group of children from their nursery, or couple of families with kids of a similar age. They run to the museum entrance, or do their new funny walk they invented on the way here, or sit in a pushchair messily eating a biscuit. Perhaps they pause at the threshold, a little uncertain. Or they run inside, and down a corridor before their grown up has had a chance to remove their coat. A young child has entered a museum and something is going to happen.

Increasingly (in the UK and globally), more young children seem to be entering museums than ever before. From the point of view of museum professionals, there is an increasing interest in how to programme exhibitions, events, activities and practical considerations to best serve this audience. Planning spaces, activities, encounters or visiting experiences for any audience begins with imagination and, coupled with this, are particular ideas and assumptions about the child, the museum and who and what else might come into play when young children visit museums. Reflecting on how well a museum or gallery caters for an audience involves processes of observation and reflection. It involves wondering, asking and experimenting. When observing what children do in museums, sometimes predictable, sometimes completely surprising, researchers and museum practitioners find themselves asking different versions of the same question: *what does that mean?* This question is frequently phrased in other ways; what does this behaviour signify? What are these children learning? How successful is this exhibition for this audience? What is the value of children visiting museums?

This book provides a wide range of practical examples of how others have worked with young children in museums. In developing the title for this book, we thought carefully about the relationship between these two things; theories for thinking about or conceptualising what is happening when young children visit museums and the practices of museum professionals who work with these audiences. Rejecting words such as "*bridging*" or "*integrating*," we settled on "*weaving* theory and practice," because, as a metaphor, weaving seems to leave the question of the relationship between theory and practice a little more open, rather than assuming a separate-ness or a binary (theory on the one side, practice on the other). Whilst bridging implies joining together in a straightforward, fixed and rather permanent way, in weaving, threads can have similarities and differences that come in from different directions and starting points. When they are brought together, something new is made.

Good theories should make sense in the everyday. They should become illuminated, transformed and made to shimmer more vibrantly by practice. They should not stand apart from practice, pointing a finger and dictating how things should be organised. When some of the most frequently observed ways in which young children behave in museums are overlooked within dominant models of children's learning in museums, multiple unresolved questions are left for museum practitioners and the unique role museums play in the experiences of very young children remains vaguely articulated (Macrae et al., 2018). An important impetus for this book was our conviction that in order to consider young children's museum visiting, we (researchers *and* museum professionals) need a wider, more generous and more materially focussed framing. Many of the theories we offer in this book are "new" in the sense that the language might be unfamiliar to museum professionals and they are not the dominant "learning theories" currently within the sector. Yet part of their power and usefulness is the way in which they align (we would argue) in very resonant ways with practice, with the way in which things unfold between young children and museum spaces in the everyday.

In this book we will outline, explain and play with some of the key ideas and theories we have found to resonate with our observations of young children in museums. By making the case for the usefulness of these theories for conceptualizing young children in museums, as well as connecting these theories to practical case study examples of programming in a range of museum, gallery and heritage sites, we offer a contextualised way of thinking about these ideas.

Coming of age? Researching young children in museums

As Piscitelli outlines in the forward to this book, the field of research focussed on children in museums is fairly young. Within "the new museology" paradigm (Macdonald, 2007; Vergo, 1997), children visiting museums were understood as learners, constructing personal meanings during the visit and drawing on their own personal schemas. Within this kind of socio-cultural approach, a large body of work emerged looking at family conversations in museums, with an emphasis on construction of meanings between adults and children (Ellenbogen et al., 2004; Leinhardt et al., 2002; Leinhardt and Knutson, 2004). Meaning making was frequently conflated with talk; particularly the kind of talk that involves turn taking, clear engagement with the intended learning themes of the museum exhibition and what Leinhardt and Knutson (2004: 7) describe as "gradual enrichment of talk" (p. 7), that is, a more complicated structure of conversations, such as synthesis and analysis, as evidence of learning.

Whilst this work usefully made the case for the value of children learning in museums, the dominance of this approach within a small body of research also created some unintended consequences. Children seemed to be designated as "little learners" from the start, rather than visitors in their own right (Kirk, 2014), with the words they spoke coded against intended topics and learning outcomes of the exhibition. Even with the increased availability of video and visual data to document museum visits (e.g., Callanan and Braswell, 2006; Crowley et al., 2001), the emphasis remained on the cognitive learning of the visitors as evidenced through their talk or other actions that could be clearly interpreted as intentional communication (e.g., pointing to something of interest). This emphasis on talk-as-learning also spilled into assumptions that children and adults should ideally be deep in dyadic conversation and interaction during visits (e.g., Dooley and Welch, 2014). Overall, the child-as-learner-through-talk -with-adults seemed to be a figure strangely abstracted from the museum building, from sensory engagement with the stuff in the museum and from physical embodiment of the experience of moving through and in a museum space.

As interest grew in young children and their families as museum audiences in their own right (Graham, 2011), interesting approaches to consulting with children and families about provision and exhibition design have been developed (Cape UK, 2011; Kelly et al., 2006), together with evaluation of existing provision (Graham, 2012; Hancock and Cox, 2002). Around the same time, some of the first research projects that attended in particular to younger children in museums began to gesture towards the need for a different kind of conceptual framing. In Australia, the QUT Museums Collaborative Research project (Piscitelli and Anderson, 2001) was amongst the first to focus on younger children (4–6 years), emphasising the importance of full body engagement and "hot and sweaty learning" (Weier and Piscitelli, 2003). In the UK, MacRae (2007) drew on phenomenological perspectives to describe a museum-practitioner-led session for pre-school children in an art gallery, with a focus on the sensory and embodied experience of engaging with objects. More recently, research in New Zealand has examined the experiences of pre-school children (2.5–5 years) visiting a range of museums and galleries (Carr et al., 2012), noting how nursery children noticed and interpreted museum-specific practices, such as standing behind a yellow line to view artwork, and then reincorporated these practices in their own activities in the nursery (Clarkin-Philips et al., 2013).

In the UK, two doctoral studies completed around the same time attended closely to the experiences of young children visiting museums with their families (Kirk, 2014; Hackett, 2014). Both Hackett and Kirk emphasised movement, and the experience of a body moving around a place, as a key characteristic of young children's museum visiting. Hackett (2016) offered Ingold's (2007) notion of wayfaring as a way of describing and valuing the way in which young children's museums experiences unfolded through lines of movement. Over time, thickening lines of wayfaring led to deep embodied knowledge, memories and rituals attached to museum spaces by the children and families. Kirk (2014; Kirk and Buckingham, 2018) mapped the importance of young children navigating and negotiating the museum as an important part of the process whereby they encountered places or exhibits they connected with and from which they could make sense.

From this work so far, the importance of movement as a key way in which the museum is experienced (Hackett, 2016; Kelton et al., 2018) has emerged as a major force shaping thinking about young children in museums. A lens of movement, body and place have encouraged researchers to attend to the sensory nature of museum experience (Dicks, 2013; MacRae, 2007) and the way a museum is experienced through the body (Hackett et al., 2018; Macrae et al., 2018; Yamada-Rice, 2018). The importance of sufficient time for children to become familiar with and develop their own ways of being in and using museum spaces has been increasingly recognised as key (Clayton and Shuttleworth, 2018; DeWitt et al., 2018). In turn, this more expansive way of considering children's presence in museums has enabled researchers to attend more closely to the diverse and often unexpected way in which things unfold in the moment and in unexpected directions (Birch, 2018; Lester et al., 2014; Piscitelli and Penfold, 2015).

Children in museums as more-than-human

The emphasis on movement (Hackett, 2016; Kirk and Buckingham, 2018), place and sensory experience in the research outlined above all point towards the potential of theories beyond socio-cultural theory to account for young children's museum experiences in a more expansive way. Tracing the possibilities of understanding a child's experience in a museum through, alternatively, a cognitive, a socio-cultural and a posthuman lens, Macrae et al. (2018) advocate for posthuman theories (also referred to as more-than-human theories, post-qualitative theories, new materialism, Deleuzian and so on) for two reasons. First, to enable a fuller consideration of place, materials and objects, the things that actually often constitute what is unique and special about being in a museum from the point of view of a child. Second, these theories allow us to escape from the idea of representative meaning; instead of only valuing things we observe and are able to explain (for example, in terms of a child's learning), these theories allow us to pay attention to things that happen that seem important whilst also seeming to escape or evade easy descriptions or neat explanations.

Research methods and theories centred on talk and learning shaped and framed what researchers and professionals were able to notice, value, interrogate and story with regards to what happens when young children visit museums. While we do not dispute that visitors (young children and the adults they come with) often use prior knowledge and experiences in order to make sense of the museum, and sometimes express this through talk, the experiences of young children in museums extend beyond this in several different directions. Beyond talk and adults, young children in museums are also deeply entangled with and co-exist alongside spaces and things, with the more-than human, so that all these things lose their clear boundaries. The case studies in this book are replete with examples of this, as young children spin around in a revolving door (Chapter 10), place a colander on their head (Chapter 22) or dump a cardboard box on their baby brother (Chapter 22). Crawling or running across surfaces and rolling around on a wooden polished floor (Chapter 12), young children *and* their ideas seem frequently to be in constant motion, rigorously resisting the fixing down of meanings, yet still with a sense of purpose, of something special unfolding. Whilst we are not suggesting that these kinds of moments are the *only* thing to value or pay attention to when working with young children in museums, we are arguing that an account of young children in museums that disregards these frequent and common practices is insufficient. Further, we would suggest that the possibilities for becoming entangled with different and unique kinds of objects, spaces, sensations, architectures, is a large part of where we see the value in children visiting museums (Macrae et al., 2018). This entanglement is an important part of the answer to "*what does that mean*?" when children visit museums.

Theories that we find helpful for attending to the body, movement, experience of spaces in museums can broadly be described as more-than-human theories. By more-than-human we refer to a theoretical lens that does not truncate the child and the adult human accompanying them from the building, objects, smells, movements, atmospheres and sensory experiences which are also bound up in museum visiting. These theories offer more expansive ways to take seriously about the way in which museum visits always extend beyond talk, humans, the notion of children as "learners" and the kinds of behaviour that are easy to explain or rationalise. Although the literature on the more-than-human is extensive, we have focussed in particular on theories that help us to rethink objects, spaces and time during children's museum visiting. More-than-human theories are useful for helping us to reconceptualise how we understand objects, space and time within our research and practice. At the same time, objects, space and time have become vehicles for us to use when looking at what these different theories might afford our thinking in terms of children in museums.

Across the three Parts of the book, we engage with theories of objects, space and time in the following ways.

1 Thing-ness and the power of objects

This Part will make the case for taking objects themselves seriously when considering children's experiences in museums. Whilst in the wider museum literature Dudley (2014) has made a case for museum artefacts as "complex material objects" rather than only mediums for generating human learning, the full potential of the materiality of museum objects is rarely considered when working with young children in museums (Macrae et al., 2018). Rather than being inanimate tools to be put to use to stimulate children's learning, objects themselves have what Bennett (2010) calls "thing-power," that is, the capacity to drive action and have unanticipated effects above and beyond what humans might envisage for them. This Part will focus on the inter-related material processes that produce or are produced by the *affects*, *assemblages* and *agency* of objects as they flow together/apart, generating a backcloth to the case studies in this Part, each of which carefully and slowly focus on the thing-power of objects in museums.

2 Museum spaces

The theories and case studies in this Part begin with the premise that people experience the world through their bodies and these bodies are inseparable from the place in which they are located (Pink, 2009). Tracing the importance of sensory experience, movement and bodily memory in how children experience place, this Part explores how we might understand a museum visit in new ways when we take seriously the dynamic role place plays in what unfolds (Massey, 2005). Disrupting the assumption that the child is a bounded individual with a distinct impermeable membrane, we consider instead the potential for child and museum to leak into each other, to become entangled with each other, and the bodily experimentation between child and museum as they playfully explore together what the possibilities of this kind of entanglement might be. Children's presence can change museums, but equally the experience of being in a museum changes a child, as new ways of knowing and being in the museum gather and are stored in the body. Children can know museums through their bodies. We cannot think of bodies and place without also thinking of movement, so, finally, this Part will draw on Ingold's (2007) work to introduce the concepts of wayfaring and dwelling in order to offer new ways of conceptualising young children's movement in museums.

3 Time, new experiences and repeat visits

In this final Part of the book, the case studies variously touch on ways that experience, duration, time and memory are entangled when young children and their families visit museums. It brings together case studies that highlight a range of themes connected to time in the context of young children and families visiting museums and galleries. A significant aspect of this is the experience of encountering new places and objects for the first time. When children visit museums, they meet with the unfamiliar: the buildings themselves are often strange, large-scale and overwhelming to first-time visitors and many objects in the collections are unlike anything children might encounter elsewhere. The way that children respond in-the-moment to these new encounters and the question of how to balance the excitement and wonder in response to the new, whilst at the same time providing a safe space in which to create familiarity and attachment, is discussed in different ways through the case studies. Many pick up on how the repeat visits and routines within the visit can establish a sense of connection and belonging. At the same time, many cases document the spontaneous rituals and routines produced by children and their families as they encounter these unfamiliar spaces. These acts of noticing give attention to the lively and unpredictable ways that the duration of a visit might unfold: they make these everyday practices visible and this gives value to this creative and inventive force that catalyses when children move through museum space. Furthermore, this practice of attending actively shapes the ways that museum practitioners respond in singular ways to children and families. The introduction to this Part will offer a range of theories inspired by Deleuze and Guattari's thinking to help museum practitioners consider the significance of time, memory and meaning making during young children's museum visiting.

How to use this book

Within each of the three Parts of the book, the reader will find an accessible introduction to key theoretical ideas, followed by a series of practical case studies from museums and galleries around the UK and beyond. Each Part concludes with a reflective commentary from leading international academics whose research has a synergy with the themes of the Part. Whilst the introductory chapters seek to orientate the reader and offer clear guidance on the relationship between the theoretical ideas and the case studies, the commentary chapters serve a different purpose. Offering our theories and case studies to a fresh pair of eyes, we asked these academics "Where else do these ideas take you? Where else could our thinking go?" Pulling apart threads from the different case studies and theories of that book Part, the commentaries show how the threads could be arranged in a different way, or viewed from multiple different angles, if we continue to ask "what if?"

In selecting the case studies for this book, we thought really widely in terms of what defines a museum from the point of view of young children. Whilst most definitions of "museum" centre on the collection, care and interpretation of objects, young children in museums can often decentre these objects. Spaces, atmospheres, possibilities for moving, for interacting with light or materials or architecture, all these things and more can become the focus of a visit with young children to a museum. Therefore, it is particularly pertinent to look at how young children's experiences of other kinds of spaces might inform both theory and practice for working with young children in museums. The case studies in this book include outreach activities with children and families in their own familiar settings, and explorations of the possibilities of libraries and art centres for this audience as well as more traditional museums. The case studies encompass work done in spaces dedicated to and designed for young children and work taking place in spaces used by many different audiences.

More-than-human theories help us to attend to children's lived experiences of visiting museums in particular ways that the other theories do not. Any concept will tend to condition what we are able to recognise or notice in research (St Pierre, 2017). Whilst this is unavoidable (we cannot research children in museums with *no* pre-existing ideas or assumptions), the role of concepts in shaping what can be noticed is worth remembering. We invite readers to approach this idea playfully; spend time in your own or a local museum together with one or more of the concepts introduced in this book and notice what aspects suddenly become noticeable where they were not before.

The three Parts of this book can be read in any order. We are interested to note how the three Parts correspond with tasks and decisions museums professionals might be engaged with whilst working with young children. For example, a focus on objects aligns with the work of curators, interpreters and learning teams making decisions about which museum objects are most likely to appeal to young children, which could be handled by children, or could provide a focus for an activity, challenge, story or some other form of engagement. The Part on place will resonate with those who are tasked with thinking about the design, layout and interpretation of museum spaces for young children; from designing entire new exhibitions to making small additions to existing spaces to make visiting with young children more comfortable, enjoyable or appealing. The third Part of the book is concerned with time and we see the relationship here with audience development. Whether museum professionals are aiming to attract new (perhaps "hard to reach?") audiences or encourage repeat family visits or lifelong museum advocates, this Part will offer some ideas to think about the layered experiences that can occur when museums start off as strange and unfamiliar spaces to young children and develop into familiar ones. Therefore, whilst readers will not find checklists, recommendations for best practice or "how to" guides in any of these Parts (we discuss in more detail below why the book does not offer that!), it might be that starting with a Part of this book closely aligned to whatever is most urgent or significant in your current work will offer some interesting resonances and fresh ways to think.

Why isn't this book a "how to" guide?

In inviting the range of perspectives and ideas represented in the diverse case studies within this book, we embrace the multiple voices on "how" to work with young children in museums. In weaving theory and practice, we seek to embrace and celebrate the range and uniqueness of different kinds of practice, together with numerous exciting and inspiring theories that seem related to these practices. We firmly believe that there is not one "right" way to work with young children in museums, or even any one "right" theory to guide thinking. Rather, knowledge and expertise of any sort is contingent and situated.

In other words, it depends; on audiences, spaces, collections, priorities and even on what seems to work or not on any particular day.

There is some fantastic practice already being developed in the UK, and beyond, around working with young children in museums, including some excellent toolkits that act as starting points of a more practical nature for "how to" work with young children in museums, written by those who are doing this work every day. We recommend as a starting point:

Museum of London Early Years Toolkit
www.museumoflondon.org.uk/supporting-london-museums/information-services/early-years-toolkit.
Humber Museums Partnership Under Fives project
http://humbermuseums.com/under-5s.
IVE Creative Families Award
https://weareive.org/bridge/creative-families-award.

More than any other audience, young children surprise us in terms of what they gravitate towards, or what objects or ideas or movements spark something on any particular day. Olsson (2013) stresses the genuine creativity and productivity of young children, their "longing for invention of the yet not known" (p. 230). This kind of genuinely original thinking is "Far away from already formulated questions with given and corresponding answers. Far away from already constructed problems with given and corresponding solutions" (p. 230). As Deleuze points out, truly original thoughts are rare; most thinking involves going in circles over things already thought, so that "to get an idea is like a party" (Deleuze, in Olsson, 2013: 231).

We hope this book supports the sector to successfully avoid the danger of deploying any strategy or idea for working with young children as an "*apparatus of capture*" (Manning, 2016: 32), that is, a fixed and reproducible formula that one can begin relying on and stop thinking about. The effect of trying to generalise or assuming that the formula for working with young children in museums is now "solved" or "fixed" is likely to be that what counts as meaning and thought is narrowed and reduced to "already formulated questions with given and corresponding answers." Improvisation should be absolutely at the heart of working with young children in museums. Instead of asking how museums could ensure certain kinds of educational outcomes, we could focus our energies on creating spaces and experiences that anticipate and are sensitive to the potential for emergent connections.

References

Bennett, J. (2010) *Vibrant Matter. A Political Ecology of Things*. Durham: Duke University Press.

Birch, J. (2018) Museum spaces and experiences for children – ambiguity and uncertainty in defining the space, the child and the experience. *Children's Geographies*, 16(5), 516–528.

Callanan, M. A. and Braswell, G. (2006) Parent-child conversations about science and literacy: links between formal and informal learning. In Berkerman et al. (ed) *Learning in Places: The Informal Education Reader*. New York: Peter Lang Publishing Publishing, pp. 123–138.
Cape UK (2011) *In the Gallery: Children, Young People and Families Co-researching Their Experience in Museums*. Leeds: MLA.
Carr, M. Clarkin-Phillips, J. Beer, A. Thomas, R. and Waitai, M. (2012) Young children developing meaning-making practices in a museum: The role of boundary objects. *Museum Management and Curatorship*, 27 (1), 53–66.
Clarkin-Philips, J. Carr, M. Thomas, R. Waitai, M. and Lowe, J. (2013) Stay behind the yellow line: Young children constructing knowledge from an art exhibition. *Curator: The Museum Journal*, 56 (4), 407–420.
Clayton, E. and Shuttleworth, J. (2018) Spaces In-between. *Children's Geographies*, 16(5), 539–542.
Crowley, K., Callanan,M. A., Jipson, J. L., Galco, J., Topping, K., and Shrager, J. (2001). Shared scientific thinking in everyday parent – child interaction. *Science Education*, 85(6), 712–732.
DeWitt, J. King, H. Wright, D. and Measures, K. (2018) The potential of extended cultural residencies for young children. *Museum Management and Curatorship*, 33 (2), 158–177.
Dicks, B. (2013) Interacting with … .what? Exploring children's social and sensory practices in a science discovery centre. *Ethnography and Education*, 9 (3), 301–322.
Dooley, C.M. and Welch, M.M. (2014) Nature of interactions among young children and adult caregivers in a children's museum. *Early Childhood Education Journal*, 42, 125–132.
Dudley, S. (2014) What's in the drawer? *The Senses and Society*, 9 (3), 296–309.
Ellenbogen, K.M., Luke, J.L. and Dierking, L.D. (2004) Family learning research in museums: An emerging disciplinary matrix? *Science Education*, 88 (1), 48–58.
Graham, J. (2011) Early years: a growing audience for museums and galleries. *Journal of Education in Museums*, 32, 54–62.
Graham, J. (2012) *Museums and children under 2*. Accessed 19 May 2015 at www.learning-unlimited.co.uk/page4/page4.html.
Hackett, A. (2014) *How do families with young children (2–4 years old) make meaning in a museum?* PhD thesis, University of Sheffield.
Hackett, A. (2016) Young children as wayfarers: learning about place by moving through it. *Children and Society*, 30, 169–179.
Hackett, A. Holmes, R. MacRae C. and Procter, L. (2018) Young children's museum geographies: spatial, material and bodily ways of knowing. *Children's Geographies*, 16(5), 481–488.
Hancock, R. and Cox, A. (2002) 'I would have worried about her being a nuisance': Workshops for children under three and their parents at Tate Britain. *Early Years*, 22 (2), 105–118.
Ingold, T. (2007) *Lines. A Brief History*. London: Routledge.
Kelly, L., Main, S., Dockett, S., Perry, B. and Heinrich, S. (2006) Listening to young children's voices in museum spaces. Paper presented at the Australian Association for Research in Education Conference. Available from: www.aare.edu.au/publications-database.php/5105/Listening-to-young-children's-voices-in-museum-spaces [accessed 18 April 2014].
Kelton, M. L., Ma, J. Y., Rawlings, C., Rhodehamel, B., Saraniero, P. and Nemirovsky, R. (2018) Family meshworks: children's geographies and collective ambulatory sense-making in an immersive mathematics exhibition. *Children's Geographies*, 16(5), 543–557.
Kirk, E. (2014) Crystal Teeth and Skeleton Eggs: Snapshots of Young Children's Experiences in a Natural History Museum. Unpublished thesis.

Kirk, E. and Buckingham. W. (2018) *Snapshots of Museum Experience. Understanding Child Visitors through Photography*. London: Routledge.

Leinhardt, G., Crowley, K. and Knutson, K. (2002) *Learning Conversations in Museums*. London: Routledge.

Leinhardt, G. and Knutson, K. (2004) *Listening in on Museum Conversations*. Oxford: Altamira Press.

Lester, S. Strachan, A. and Derry, C. (2014) A more playful museum: exploring issues of institutional space, children's play and well-being. *International Journal of Play*, 3, 24–35.

Macdonald, S. (2007) *A Companion to Museum Studies*. London: Wiley-Blackwell.

MacRae, C. (2007) Using senses to make sense of art: Young children in art galleries. *Early Years*, 27 (2), 159–170.

Macrae, C. Hackett, A. Holmes, R. and Jones, L. (2018) Vibrancy, repetition, movement: Posthuman theories for reconceptualising young children in museums. *Children's Geographies*, 16 (5), 503–515.

Manning, E. (2016) *The Minor Gesture*. London: Duke University Press.

Olsson, L. (2013) Taking children's questions seriously: The need for creative thought. *Global Studies of Childhood*, 3 (3), 230–253.

Massey, D. (2005) *For Space*. London: Sage.

Pink, S. (2009) *Doing Sensory Ethnography*. London: Sage.

Piscitelli, B. and Anderson, D. (2001) Young children's perspectives of museum settings and experiences. *Museum Management and Curatorship*, 19 (3), 269–282.

Piscitelli, B. and Penfold, L. (2015) Child-centered practice in museums: Experiential learning through creative play at the Ipswich Art Gallery. *Curator*, 58 (3).

St Pierre, E. (2017) Haecceity: Laying out a plane for post qualitative inquiry. *Qualitative Inquiry*, 23 (9), 686–698.

Vergo, P. (ed) (1997) *The New Museology*. London: Reaktion Books.

Weier, K. and Piscitelli, B. (2003) Hot and sweaty in the museum: Young children learning about nature, culture and science. *Journal for Education in Museums*, 24, 19–23.

Yamada-Rice, D. (2018) Licking planets and stomping on buildings: children's interactions with curated spaces in virtual reality. *Children's Geographies*, 16(5), 529–538.

PART I

Thing-ness and the power of objects

2

INTRODUCTION TO PART I

Rachel Holmes, Christina MacRae and Abigail Hackett

This chapter introduces meshwork thinking (Ingold, 2008) as a way to understand children's relationships with objects in museums. The processes and flows between "things" (be it (in-)between young humans, artefacts or objects, times of the day, the bricks and spaces of the museum building) that Ingold describes as a "gathering together of the threads of life," are expressed as connected and always in relation to one another. Karen Barad (2007) writes about these relations as an enmeshment of matter and discourse, that is, of things and ideas, interconnections between many diverse and differentiated entities that form the basis of life. Our writing about children's relationships with objects is not just a text but also has a *texture* (Ingold, 2008); an enmeshment of many different threads, folds, creases and crevices that knot, pleat and pour into our labyrinthine story of objects. Threads from a range of disciplines such as philosophy; museology and archaeology; art and crafts; anthropology; developmental psychology and early years education inform the ways we think about and choose to interpret young children's relationships with objects in the museum. This chapter will focus on the inter-related material processes that produce or are produced by the *affects*, *assemblages* and *agency* of objects as they flow together/apart, generating a backcloth to the case studies in this Part, each of which carefully and slowly focus on the thing-power of objects in museums. Jane Bennett writes about her distinction between objects and things, "thing-power rises to the surface … objects appear more vividly as things, that is, as entities not entirely reducible to the contexts in which (human) subjects set them, never entirely exhausted by their semiotics" (2004: 351). "Things" are less tied to stable meanings, fixed words and common sense ideas. "Things" might be more likely to escape definition and consistency, baffle and provoke, as well as incite curiosity and intrigue.

We write this introduction already sensing the vibrating threads we are part of and caught up in, not only from the other Parts in this book and the case studies we are about to introduce, but from across disciplinary boundaries, fraught historical eras and diverse political challenges faced by those who engage in Early Years museum practices. Museum practices of collection and exhibition, curation and education, are all processes of transformation that evolve simultaneously with past, present and future reconfigurations of the world (Barad, 2007). This chapter re-presents something of the museum as meshwork of multiple past-present-future entanglements and encounters. Seemingly unrelated ideas about object relations come together to generate the museum as an important hybrid space for thinking differently about relations between and in-between things and young humans.

Mapping the world: collecting and categorizing objects

Objects in young children's lives have always been powerful as well as contested: mostly identifiable, named and unfamiliar artefacts all carry a sense of other worlds; soft toys and blankets that attach themselves to children and children attach themselves to; wooden bricks, puzzles and rulers that help learning; sticks, stones and conkers that sustain fascination; vases, sandals and jewellery that tell stories of past communities; eclectic home collections of things for decorative purposes. Each has a story to tell that shapes the ways we relate to children and objects.

The collection of objects in museums arguably began with the Victorian bric-à-brac collections of objects and the emergence of Cabinets of Curiosity in the 17th and 18th centuries that sought to categorize and map the world and all its contents. Moore (2013) notes that such curated collections of objects were the precursors to the modern museum, for example the private collections of the naturalist John Tradescant formed the foundation of Oxford University's Ashmolean Museum and Sir Hans Sloane's became the start of the British Museum. At the time of their emergence, such collections were perceived as products of an era of exploration, in both physical and intellectual discovery, comprising eclectic, juxtaposed assemblages of natural wonders, scientific instruments, art works, trophies of ethnographic adventures and inexplicable objects. They symbolised how the mind, with its capacity for knowledge, was able to get to know a world that seemed increasingly inexplicable. This history and practice of collecting objects also has a deeply troubling colonial foundation as the collections themselves created " … a corpus of imagery of the Other which manufactured and permanently defined the Other" (Blanchard, 2011: 72). Artefacts and objects brought back from journeys around the world portrayed and somehow infused the public's imagination with particular exotic and oriental images of far off lands and tribal communities. The collections have come to represent an era of Cartesian domination (mind/body, subject/object split) and scientific imperialism – yet interestingly, the objects collected did not necessarily express something of what Ingold might describe as a *fait accompli* (2008: 4), often refusing to be recognisable, legible entities that, for their audience, were immediately functional or instrumental. Carroll asks, "What should we call an object whose 'thingness' appears so removed from our own understanding of a commodity?" (2008: 206). It is to the idea of children's relationships with "things" in the museum that we now want to turn.

Caught in a spin: wild, affective things

The following section considers the importance of "affect" in understanding the relationship between children and objects:

> affect is found in those intensities that pass body to body (human, nonhuman, part-body, and otherwise), in those resonances that circulate about, between, and sometimes stick to bodies and worlds ... affect is in many ways synonymous with ... *forces of encounter.*
>
> *(Seigworth and Gregg, 2010: 1)*

Affect is the complexity of the world in movement. Objects always leak, they are never passive. They ooze the potential to be both "object" and "thing" in that they may be legible in particular places and times, but are simultaneously rendered indescribable and indeterminate to universal sense-making. At times, they may resist being comprehensible at all, "thing-power ... seeks to acknowledge that which refuses to dissolve completely into the milieu of human knowledge" (Bennett, 2010: 3). Although an "object" as part of a cabinet of curiosity may seem like a congealed material effect of particular historical and geographical times, places and living practices, its "thingness" means it does not give itself up readily to human understanding or control, there is a wildness, "an existence peculiar to a thing that is irreducible to the thing's imbrication with human subjectivity" (Bennett, 2004: 248). Drawing on Thoreau, Bennett remarks that this wildness gives things the power to rearrange thoughts and perceptions.

With a focus on this potential of the wildness of a thing to rearrange thinking, we turn to Barad (2007) to focus on the notion of entanglement. The usual notion of *inter*action assumes that there are individual, independently existing entities that pre-exist their encounters with one another; a young child pre-exists the museum objects she encounters and the objects pre-exist the child. If we assume that things and people are both recognizable, stable entities before they meet, we want to focus on what is produced as they enter into a process of encountering each other that changes both child and thing. As the child's body encounters the Degas spinning wax sculpture in the case study at the Fitzwilliam Museum, Nicola Wallis documents how "Some children began spinning around themselves, or circling around objects," infectious, contagious responses as they affect and are affected by the vibrancy of museum matter (Bennett, 2010). The wax figure, the children's knowledge of dancing, flowing air, spinning bodies and space of the museum participate in a form of touching of each other, sensory exchanges, forces of encounter where knowing the thingness of the sculpture does not rely on vision alone. Barad uses the term *intra*-action to suggest an entanglement of inseparable entities, as the child's spinning body produces faster streams of air flow, a tiny current also stirs the fluid in her inner ear, connecting physically and physiologically, with the wax figure in motion. Swirling electrical energy flows to the child's brain, tingling at her fingertips and stirring the museum floor and walls in a mutual dance. The power of the wildness of the thing to rearrange thoughts and perceptions does not only happen inside the child's skull, in her eye or brain, but as Elizabeth Grosz writes,

> every organ functions as an eye, the very entrails see and look ... every organ and pore of the body functions as an ear attuned to rhythm ... the body is, for a moment at least, directly touched by the forces of chaos.
>
> *(2008: 23)*

The brain is all over the child's body, there is no mind/body split. The child's body is deeply entangled with the museum, its objects, spaces, time, sensations. Although physically, the organ/matter of the brain is located in the skull, its sensations, nerve triggers, are felt and spill out all over the body and into the atmosphere. The atmosphere, filled with musty objects, vibrant colours, strange acoustics, rough and smooth textures seep into every pore. The brain requires feedback from air pressure, fingertips, light, skin, decibels and more to respond and those stimuli are sensed through a child's entire network of bodily sensors, as Bennett goes on to write, "the nonhumanity that flows around but also through humans" (2004: 349). So, to observe children as they encounter things in the museum allows you to wonder *where* thought and perception happens, as Louise Phillips and Roxanne Finn in The Corner case study note, "Scenes never rest, but are reconfigured within, dispersed across, and threaded through one another ... the hauntological nature of quantum entanglements" (Barad, 2010: 240). Lucy Hill & Aisling O'Gorman note how,

> In the unique context of a 45 minute workshop where the adult to child ratio is an undistracted, phone free and focussed one to one, it is possible to explore the innate and intense desirability of tiny things and even to extend their possibilities beyond the potentially forbidden (as perhaps, precious, dirty or dangerous).
>
> *(Chapter 7, page 64)*

Bewildering sensation: assembling ordinary objects

Museums often invite young children to engage with art materials or everyday artefacts in the process of responding to art or museum collections. The notion of "assemblage" can be helpful as we wonder how encounters with such ordinary objects can challenge the idea of the subject/object split, whereby an active subject (child) animates an otherwise passive object. Particularly we are interested in rethinking how we might become more aware of the dense web of connections that objects have with each other, as well as with human bodies (Bennett, 2004: 349), "it is not only the human beings who educate and are educated, but that objects and spaces participate in these exchanges as well" (Nicola Wallis, Chapter 3, page 28). Assemblage is the way in which Deleuze and Guattari (2004) describe the non-hierarchical relationship between discourse and matter in the world, whereas Barad (2007) may refer to this as entanglement.

Inspired by the Surrealist artists with an interest in readymades, found objects and assemblages, many mundane objects can find new resonances when they are re-arranged in unexpected juxtaposition and provocative configurations. This process of re-arranging can " … aid the systematic derangement of all the senses … we must not hesitate to *bewilder sensation* …" (Breton, 1969: 263).

The Surrealists had a much less rational or logical relationship with objects than the early anthropologists and archaeologists who were collecting objects and artefacts for scientific advancement, historical preservation and restoration. There is a sense that Surrealist "objects ultimately lose their otherness, their externality, in the process of becoming enfolded into the subject" (Rothman, 2016: 6). Oppenheim's *Object* (fur-covered cup, saucer and spoon, 1936) is an interesting example of how the object in Surrealist art becomes enfolded into, or decomposed with the human body. The alchemic transformation of ordinary, mundane things such as a cup, saucer and spoon evokes visceral, bodily responses; an otherwise everyday functional object re-presents something deeply personal, perhaps resonating a moment where "realities" mesh, as described by Breton in his first Manifesto of Surrealism.

Joseph Cornell elevated the found object to the centre of his work. His glass-fronted boxes used very particular collections of Victorian bric-à-brac, cheap trinkets, old photographs and other found things. These miniature assemblages inspire the viewer to see each element anew, often exploring recurrent themes of interest such as childhood, space and birds. In Lucy Hill's experimentations with a range of objects brought in by the children at The Ark in Dublin, there is a strong sense of collaborative art-in-the-making (Figure 2.1). Drawing on the works of Jane Bennett and Barbara Bolt, David Rousell discusses the idea of collaboration,

> To collaborate, then, is to become entangled with 'the shared materiality of all things […] of which we are all composed' (Bennett, 2010: 12–13) … art is a 'co-collaboration' in which 'matter as much as the human has responsibility for the emergence of art' (Bolt 2013: 6).
>
> *(Rousell, 2018: 93)*

Lucy's and Aisling's case study draws from activities using photograms. This, together with their string activity, bear a resemblance with the disorienting and bewildering assemblage work of Surrealist artists; the sun print cyanotypes, collections of children's objects from home, evoke Man Ray's rayographs that exploit the elasticity of light and its affects on surfaces. Large-scale light projections have been used in a number of Piscitelli's museum projects where she notes how many children are energized by the large-scale projections, racing around open spaces in response to images on the walls, and demonstrating a visceral, full-body reaction to the sensations of play spaces (Piscitelli et al. 2003). Such projections interestingly entangle children's bodies in the case study at Ipswich Art Gallery in Chapter 5.

Returning to Lucy's and Aisling's case study at The Ark, the Tangle/Wrap/Knot/Wriggle adventure (Figure 2.2) where "Attachments were formed with particular balls of string," resonates with Duchamp's mile of string,

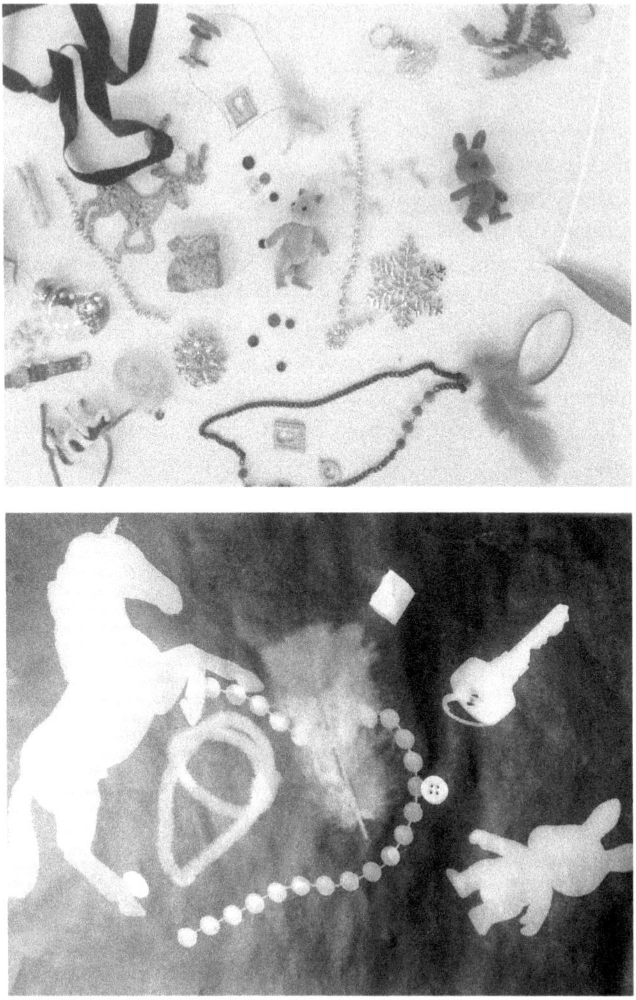

FIGURE 2.1 "Cyanotypes – for the love of small stuff" – table set up and a cyanotype using the objects. Photos by Lucy Hill.

> Visitors to the opening of the *First Papers of Surrealism* exhibition in New York in 1942 were disorientated, not only by Marcel Duchamp's famous 'mile of string' installation, but also by the presence of a group of children who, at Duchamp's instigation, bounced balls and played hopscotch among them … the criss-crossing twine prohibited engagement with the art on show … a number of children wove in and out of the guests, eventually carving out a space for themselves in the central area of the exhibition.
>
> *(Hopkins, 2014, www.tate.org.uk)*

Lucy notes how, "The string took us into parts of the space we would never have spent time in. At the end, together we had created a whole room tangle,

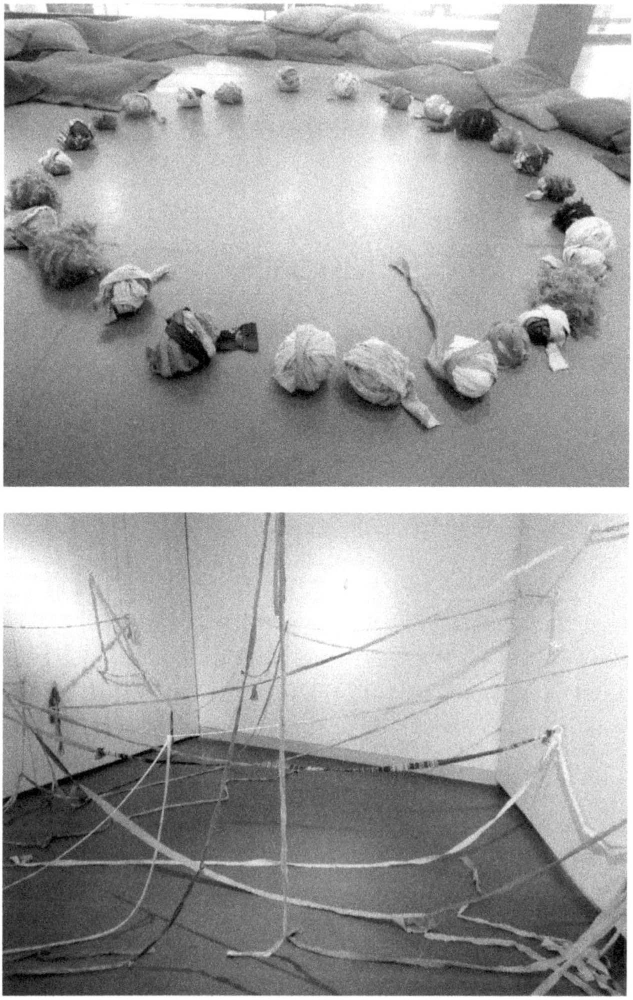

FIGURE 2.2 "Tangle/Wrap/Knot/Wriggle" – The Ark, Dublin, by Lucy Hill.

mapping our movements with looping, tying, weaving and wrapping" (Hill & O'Gorman, Chapter 7, page 69).

Collaborative webs of matter and materials – string, sun prints, bodies and processes such as light in complex relationship with space and time are produced in museums; objects and bodies flow into and out of each other's edges, involving "collaboration, cooperation or interactive interference of many bodies and forces," including human bodies as "vital materialities" (Bennett, 2004: 21). The museum and its objects are all part of a complex, moving, pulsating assemblage, generated by and generating what Bennett refers to as "distributed agency" (2004: 21); the materials collaborate with the children in their work, "the entire gallery space came alive with jumping as if by itself" (Hill & O'Gorman, The Ark, Chapter 7, page 69).

The bewildering sensations provoked by peculiar shadow collections of the children's ordinary objects from home, together with the immersive entangled stringing event help us wonder "what it might mean to become a work of art collaboratively?" (Rousell, 2018: 93).

Distributed agency: encounters with pointless, wondrous objects

Agency is defined by various New Materialists as, "the actions that produce the social world – extend[ing] beyond human actors to the non-human and inanimate (Braidotti, 2006; DeLanda, 2006; Latour, 2005) …" (Fox and Alldred, 2016: 4). MacLure describes "the wonder of objects" as "the intimate and clandestine bonds that objects are capable of contracting with children (and with adults)" (2013: 230). Objects in the museum have long been seen as replete with powers to compel, teach, question, provoke. They are thought to be imbued with the knowledge of past communities, different cultures, techniques of making, ways of living, habits and routines of otherwise unreachable peoples, times and places. The object, if examined, probed and analytically deconstructed carefully enough alongside more knowledgeable adults, would teach young children about lives and processes of living (MacRae et al., 2018). MacRae writes of, "a long educational tradition where objects are harnessed in terms of their ability to instruct. With the object rendered docile in the service of 'learning' from it" (2012: 123).

Moving with and away from cognitive and socio-constructivist ways of understanding the role of objects in young children's learning in the museum, New Materialist orientations to Bennett's notion of "distributed agency" open up new ways for considering the relations in-between things. "By allocating agency to the space in-between children and the material world, agency becomes something that arises out of complex encounters rather than something that is solely located in humans (Rautio, 2013) …" (Arvidsen, 2018: 281).

We are able to ask how can museum experiences give an object's account of what it means to be in the world? How do museums allow us to see objects as they are, as imbued with their own language, interests, and will? (Simon, 2011). Thinking of the forces of *agency*, *affect* and *assemblage*, how can the object or thing be perceived differently in relation to the process of learning in the museum?

Lisa Howarth in her case study in the North Lincolnshire Museum Service explores the open potentialities of wood chippings, "unexpectedly it was the wood chippings that seemed to have a kind of a pulling power for both the children and adults during the visits" (Chapter 4, page 36). The wood chippings are "in lieu" of soil in the museum's child-friendly "archaeological dig" and rather than them remaining a contextual feature that nested the archaeological finds, for some children experiencing the wood chippings became what Rautio writes of as autotelic activity, "something that escapes instrumentalist value claims: it seems to be an end in itself rather than a means to an end. The activity is enjoyed in itself and sustains itself" (2013: 399). Far from the intended activity of searching through the chippings for archaeological treasures, there was "[a] movement or process by which something escapes or departs from a given territory" (Patton, 2010: 190) as some young children attend carefully and closely to the wood chippings themselves and the wood chippings responded, producing textures, multiplicity, density and sounds that entangle the relations in the "visceral immediacy of bodily encounters" (Woodward and Lea, 2010: 165). MacLure describes how,

> Choosing and chosen by an object, a child forms a bond that is not amenable to adult intervention. Moreover the engagements that objects invite and receive are multisensory, and touch is often especially important. The intimate contact that this involves between objects and children's bodies amounts to a kind of *secrecy* from the viewpoint of ideology and surveillance.
>
> *(2013: 230)*

The melée of mutual and layered sensations of touch and sound sweeps the activity somewhere other than the logic and "educational" quality of the archaeological dig, as the bodies of the children and the bodies of the wood chippings "enter into relations … in order to do things, in order for things to happen" (Lim, 2010: 2401), as Roberts proposes, "The full viscerality of a body submerged in the push and pull of its material milieu always escapes representation, precisely because the world is more excessive than we can theorise" (2012: 2517).

Nicola Wallis at the Fitzwilliam similarly notes how things may "feel familiar, but still set apart from the ordinary, everyday world," their thing-power drawing children "towards particular objects for complex, multidimensional and perhaps unknowable reasons" (Chapter 3, page 28). Louise Phillips and Roxanne Finn in their case study of The Corner for 0–8 year olds in the State Library of Queensland, Australia, document how, "Things and actions don't have to have meaning. There is joy in being and doing" (Chapter 6, page 59). Objects are in themselves full of wonder, they call to us, relate to us, reach out and into us, they grasp us through their textures, vibrations, odours and tastes. Lisa Howarth also notes how children

> enjoyed collecting objects, banging them together to make different sounds ... This has shown us how important it is to have a wide variety of objects and things in the museum that are of different materials and textures. It is also important not to have too many rules or instructions when it comes to different activities in the galleries.
>
> *(Chapter 4, page 38)*

> Vibrations traverse architectural spaces, the bodies that circulate within them, and the vague moods that haunt them. Resonating at subaudible frequencies, the cavernous interiors of large spaces such as [museums and galleries] … can create atmospheres of awe and foreboding, as vibrations enter into impersonal relations with the capacities of the human skin, preparing the body for action.
>
> *(Roberts, 2012: 2517)*

The mingling between bodies can produce enchantment as well as bewilderment. Children are attuned to a non-hierarchical, non-linear way of being with objects. Relinquishing adult intentionality to use objects to instruct and educate allows for other potentialities to erupt into the museum. Paying attention to those things that might otherwise pass us by opens other worlds of assemblages, intra-actions, affect and agency.

Meandering musings

In Chapter 3, Nicola Wallis asks "Why are we so enchanted by these instances of connection which we recognise as meaningful?" Seeing the potential for enchantment and of being enchanted by connections, Bennett's work (2001) notes the ways everyday attachments diversify and enrich life. Children's intra-active relations with material objects in the museum can be understood as affective engagements with the wondrous nature of matter. Concepts such as affect, assemblage and agency offer us ways to re-organise our thinking about the young child's relationship with objects in this way. Against the subject–object divide, Braidotti notes how Haraway (1992) calls for a wider recognition of "a kinship system, radicalized by affectionate (or affective) ties to the non-human 'others' …" (2006: 200), objects or things of the world. "The thing, however, is not just one thread but a certain *gathering together* of the threads of life" (Ingold, 2011: 10), returning us to a world that is always moving and full of textures. As children move through and with objects and things in the museum, they are "treading their own paths through the meshwork [and thereby contributing] to its ever-evolving weave" (Ingold, 2011: 71).

References

Arvidsen, J. (2018) Growing dens. On re-grounding the child–nature relationship through a new materialist approach to children's dens, *Children's Geographies*, 16:3, 279–291, doi: 10.1080/14733285.2018.1425371.

Barad, K. (2007) *Meeting the Universe Halfway: Quantum Physics and the Entanglement of Matter and Meaning*. Durham, NC: Duke University Press.

Barad, K. (2010) Quantum entanglements and hauntological relations of inheritance: dis/continutities, spacetime enfoldings, and justice to come, *Derrida Today*, 3:2, 240–268.

Bennett, J. (2001) *The Enchantment of Modern Life: Attachments, Crossings, and Ethics*. Princeton: Princeton University Press.

Bennett, J. (2004) The force of things: steps toward an ecology of matter, *Political Theory*, 32:3, 347–372.

Bennett, J. (2010) *Vibrant Matter: A Political Ecology of Things*. Durham, NC: Duke University Press.

Blanchard, P. (2011) Human zoos: the invention of the savage, in G. Boetsch, N. J. Snoep and P. Blanchard (eds) *Human Zoos. The Invention of the Savage*, pp. 34–75. Paris: Musée du quai Branly.

Bolt, B. (2013), 'Toward a "New Materialism" through the arts', in E. Barrett and B. Bolt (eds.), *Carnal Knowledge: Towards a 'New Materialism' through the Arts*, pp. 1–14 London: I.B. Tauris, pp. 1–14.

Braidotti, R. (2006) Posthuman, all too human towards a new process ontology, *Theory, Culture & Society*, 23:(7–8), 197–208.

Braidotti, R. (2013) *The Posthuman*. Cambridge: Polity.

Breton, A. (1969) *Manifestoes of Surrealism*. Translated from the French by Richard Seaver and Helen R. Lane. Ann Arbor: University of Michigan Press.

Carroll, K.Z. (2008) Curating curiosity: wonder's colonial phenomenology, in T. Mehigan (ed) 2008 *Frameworks, Artworks, Place: The Space of Perception in the Modern World*, pp. 206–223. Netherlands: Rodopi B.V.

DeLanda, M. (2006) *A New Philosophy of Society*. London: Continuum.

Deleuze, G., & Guattari, F. (2004) *A Thousand Plateaus*, translated by B. Massumi. London: Continuum.

Fox, N., & Alldred, P. (2016) *Sociology and the New Materialism: Theory, Research, Action*. London: Sage.

Grosz, E. (2008) *Chaos, Territory, Art: Deleuze and the Framing of the Earth*. New York, NY: Columbia University Press.

Haraway, D. (1992) 'The Promises of Monsters: A Regenerative Politics for Inappropriate/d Others', in Lawrence Grossberg, Cary Nelson and Paula A. Treichler (eds) *Cultural Studies*, London and New York: Routledge.

Hopkins, D. (2014) Duchamp, Childhood, Work and Play: The Vernissage for *First Papers of Surrealism*, New York, 1942, accessed 23. 11.18at www.tate.org.uk/research/publications/tate-papers/22/duchamp-childhood-work-and-play-the-vernissage-for-first-papers-of-surrealism-new-york-1942.

Ingold, T. (2008) When ANT meets SPIDER; social theory for arthropods, in C. Knappett and L. Malafouris (eds) *Material Agency: Towards a Non-Anthropocentric Approach*, pp. 209–215. New York: Springer.

Ingold, T. (2011) *Being Alive*. New York, NY: Routledge.

Latour, B. (2005) *Reassembling the Social*. Oxford: Oxford University Press.

MacLure, M. (2013) The wonder of data, *Cultural Studies ↔ Critical Methodologies*, 13:4, 228–232.

Lim J, 2010 "Immanent politics: thinking race and ethnicity through affect and machinism" *Environment and Planning A*, 42, 2393–2409.

MacRae, C. (2012) Encounters with a life(less) baby doll: rethinking relations of agency through a collectively lived moment, *Contemporary Issues in Early Childhood*, 13:2, 120–131.

MacRae, C., Hackett, A., Holmes, R. & Jones, L. (2018) Vibrancy, repetition and movement: posthuman theories for reconceptualising young children in museums, *Children's Geographies*, 16:5, 503–515.

Moore, S. (2013) Links between the Renaissance cabinet of curiosities and contemporary artists' works. *Financial Times*, accessed 17 October 2018, www.ft.com/content/55f966a4-2cfd-11e3-8281-00144feab7de.

Patton, P. (2010) *Deleuzean Concepts: Philosophy, Colonization, Politics*. Palo Alto, CA: Stanford University Press.

Piscitelli, B., Weier, K., & Everett, M. (2003). Museums and young children: Partners in learning about the world. In S. Wright (Ed.), *The Arts and Young Children*, pp. 167-192. Frenchs Forest, NSW: Pearson Education Australia.

Rautio, P. (2013) Children who carry stones in their pockets: on autotelic material practices in everyday life, *Children's Geographies*, 11:4, 394–408, doi: 10.1080/14733285.2013.812278.

Roberts, T. (2012) From 'new materialism' to 'machinic assemblage': agency and affect in IKEA, *Environment and Planning A*, 44, 2512–2529.

Rothman, R. (2016). 'Object-oriented Surrealism: Salvador Dalí and the poetic autonomy of things, *Culture, Theory and Critique*, doi: 10.1080/14735784.2016.1143333.

Rousell, D. (2018) Becoming a work of art: collaboration, materiality and posthumanism in visual arts education, *International Journal of Education Through Art*, 14:1, 91–110.

Seigworth, G., & Gregg, M. (2010) An inventory of shimmers, in M. Gregg and G.J. Seigworth (eds) *The Affect Theory Reader*, pp. 1–28. London: Duke University Press.

Simon, J. (2011) Neo-Materialism, Part I: The Commodity and the Exhibition, *e-Flux Journal*, Volume 20, www.e-flux.com/journal/23/67825/neo-materialism-part-ii-the-unreadymade.

Woodward K., & Lea J. (2010) Geographies of affect, in S.J. Smith, R. Pain, S.A. Marston, and J.P. Jones III (eds) *The Sage Handbook of Social Geographies*, pp. 154–175. London: Sage.

3

THE POWER OF OBJECTS

Little things please little minds?

Nicola Wallis

Introduction

Through vignettes drawn from my experiences as a gallery teacher at the Fitzwilliam Museum, this chapter describes ways in which young children have connected with art objects in our collection. I consider factors that might support children in developing these personal connections and the ways in which they might be expressed.

Context

The Fitzwilliam Museum is the principal art and antiquities museum of the University of Cambridge. The Museum collections include: illuminated manuscripts; printed books; sculpture; artefacts from Egypt, Greece, Rome, Ancient Near East, Africa and Asia. There are also collections of paintings and drawings, coins, armour, ceramics, textiles and musical instruments.

The Early Years programme at the Fitzwilliam Museum aims to give young children authentic encounters with incredible artworks. The various facilitated sessions on offer consist of invitations for young children to discover aspects of the collection through stories and playful sensory exploration.

Core values

In the *Review of the Value of Museums and Galleries*, Scott et al. (2014) argue that in these changing times the user will play a more active role than before. This chapter will explore the role that foregrounding the interactions between young children and objects might have within this context. The aspirations above compel us to take time to allow relationships to develop between people, spaces and objects in the Museum, to welcome and to value these, and to consider how these new understandings might influence practice.

Rinaldi (2001) suggests:

> There is a constant relational reciprocity between those who educate and those who are educated, between those who teach and those who learn. There is participation, passion, compassion, emotion. There is aesthetics. There is change.
>
> *(p. 44)*

Our work with young children at the Fitzwilliam Museum shows that it is not only the human beings who educate and are educated, but that objects and spaces participate in these exchanges as well.

Sustained engagement with cultural spaces such as museums promotes greater confidence and willingness to participate actively (DeWitt et al., 2018). With this in mind, we work in partnership with families and community organisations to enable young children and their adults to have multiple opportunities to engage with the Museum. With repeated encounters, the Museum becomes a place that feels familiar, but still set apart from the ordinary, everyday world. The spaces, objects and activities, including expressive art making and documenting, provide an opportunity for adults and children to become immersed in a comfortable "otherness" and thereby tune into each other. As adults and children move through Museum, their experiences and emotions become contextualised. This is a place where it is normal to encounter a chair that is not for sitting on, a cup that has never been drunk from, or a naked body that is not remarked upon. This is a place where it is normal to stare, to be surprised, to be uncertain. While many of the objects they encounter may have elements of familiarity, bringing with them a sense of security, the new context reveals uncharted territory through which adults and children negotiate their explorations together. Below are some examples of how these ideas are manifested in our pedagogy.

Moving through space and time

During a pre-school session, families were exploring the: *Degas: a passion for perfection* exhibition. This showcased a range of Degas' works including preparatory sketches and wax maquettes alongside finished pieces. One of the themes of the exhibition was Degas's fascination with repetition and rehearsal.

A story had been created for the exhibition about a young dancer meeting Degas and being encouraged by him to practice and repeat her steps over and over again in order to succeed. The story introduced the group to pieces in the exhibition and included time for the children to explore and respond freely to what they saw. Some of the children were mesmerised by particular works, moving close to them and looking intently for extended periods. Others were captured by the physicality of what they saw, particularly the idea of spinning movement which had been featured in the story and was shown by a wax model mounted on a spinning plinth in order that it could be viewed from all sides. Some children began spinning around themselves or circling around objects.

One child, David, did not want to explore the works on display, although he had listened with interest to the story. Instead, he stayed close to his grandmother, pulling her arm towards the exit. Rather than trying to redirect his attention back towards the exhibition, I felt it was important to acknowledge his emotions and thinking at this moment, by crouching down to his eye level and offering him the opportunity to voice his thoughts.

> "Are we going to the studio now?" he asked.
> "Would you like to?"
> "Yes, please."
> "Do you have some ideas?"
> "I'm going to make some things. You can see them if you want."

David has attended these sessions before, so he knows that we always visit the studio after the galleries. This time, the children were offered modelling wax, scrim and everyday materials such as corks and cotton reels to give a sense of the materials that Degas used in his wax models. They also had pipe cleaners and we invited them to combine these items into figures. Many of the children and their adults made dancing figures, as we might expect following the exhibition. Some transformed into footballers as the joy of rolling the modelling wax into a sphere became apparent and the children wanted to include these with their figures.

David did not speak to his grandmother or any of the other children or adults during the workshop. Instead he spent most of the session threading pipe cleaners through a cotton reel. After a while he realised it was possible to thread more than one through at a time and finally, when he had pushed four through and the cotton reel had wedged in the middle, he held it up delightedly.

> "Look!"
> "It looks like a spider!" smiled another of the adults, recognising his pleasure in what he had produced.

David put this "spider" to one side and began work on another, and another and another, until we needed to find more pipe cleaners. When asked to reflect on why he was making so many spiders, David said: "I'm practising, like Degas."

The responsive way in which we create and acknowledge these connections between children, adult, objects and spaces is part of all effective pedagogy, but is especially pertinent in the context of an informal learning setting such as a museum. Above is an example of how being open and welcoming to allowing children time and space to develop their ideas facilitates their understanding.

A focus on outcome, or a concern that the children should experience the exhibition in a certain way, could have stifled David's thinking here. Instead, the opportunity for him to express his ideas creatively through materials and the tacit acknowledgement that his ideas and experiences were valued and in a state of development rather than fully-formed, meant that within the guided structure of the group session he could be supported to explore his own individual connection with Degas.

Ways of knowing

A mother and ten-month-old baby were spending time in the Arts of the Far East gallery as part of a young parents' course at the Museum. The glass cabinets reach all the way to the ground and the pair had seated themselves on the floor in front of a display of porcelain.

Aaron reached towards the glass, opening his fingers onto the pane and then scrunching them in towards his palm. He did this a number of times – stretching and scrunching. He then turned his attention to the wooden floor and repeated the same movement: opening his fingers to touch the floor and then scrunching them inwards again.

"Oh, he's always doing that at the moment," said his mother. "Aren't you? You're always scratching things. Like his highchair tray. Scrape, scrape, scrape; scratchy, scratch, scratch."

I asked whether he was maybe investigating the different sounds he could make using his hands in contact with different materials and his mother thought that this could be possible, remarking that he was very interested in sounds and songs.

Later in the session we were reminded of this when Aaron made loud, excited and inquisitive shrieks on entering a new space with a high ceiling. "I think he likes the echo," said his mother, who was interested in this response from her child, but seemed a little uncomfortable about the noise he was making. To demonstrate to Aaron and to his mother that using his voice to explore the space was an interesting and useful thing to do, the adults working with the group began making similar noises with their voices and stamping their feet to create echoing sounds.

Noticing and validating these small moments that show what young visitors (and those who know them well) bring into museum spaces is a way in which connections can be formed. Children and babies can use the understandings they are developing elsewhere and try them out in a new place. Materials, objects and spaces have an active role to play in holding and shaping these understandings (Procter and Hackett, 2017). As educators, we can be alert to these non-verbal invitations into the child's world and facilitate personally relevant experiences for them. The above example, for instance, led on to a much more in-depth exploration of sound and texture, based on Aaron's actions and his mother's reflections.

Connections and contexts

Sometimes these connected moments are about direct (although not necessarily physical) contact.

A group from a local playgroup had spent the morning at the museum. After about half an hour we entered the Armoury. One of the children in the group gasped, "a real horse!" The adults smiled to each other, before trying to explain to the child: "It's not really real, but I know what you mean: it's really a horse and it really is there!"

The feeling of being "really there" with an object, of being able to relate to it in terms of one's own body, is something that we have observed time and again in our Early Years Programme at the Fitzwilliam Museum. The children use their bodies to understand the objects and their reactions to them: how big am I compared with this thing? How does the space around it compare with the space around me? This is explored in more detail in the University of Cambridge Museum's "nursery in residence" chapter (Chapter 10) in this volume.

Equally, we have found that being able to give objects a name is another important way to build these personal connections. Sometimes these names are mediated by others: parents very consciously teaching new vocabulary ("It's a sarcophagus – can you say that?") or Museum Educators introducing objects through stories with named characters. Anderson et al.'s (2002) important study found that objects presented within a storytelling context were particularly memorable for the children and this has also been our experience as practitioners, with families regularly mentioning to us that children have remembered details described in object-based story sessions long after visiting the museum.

Of course, the social and cultural context in which the children encounter these objects is also important in whether they are experienced as significant. The socio-cultural interpretation alone, however, does not sufficiently explain those moments when children spontaneously make connections with museum objects or features that do not command the attention of other visitors, but which seem meaningful for children.

As Anderson et al. highlight, a visit to a museum is multidimensional. The socio-cultural aspect is important, but there are also aesthetic, cognitive, motivational and collaborative factors in play and, of course, this is taking place in a physical space where humans and non-humans interact. Physical bodies and physical objects are also sites of emotional interactions, so this is another consideration when trying to understand what is happening when young children and museum objects come together. Vygotsky (1986) conceptualised children's external actions such as talk, drawing or movement as "tools of thought" (p. 102). This is helpful as we observe young children and their activities in museums, which we recognise as important but find hard to understand or explain.

Why are we so enchanted by these instances of connection which we recognise as meaningful, sometimes without knowing why? MacRae et al. (2017) refer to "sticky data" – episodes that draw us in but which we struggle to explain logically – while Albon and Rosen (2014) highlight "critical moments" which bring us up short, urging us to reconsider what was previously taken for granted. Similarly, MacLure's (2013) "data that glows" (p. 661) is yet another way of speaking of these moments which fix themselves in our emotional and physical selves, resisting the clutches of our logical reasoning.

This element of surprise, of unpredictability and magical revealing seems to be valued by parents seeing their children in a new context:

> An extraordinary opportunity to connect very young children to art, and to be astonished and humbled to witness as a parent how perceptive and engaged pre-schoolers can be when studying a complex object in a museum context.
>
> *(Mother of a four year old at an It's Magic session)*

These moments cannot happen in isolation. They are a result of a coming together – of people, objects, spaces and ideas. The observers of these moments are not neutral – they are also drawn in, connected.

Final thoughts and implications for practice

- We have seen that children's relationships with objects are surprising, diverse and intriguing.
- Welcome this unpredictability and be open to the development and expression of these relationships.
- Embrace new ways of viewing children, objects and how they are enmeshed with each other in the unique context of a museum gallery
- Child–object relationships may be mediated – through stories or materials – and it is possible to do this democratically, in a way which does not privilege adult ways of knowing over children's (Carr et al., 2018).
- Consider collapsing the rigid distinctions between children's and adults' experiences (Birch, 2018) to gain freedom from low expectations and the tendency to make assumptions about our youngest visitors.
- Acknowledge the ability that children have to create their own individual and significant connections with our spaces and collections, with as much right as any other stakeholders to access, construct meanings about and participate in decision making regarding what our museums should be like. Our job as educators of these young children is to make this a reality.

References

Albon, D. and Rosen, R. (2014) *Negotiating Adult-Child Relationships in Early Childhood Research*. London: Routledge.

Anderson, D., Piscitelli, B., Weier, K., Everett, M. and Taylor, C. (2002) Children's museum experiences: identifying powerful mediators of learning. *Curator* 25 (3), 214–229.

Birch, J. (2018) Museum spaces and experiences for children – ambiguity and uncertainty in defining the space, the children and the experience. *Children's Geographies* 16 (5), 516–528.

Carr, M., Clarkin-Phillips, J., Soutar, B., Clayton, L., Wipaki, M., Wipaki-Hawkins, R., Cowie, B. and Gardner, S. (2018) Young children visiting museums: exhibits, children and teachers co-author the journey. *Children's Geographies* 16 (5), 558–570.

DeWitt, J., King, H., Wright, D. and Measures, K. (2018) The potential of extended cultural residencies for young children. *Museum Management and Curatorship* 33 (2), 158–177, doi: 10.1080/09647775.2018.1442241.

MacLure, M. (2013) Researching without representation? Language and materiality in post-qualitative methodology. *International Journal of Qualitative Studies in Education* 26, 658–667, doi: 10.1080/09518398.2013.788755.

MacRae, C., Hackett, A., Holmes, R. and Jones, L. (2017) Vibrancy, repetition and movement: posthuman theories for reconceptualising young children in museums. *Children's Geographies* 16 (5), 503–515, doi: 10.1080/14733285.2017.1409884.

Procter, L. and Hackett, A. (2017) Playing with place in early childhood: an analysis of dark emotion and materiality in children's play. *Contemporary Issues in Early Childhood* 18 (2), 213–226.

Rinaldi, C. (2001) *Infant-Toddler Centers and Preschools as Places of Culture Making Learning Visible: Children as Individual and Group Learners*, 38–46. Reggio Emilia, Italy: Reggio Children and Project Zero.

Scott, C., Dodd, J. and Sandell, R. (2014) *User Value of Museum and Galleries, A Critical View of the Literature*. Leicester: AHRC and RCMG.

Vygotsky, L. (1986) *Thought and Language*. Cambridge, MA: MIT.

4

THE THING-NESS OF WOOD CHIPS

Lisa Howarth

This case study draws on some of the work of the Humber Museum Partnership (HMP), who were tasked by the Arts Council to increase the usage by families with under-fives. In order to do this we needed to understand how families engage with a museum and what is needed to make the visit a good experience. The Humber Museum Partnership is a consortium between Hull Museums, East Riding of Yorkshire Museums and North Lincolnshire Museum Service, funded as a Major Partner Museum through the Arts Council from 2015 to 2018. My role at the time was as the Learning Manager for North Lincolnshire Museum Service and I co-ordinated the under-fives project on behalf of the Humber Museum Partnership.

Our work with young children at North Lincolnshire Museum during this project has been characterised by unexpected and surprising entanglements between children and objects. One of the best ways to understand how families with children under five experience a museum is through observations. The partnership commissioned Dr Abigail Hackett, Dr Lisa Procter and Dr Christina MacRae from the Manchester Metropolitan University to facilitate some research involving participant observations at three sites, including North Lincolnshire Museum, a local museum in the small town of Scunthorpe near the east coast of England. North Lincolnshire Museum is funded by North Lincolnshire Council and has two floors of interactive galleries and exhibitions focussing on the history of North Lincolnshire through geology, archaeology and social history. It also has an under-fives learning space called "Dudley's Den," opened in 2016, which was funded as a part of the Arts Council project. Many of the galleries have been redeveloped to become more accessible over the last ten years as funding has become available.

Description of the project

A small group of families who had never visited North Lincolnshire Museum before were recruited through an existing partnership with the Local Authority Adult Community Learning service and a local community centre. The families came as a group to the museum on a minibus provided by the community centre once a week for a total of four visits. They all had at least one child under the age of five and most of the children were around the age of three. Each visit lasted 90 minutes, beginning in Dudley's Den, before exploring the rest of the museum. At the end of each visit a drink and a snack was provided before the families travelled home on the minibus. The visits were facilitated by the Museum Learning Officer (under-fives) and the families were accompanied by a Family Learning Development Assistant from the Adult Community Learning Service, whom they knew really well. Field notes were written for each visit and still images and video footage collected on the latter three visits. The families were visited in their community some months later to present them with certificates and a copy of the interim findings of the research.

As new visitors to our museum, the young children and families involved in the study encountered a range of objects; material things, some of which were familiar to them and some mysterious, some of which they were able to hold and play with, others that were displayed behind glass. By describing close and careful observation of what happened between children and some of these objects during the visit, this chapter will explore the possible roles objects in museums can play for young children.

The following sections summarise observations made during the research, some of which are drawn from the end-of-project report (Hackett et al., 2017).

Importance of being comfortable

"Dudley's Den," a newly developed dedicated under-fives space in the museum, was important to families during the visit. It was created to be a neutral comfortable space on the ground floor of the museum in which families could explore, play and engage with their children. It is one of the few areas in the museum that has natural light and everything in there is suitable for children under five. As such, it was reassuring, easy and offered a space where the children and families felt comfortable. One of the families' biggest concerns before beginning the visit was that their children might break things in the museum. The parents knew that the children could touch everything in this space and would not break anything too delicate. This enabled them to engage with the objects and activities that were in there and explore them in their own way, without feeling a need for constant vigilance. Dudley's Den was always a starting and ending point for the families, so both parents and children felt comfortable in the space and knew how to behave in it.

Dudley's Den was designed to replicate some of the themes in the museum so there is an archaeological dig, dinosaur den, museum wall with real and replica objects, reading cubby hole and soft baby space with an under-the-sea theme. Some of the activities are static and other smaller activities are rotated so there is often something different to see. It is always open to the public, except when there is a led under-fives session in there.

One child in particular enjoyed playing with the objects on the museum wall, picking them up and carrying them around the room. The museum wall is an area with full length shelves divided into compartments in which historical and play objects are placed, such as shells, buckets, cups and a train. The activity was designed so that children could move objects around so the objects chosen were quite robust and suitable for this purpose.

> Later A picks up two buckets, places them in the reading cubby and climbs in. Then gets out, goes to fetch one more bucket, places it in the reading cubby, climbs in again.
>
> *(Field notes, Abigail Hackett)*

Although we had thought about the objects that went into the space, it didn't seem to really matter to the children what the objects were. It seemed to be more the process of independently moving them around that was important. One boy did this on several visits. In this way, it seemed like it was more important to the children what the objects could *do* (be moved around), rather than what they were or what learning messages they were connected with (for example, archaeology, life in the past). This is a surprising finding and a challenge for museum work, which tends to consider objects in terms of the messages and information they signify (Dudley, 2014; Macrae et al., 2018).

Unexpected touch

Frequently during the visits, certain objects had an impact on how children responded which was different to the intended purpose. The archaeological dig in Dudley's Den had real and replica objects (such as a flat iron, replica Iron Age torc and a Victorian shoe) covered with wood chippings (in lieu of soil) which could be "unearthed" using trowels and brushes. The activity was designed to give children a chance to experience archaeology by uncovering objects like archaeologists do. However, unexpectedly, it was the wood chippings that seemed to have a kind of pulling power for both the children and adults during the visits. Gathering in Dudley's Den at the start of each visit, children and adults would congregate around the archaeological dig and reach for the wood chips, running them through their fingers, picking them up, brushing them and scrunching them in their hands. One child was continually attracted to the dig on each visit and enjoyed immersing herself in it.

> La is very happy sitting in the archaeological dig for a really long time. She picks up the wood chippings, the magnifying glasses and the brushes in turn and places them down again. I sit near her and scrunch wood chippings in my hands – she looks at them intently. La brushes them all off my hand, first with her brush and then with her fingers, and then waits, as if to prompt me to put some more onto my hands. We do this a couple of times. L is so content to sit in the dig. I say to her mum does she like things like sand pits and water, she says she does.
>
> *(Field notes, Abigail Hackett)*

Some of the children used the wood chippings to play with other objects they had taken from the object wall, such as putting the chips down the funnel of a train or filling a metal goblet with them. We did not intend for the children to play with this material in this way, it was just intended to cover the objects in the archaeological dig. Bennett (2010) writes about how objects can exceed their original intended use, but also about how objects can produce or shape people, just as people can produce or shape objects. The wood chips seem to invite the children to experiment in these ways, yet, at the same time, in diverting from the intended purpose and distributing the wood chips more widely than intended around the room, these experimentations seem to sit on the cusp of creativity and "naughtiness."

We have since explored using different materials in the dig such as rubber pellets and sand to see how the children use these materials. The different materials, due to their varied texture and size, are all used in different ways. The other two materials are moved around less as they are much less tactile than the wood chips. The pellets are quite light and children would throw them into the air and allow them to fall everywhere, whilst the sand tends to stay in the dig and be explored with the tools.

Real or not

Despite spending quite a lot of time in the under-fives space, the children also enjoyed exploring the rest of the museum on each visit. They often did this fast paced, looking at and touching cases that had something that appealed to them and making brief comments such as "hey look at that dice" or "pennies."

It was interesting how the children tried to make sense of the museum objects they discovered, including trying to understand whether things were real or not. The Bronze Age skeleton in the archaeology gallery caught one boy's attention. He thought it must be broken as it was lying on the floor and commented that it wasn't real. This was around Halloween, when perhaps he had seen lots of other skeletons out and about, but most of these would be suspended vertically.

The same boy encountered taxidermy specimens in the natural sciences gallery, where a bird of prey was suspended from the ceiling and a mouse was embedded into the floor, to be viewed through Perspex,

> Z wanders, playing with the wooden bead chaser and the coloured shapes on the light box. Me and his mum point out the owl in the air and the mouse in the floor. Z's mum says "The bird is going to fly down to get the mouse." Z looks amazed – "when?" We explain this is a model. He looks again suspiciously at the mouse, I say something like "you like that don't you" and Z asks "why isn't it walking?"
>
> *(Field notes, Abigail Hackett)*

It was surprising to witness how much it mattered to the children if something was real. Trying to make sense of such objects also seemed to be an emotional and deeply engaged response. This interest in the "real-ness" of skeletons and taxidermy has been noted by other studies, including by Kirk and Buckingham (2018) and Procter and Hackett (2017) who all suggest that playing with ideas of real-ness, danger and fear in their encounters with, for example, a taxidermy bear or a dinosaur skeleton with large teeth, are important aspects of children's imaginative and visceral entanglements with museum objects. The children had unfamiliar emotional encounters in the museum, including with the skeleton, which one boy called "creepy," and an air raid siren noise, which many of the children did not like. This contrasted to the familiar space of "Dudley's Den" and made the visit more engaging for them. The parents quickly reassured the children if they were unsure of something and this seemed to help the children develop confidence during the visits.

Reflections

The way the children engaged with particular objects was the most surprising part of the project. They didn't always use the activities or objects in the way they were intended and created their own experiences using the materials on offer. They enjoyed collecting objects, banging them together to make different sounds and sometimes just looking and touching them. This has shown us how important it is to have a wide variety of objects and things in the museum that are of different materials and textures. It is also important not to have too many rules or instructions when it comes to different activities in the galleries. The children will often engage with the activity or object in the way that is best for them and not always in the way it was intended.

The environment was important to the experience that the families had with the objects. Parents felt much more relaxed when they knew how to behave in the different spaces and what was expected from them. Knowing that objects were intended to be handled and wouldn't easily break made the families more comfortable in the museum. This then had a positive impact on the children. Having a familiar space such as Dudley's Den with lots of objects and activities in was important as it built up their confidence to explore the museum.

We have used the evidence in this project to inform our new galleries which opened in 2017. We have introduced "please touch" signs in areas of the museum that have objects which people can touch. This was to make it clearer for families to know what they can touch, so they feel more comfortable in these spaces. The importance of real to the children led us to introduce real fossils for handling in the Jurassic Sea gallery. However, they are secured down to prevent them from going missing.

Final thoughts and implications for practice

Working with new audiences

One of the main challenges for the project was ensuring that enough families were committed sufficiently to return for the four weeks. Only two dropped out after the first week and most of them came to each session. Taking away barriers such as transport, having familiar faces attend the sessions and providing snacks made a big difference to encouraging families who had never visited the museum before to take part in the project. This was also down to the fact that the partnership with Adult Community Learning was already established before this project took place. Lessons had already been learnt from earlier projects, such as the importance of communicating effectively with the families and reassuring them so they knew what to expect. It was also important to go at their pace and not to try to achieve too much in the first week. Many of the families achieved a lot out of the project and two of the parents went on to do future courses with Adult Community Learning.

Observe your activities

It is important to take the time to observe how children under five engage with activities once you have launched them in the museum. We were surprised how many of the children did something unexpected with the activities we had provided, such as playing with the wood chips in the archaeological dig or collecting them and moving them around. This demonstrated how important it was to train front-of-house staff that witness this behaviour and engage with families in the galleries. They needed to understand that they could encourage this and that it is an acceptable part of the learning process.

References

Bennett, J. (2010) Vibrant Matter. *A Political Ecology of Things*. Durham: Duke University Press.

Dudley, S. 2014, What's in the Drawer. *The Senses and Society* 9 (3), 296–309.

Hackett, A. Procter, L. and MacRae, C. (2017) How do families with under fives experience museums? Research report for Humber Museum Partnership. Unpublished.

Kirk, E. and Buckingham, W. (2018) *Snapshots of Museum Experience Understanding Child Visitors Through Photography*. London: Routledge.

Macrae, C. Hackett, A. Holmes, R. and Jones, L. 2018, Vibrancy, repetition, movement: posthuman theories for reconceptualising young children in museums. *Children's Geographies* 16 (5), 503–515.

Procter, L. and Hackett, A. 2017, Playing with place in early childhood: an analysis of emotion, agency and materiality in children's 'dark' play. *Contemporary Issues in Early Childhood* 18 (2), 213–226.

5

BRIGHT AND SHINY

Infants, toddlers and contemporary art at the Ipswich Art Gallery

Barbara Piscitelli

Background

Young children have been a main focus of attention at the Ipswich Art Gallery since 1999 when they opened Australia's first dedicated gallery space for young children (Piscitelli, 1999). The Ipswich Art Gallery was established in 1980, and underwent a major renewal and expansion in 1999. During the renewal process, the entire gallery was reconceptualised in collaboration with more than 100 groups in the community of Ipswich (Henson, 1999). Ipswich is a city of 200,000 people located 45 kilometres west of Brisbane, the capital of Queensland, and is considered a moderately disadvantaged area. Young children were seen as an important audience by both the gallery and the community, so the gallery worked with external consultants and an early childhood reference group to guide thinking about how best to meet the needs of local children.

The children's programme at the Ipswich Art Gallery is known for its innovations and child-centred practice (Piscitelli and Penfold, 2015). Visitation to the Ipswich Art Gallery is consistently high with more than 100,000 people (2018) taking time to see what is happening at the gallery; it is one of the most visited galleries in regional Australia. A very high portion of the visitors are local families who come back time and again to enjoy everything the gallery has to offer. Some families are now into the second generation of gallery goers and are raising their children and grandchildren as cultural citizens.

Underpinning Ipswich Art Gallery's child-centred practice is a set of philosophical principles (IAG 2018) that inform the gallery's decision making:

Learning begins with creative play.
Creativity builds self-esteem, a necessary ingredient for success.
The spontaneous creativity within each child should be celebrated.
Children learn more in the company of adults they trust, i.e., their parents, grandparents, relatives, guardians, friends and teachers.
Children explore the environment using all of their senses, i.e., hands-on activities provide opportunities to explore and learn.
Every child deserves access to a safe, stimulating and enjoyable learning environment.
Children's exhibitions are curated for children – not for adults.
To understand and appreciate other cultures is to build community harmony.
Children are important members of our community who should be encouraged to express and develop their ideas and views, i.e., children should be seen and heard.

Infant toddler research and agenda

In 2008, the Ipswich Art Gallery developed a contemporary art exhibition and public programme for babies and toddlers. At that time, there were very few play-based programmes for this age group in art galleries. The gallery wanted to break the traditional "Toddler Tuesday" mould and develop a new type of immersive contemporary art play-space for very young children. An innovation of this type provided a rich site for researching very young children's experiences.

Four key questions informed our inquiry into how very young children engage with an innovative programme to introduce them to art in a gallery setting:

1 How do very young children (birth to four years of age) respond to contemporary art in a specially designed museum environment?
2 What kinds of social interactions (between very young children and adults) provoke responses about art and aesthetics?
3 What qualities of art do very young children prefer and why?
4 What components of the prepared environment do very young children prefer and why?

The research context included the exhibition, the play-space, the interactive programmes and the visitors, as well as the gallery staff.

The exhibition concept

Bright and Shiny: artworks

The exhibition *Bright and Shiny* incorporated six key artworks selected for their capacity to focus very young children's attention on the aesthetic qualities of the exhibition theme. The artworks were all recently made by contemporary Australian artists and they were placed strategically throughout the gallery.

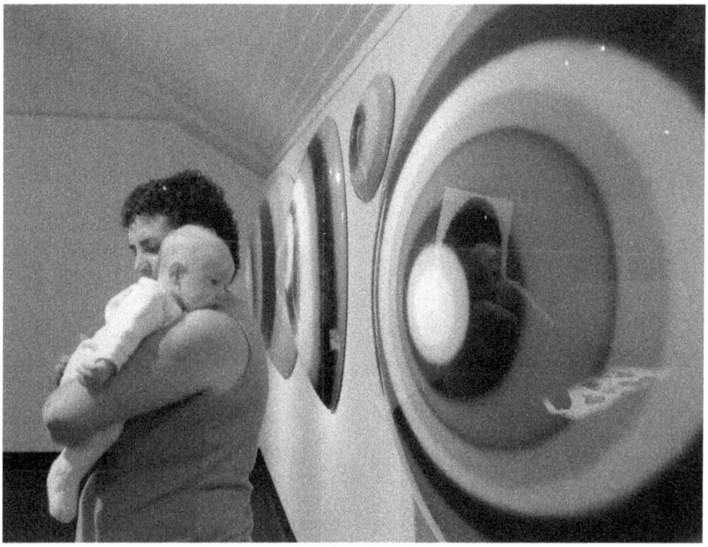

FIGURE 5.1 Grandmother gives her infant grandchild a close-up look at contemporary art. Christopher Langton, *Hypnoscope (3.009°, 49.815°, 34.987°, 99.666°, 92.638°, 96.125°, 71.329°)*, 2004. Polyurethane and pigment on PVC. (Courtesy of the artist and Tolarno Galleries, Melbourne.)

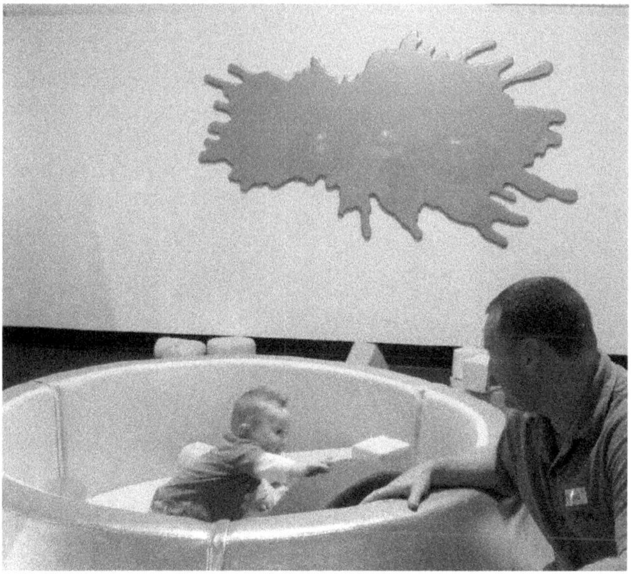

FIGURE 5.2 Father and son explore the pool and its soft toys alongside contemporary art. Sadie Chandler, *Melt No. 8*, 1996. Enamel on MDF board. (Ipswich Art Gallery Collection, 2005.)

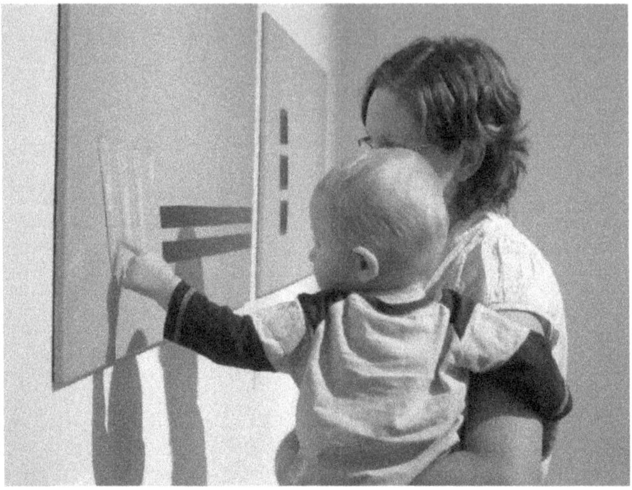

FIGURE 5.3 Mother and child explore contemporary art.

Daniel Wallwork, *Hi-way sharks, HJ GTS (Barbados Green)*, 2007. Zinc anneal, weld-in panel, 2 pack paint with mica effect. (Ipswich Art Gallery Collection, 2007.) Daniel Wallwork, *Hi-way sharks, HT Monaro GTS 350 (Indy Orange)*, 2007. Zinc anneal, weld-in panel, 2 pack paint with mica effect. (Ipswich Art Gallery Collection, 2007.)

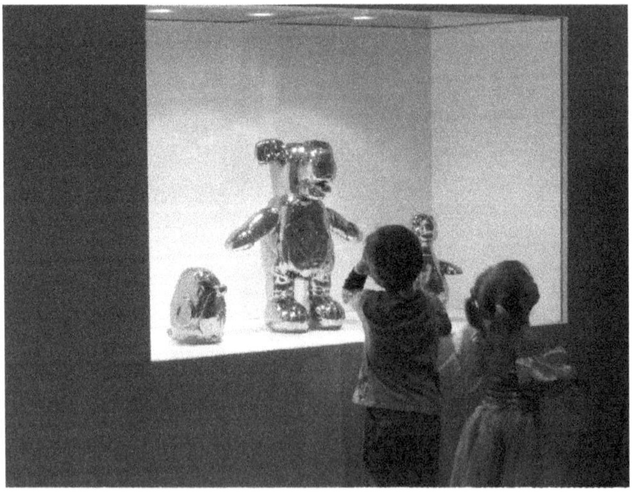

FIGURE 5.4 Toddlers explore contemporary art.

Michael Doolan, *For now and for ever (owl, dog, flower, turtle)*, 2007. Platinum lustre glazed ceramic. (Ipswich Art Gallery Collection, 2007.)

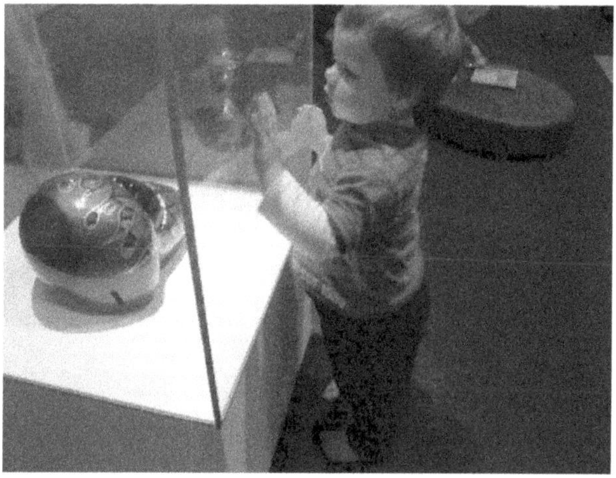

FIGURE 5.5 Toddler gazes at contemporary art.

Patricia Piccinini, *Hot head*, 2006. Fibreglass and automotive paint. (Ipswich Art Gallery Collection, 2007.)

Bright and Shiny interactive play space

The art works were installed in an infant/toddler play space of 250 square metres and were hung at a low level to accommodate the stature of very young children. Simple labels were placed alongside the work and included minimal information. The space was furnished with several movable large items (two crawl-through mirrored kaleidoscopes, a large crawl-in pool (see Figure 5.2), mirrored shape pieces, a mirrored labyrinth) and gallery-designed and built resources including a crawl-through tunnel (see Figures 5.6 and 5.7), a toddler-height light table (see Figure 5.9), three electronic paint machines (see Figure 5.11), a fire engine light installed on a low plinth with a push button activation device (see Figure 5.10) and an opaque in-floor cabinet (see Figure 5.8). Most of these items were designed and built on site and many have been in use for some time – reconfigured for new exhibitions. A large silver reflective canopy was installed over the main meeting area in the children's space and a floor-to-ceiling projection wall was set up to show various in-house-developed animations (see Figure 5.12). Finally, a range of low-cost consumable resources was added to the space: long pieces of bright and shiny fabrics; LED torches; books; musical toys; transparent colour discs; drawing and threading materials – many of the consumables were sourced from recycling centres or available in local shops.

Staff

A professional early childhood educator with extensive experience in early childhood arts education was engaged to lead the infant toddler programme. An arts trainee was involved in assisting the programme leader and staff were assigned to work in the space as usual.

Participants

More than 5,000 visitors took part in *Bright and Shiny* over a 12-week period. This included 2,894 children and 2,175 adults. Research participants were selected from visitors to *Bright and Shiny* and 224 parents and 254 children took part in the research. Signed consent forms were collected.

Research procedure

Children and parents/carers were observed during the programme and data were recorded via field notes, checklists, video and photographs. Trained observers (including the programme leader, researcher and gallery staff) gathered data. Analysis was ongoing and became the subject of team meetings at midpoint and at the conclusion of the programme.

Parents/carers completed a questionnaire to seek information about demographic details, audience characteristics, programme satisfaction and marketing.

Findings

How do very young children (birth to four years of age) respond to contemporary art in a specially designed museum environment?

In general, the literature indicates that aesthetic development starts later in life than early childhood. Parsons (1986, 1987) indicated that aesthetic development takes place in a series of five cognitive stages, starting with a visceral response of like or dislike and leading on towards a discriminating sense of art historical understanding. Parsons' studies involve children as young as five years of age. Due to the method of dialogue involved in gathering the data, his research did not include very young children.

Our findings run counter to those of Parsons and indicate that there is a strong affiliation between very young children and art and that young children are highly aesthetic beings responding to sensations and perceptions of all kinds. Our research involved naturalistic observation of very young children; we were among the children in the space on a daily basis and had the opportunity to watch them explore. We used a variety of methods for collecting information, including videos, photographs and notes.

In general, children responded with enthusiasm to the environment and scanned the space visually, both on their own and with guidance, showing attraction to the surfaces. Certain artworks attracted more attention than others: for example, the bright silver sculptural pieces by Doolan had been used in advertising promotions, so many children were familiar with the images and sought them out (see Figure 5.4). Children were drawn to these artworks and responded by eagerly investigating the shiny surfaces, gazing at the objects, having excited conversations, smiling and pointing and naming the items in the display cabinet.

Children were supported in their art observations by parents and gallery staff. Adults spontaneously carried infants around the gallery, pausing in front of artworks to allow the child to look at and absorb visual qualities (see Figures 5.1 and 5.3).

There were occasions when children engaged in spontaneously and independently looking at an artwork. One such episode involved a boy under the age of two. Captured on video, this young boy noticed Piccinini's helmet-shaped sculptural work, *Hot head*, from across the room. He crawled out of his play space and began to scamper across the room with his eyes intently focussed on the artwork. He spoke with excitement – calling out "hot head, hot head" as he clambered across the room. The toddler became distracted by the flashing light of the nearby fire engine light interactive and stopped to push the button a few times before lifting his head again, catching sight of the artwork and calling out "hot head" as he moved to the low display cabinet holding the artwork. He patted the cabinet and gazed at the work, then exclaimed "hot head" again to the nearby adults (Figure 5.5). When his mother came to join him in his discovery, she told us the child had never seen the artwork nor visited the exhibition or the gallery prior to this day. His *intuitive understanding* of the title of the artist's work shows a kind of aesthetic awareness rarely documented, yet perhaps relatively common, in early childhood.

What components of the prepared environment do very young children prefer and why?

In *Bright and Shiny*, the environment was seen as more than a space: it was viewed as both a container for social interactions and a site of educational content (Gandini, 1998). The space encompassed a large area and the adaptable room arrangements allowed for plenty of open space so children could navigate between artworks, furniture and activity areas. This wide-open quality provided plenty of room to move, work independently or cluster in small groups around various furniture components. The furniture was movable and was regularly reconfigured to create suitable arrangements for newborns, crawlers, walkers, toddlers or three year olds. Children enjoyed all the furnishings but some items were of special interest including the fire engine light, the tunnel, the light table and the floor cabinet.

An array of open-ended and multi-sensory elements was incorporated into the exhibition, including lights, bells, torches, sound-scapes and books. These added an ever-changing element to the space and afforded children with the opportunity to engage in playful interaction with the space. Bells, torches and lights offered an element of surprise.

Technology was incorporated into the exhibition by way of interactive paint machines and a wall projection (Figures 5.11 and 5.12).

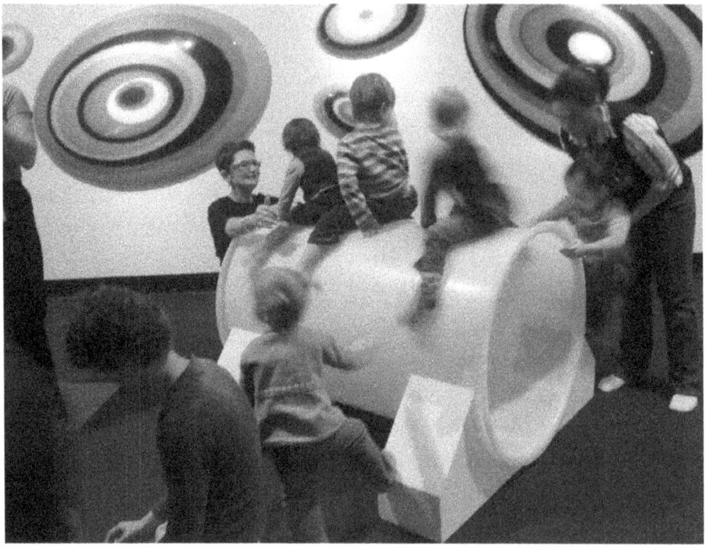

FIGURE 5.6 A group of two and three year olds play with the group leader on the tunnel installed in *Bright and Shiny*.
Designed by Ipswich Art Gallery.

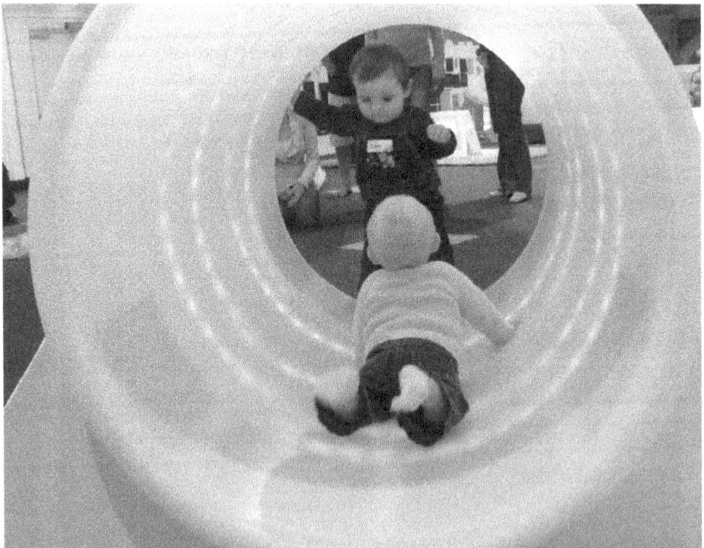

FIGURE 5.7 Toddlers play in the illuminated tunnel.
Designed by Ipswich Art Gallery.

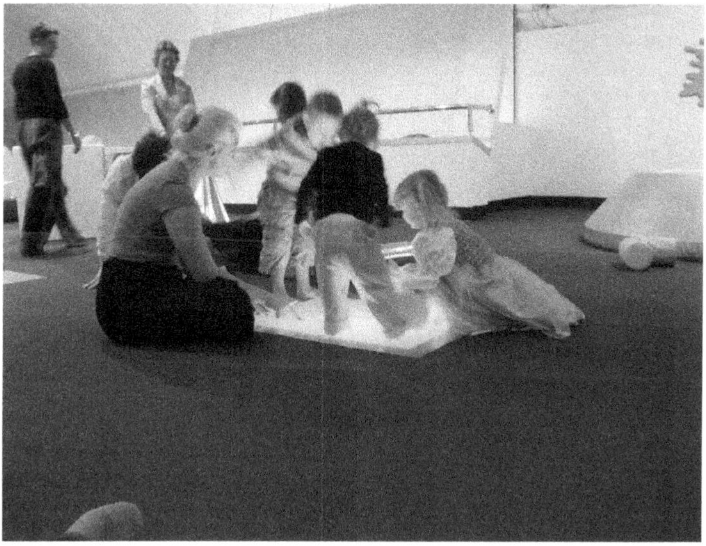

FIGURE 5.8 Children gather on the floor installation to talk, walk and look at the changing colours with the gallery assistant.
Designed by Ipswich Art Gallery.

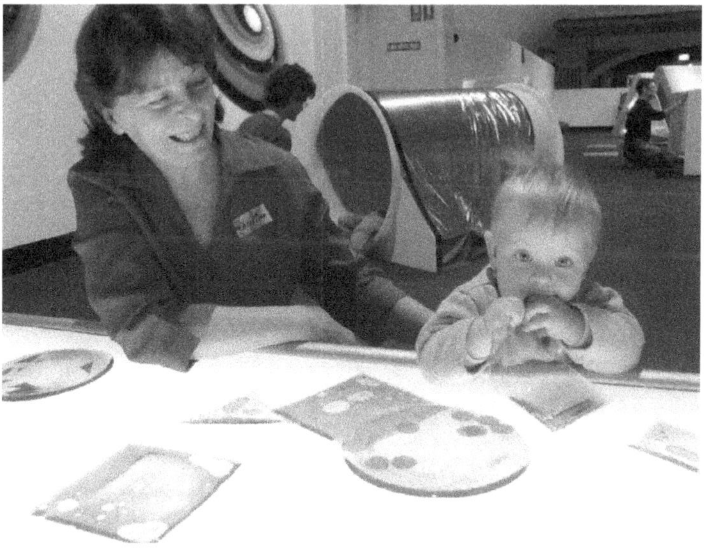

FIGURE 5.9 Grandmother and grandchild play with coloured shapes at the popular light table.
Designed by Ipswich Art Gallery.

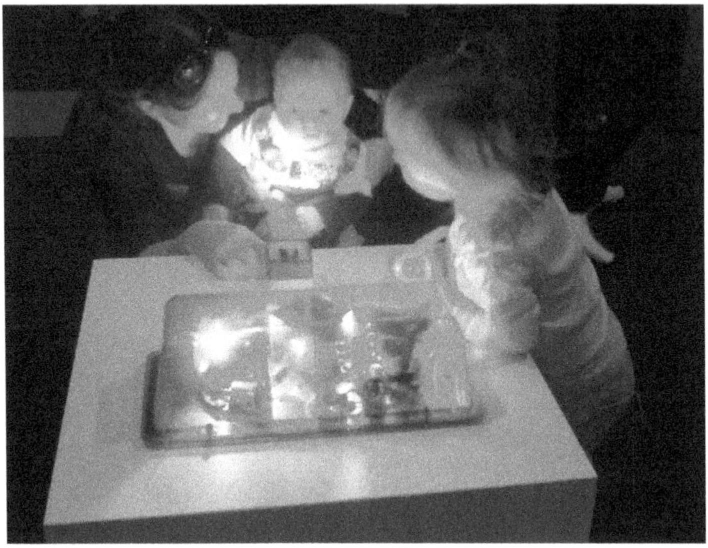

FIGURE 5.10 Infant, toddler and parent operate the flashing light installation in the *Bright and Shiny* playscape.
Designed by Ipswich Art Gallery.

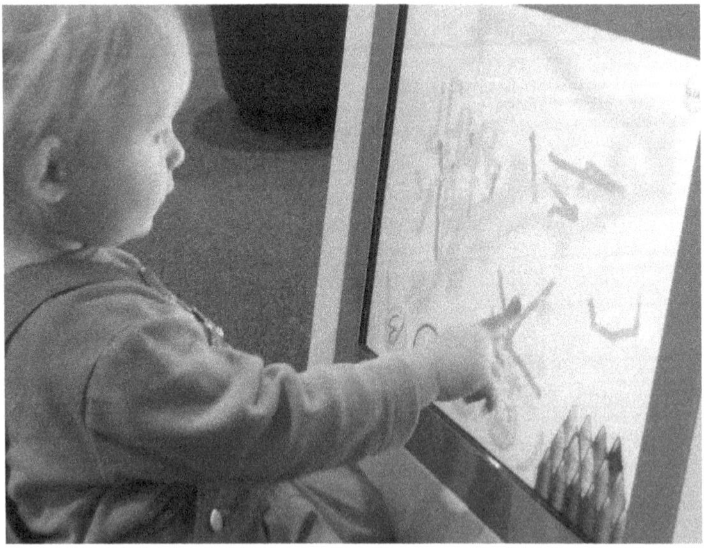

FIGURE 5.11 Toddler draws on the touch screen sketch pad installed in *Bright and Shiny*.
Designed by Ipswich Art Gallery.

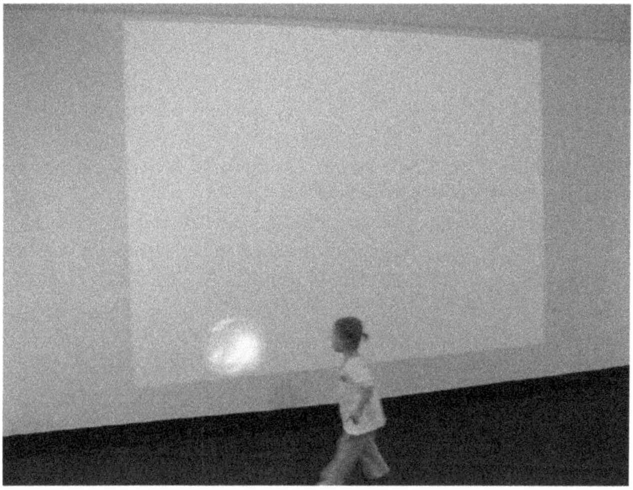

FIGURE 5.12 Young girl follows the bouncing ball wall projection in *Bright and Shiny*. Designed by Ipswich Art Gallery.

The facilitator was a key figure in the programme and her repertoire of skills led to highly engaged children and parents. Using a mix of one-on-one interactions, large group sessions and informal play, the group leader and her assistant provided the glue that held the programme together. Responses from parents indicate that the presence of the group leader was a highly important component of the programme.

Final thoughts and implications for practice

Projects like *Bright and Shiny* are worthwhile investments in cultural citizenship. Participants rate such experiences highly and seek out similar experiences for their very young children in galleries, museums and libraries. The results look impressive yet the actual costs of generating innovative play spaces for very young children are relatively low, especially if staff develop and research many of the innovations on-site and in-house.

The *Bright and Shiny* exhibition and children's responses led us to think more deeply about play-based multi-sensory engagements and to consider how best to generate such spaces for very young children in our cultural venues. These insights have been useful in generating further innovative and high quality programmes for very young children (Piscitelli and Penfold, 2015).

Thus, the regeneration of the Ipswich Art Gallery started a whole new range of opportunities for the children of Ipswich to become part of the cultural landscape of their city as consumers and as creators.

References

Gandini, L. 1998, Educational and caring spaces, in Edwards, C., Gandini, L. & Forman, G. *The Hundred Languages of Children*, 2nd Ed., pp. 161–178. Greenwich: Ablex.

Henson, B. (Ed.) 1999, *Exploring Culture and Community for the 21st Century: A New Model for Public Art Museums*. Ipswich Queensland: Global Arts Link.

Ipswich Art Gallery 2018, Philosophical principles for child centred programs, viewed 13 October 2018, https://ipswichartgallery.qld.gov.au/kids/childrens-gallery.

Parsons, M. 1986, The place of a cognitive developmental approach to aesthetic response, *Journal of Aesthetic Education*, Vol 20, No 4, 20th Anniversary Issue, pages 107–111.

Parsons, M. 1987, Talk about a painting: A cognitive developmental analysis, *Journal of Aesthetic Education*, Vol 21, No 1, pages 37–55.

Piscitelli, B. 1999, Designing galleries with children in mind, in Henson, B. (Ed) *Exploring Culture and Community in the 21st Century: A New Model for Public Art Museums*, pp. 99–101. Ipswich: Global Arts Link.

Piscitelli, B., and Penfold, L. 2015, Child centred practice in museums: experiential learning through play at the Ipswich Art Gallery, *Curator*, Vol 58, No 3, pages 263–280, http://onlinelibrary.wiley.com/doi/10.1111/cura.12113/full.

6

WHAT EMERGES IN PLAYING IN THE CORNER OF ARTIST-CURATED AND CREATED MATTER

Louise Gwenneth Phillips and Roxanne Finn

Walking in

If you come through the Knowledge Walk, you can see into The Corner on arriving, regardless of height, via floor-to-ceiling windows. You can even sit on a bench and interact through the window. It is a ground-floor corner of the State Library Queensland's (SLQ) architecture award-winning premises that opened in 2006. As you enter, you weave your way through a maze of single-seater lounge chairs, with locals reading newspapers, utilising free internet and curling and bending into folds of lounge chairs to sleep. SLQ's values of providing free and equitable access, sharing and belonging to community are immediately evident (The State of Queensland (State Library of Queensland), 2018).

Then you see a sign for The Corner and a glass display cabinet packed with child/adult/artsworker co-constructed creations with their accompanying stories. You are lured around to the right and there it is, The Corner – a sunken floor, framed by tiered seating and a zigzagged ramp filled with a "Let's play house" installation[1] of large replicas of home-made play items and varying loose open-ended play things. Before you enter the sunken floor area, there is a large television set that you can enter on one side for live television show creation. Down five stairs or along the ramp, there is a large egg carton boat – looking as if it is made from a half dozen egg cartons, with paddle pop sticks for masts and fabric for sails, but it's big enough for six children to easily sit in each egg hole. Alongside there is a large replica of a toilet roll car that you can climb on and crawl through. Then against the ramp wall is a large soft sculpture bath, about the size of two double beds, with handmade bath toys dispersed. Then up the tiered seating, by one of the windowed walls, is an array of child-sized furniture and a collection of children's picture books in line with the installation theme. Under a curtained bench against the other outside wall/window are baskets of animated household cleaning devices: dusters, dustpans, brushes and wooden spoons. Making materials are offered along the bench looking out to the Knowledge Walk, with a diorama made from household items and toy farm animals. The Corner provides a welcoming sanctuary, a curated experience, a dynamic space and an opportunity for learning through play. Being drawn into its immediate flow of activity is both inevitable and irresistible.

To further animate and ignite wonder, The Corner rosters artsworkers and programme assistants on daily.

Tiffany brings a playful approach to making
Vanessa divergent thinking
Anthea relationality
Walter playful technical expertise
Mari brings her love for making, guidance and affirmation and
Tim animates and authorizes the joy of the carnivalesque.

These roles are entities in the space to extend the invitation of playfulness and exploration with matter – a valued social affordance in the space (Gibson, 1979/2015). Volition is privileged (Barab and Roth, 2006). Artsworkers offer materials and shared attention with matter, space and relationality without coercion. They work sensitively with families to dispel confusion about how particular tasks may be undertaken. Open-ended exploration is the welcomed action/behaviour. Artsworkers and programme assistants simply begin or respond to child/family-initiated activity with song, playful characterization or offers of ideas and resources.

We spent six days (spread across two weeks) in The Corner to notice what emerges in this space of loose parts for young children and families. Our purpose was not to locate utilitarian agendas and learning outcomes, but rather to be emplaced with The Corner, to sense its rhythms; its culture; its wonderings; its energy – the ontologies, epistemologies and ethicalities of The Corner. Through agential realism (Barad, 2007, 2010), attention to what emerges in person and object actions, and ecological psychology (Gibson, 1979/2015), attention to affordances of place, we observed, listened, talked, played, recorded and wondered about the happenings in The Corner. Agential realism creates performative accounts of relationality and material phenomena (Barad, 2007), whereas ecological psychology seeks to explain relationality as co-constituted with attention to dynamic transactions of persons (or other beings) with the environment (Gibson and Pick, 2000).

We offer our poetic, pictorial and storied accounts to invite you to imagine the culture and happenings of The Corner from differing ways of knowing and naming yet from shared interests in bodies, matter and place. Through attention to being in and with The Corner, we pushed aside or muffled preconceived notions of children, play, loose parts and libraries, welcoming differing ways of seeing and understanding to emerge.

Corner happenings

Louise records

Cylindrical can offers leverage to stand.
Dustpan monster snaps at ankles (see Figure 6.1).

Small bodies lean and twist against low bench.

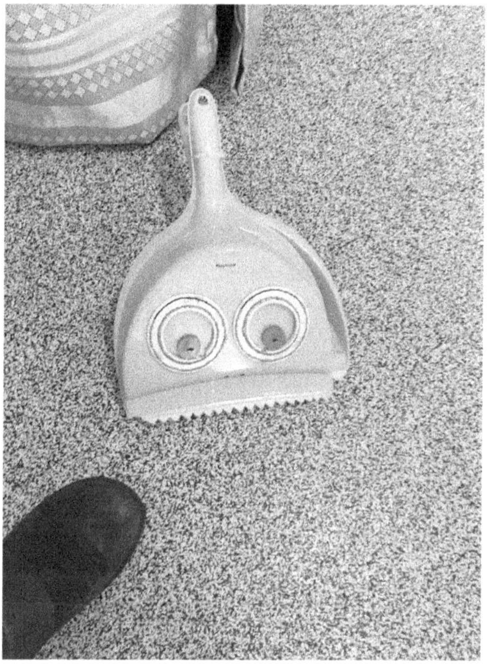

FIGURE 6.1 Animated dustpan.

Three girls seated in a row holding a paperclip each – bending them.
Sticky tape sticks to fingers.
Child bends irregular-shaped green card between both hands – each bend creates a different shape – arced, diagonal, twisted ....
Yindi (3) reads a book at my feet.
Wynnie (1) bumps head on stair rail, her face grimaces, then pats the point of contact and walks on.
Diyan (5) draws "There's the junk in the ocean ... here's a tin can."

Velveteen-covered plastic bottle fish drives large toilet roll car (see Figure 6.2).
Doll's foot pushed into velveteen-covered plastic bottle fish's mouth.
Nia takes photos with mother's phone of fish.

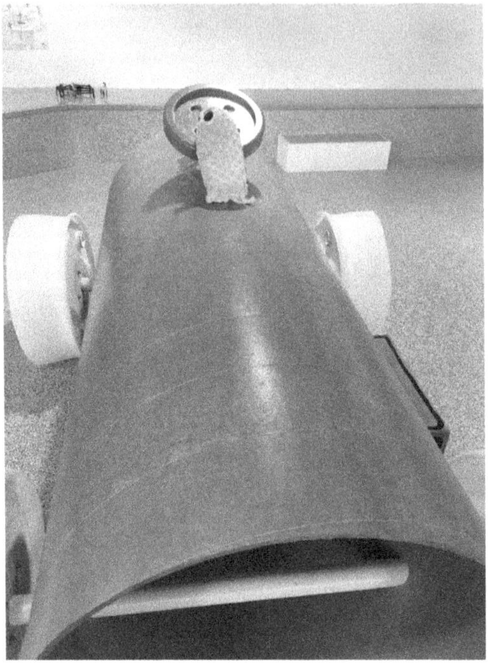

FIGURE 6.2 Fish drives toilet roll car.

Nia pulls dark blue velvet flippers onto her feet laughing with arms by her side, flapping and quacking (see Figure 6.3).

Fish nibbles at her legs.
Aikito (1) holds a spongy ball in one hand and a plastic persimmon in the other.
Persimmon drops (see Figure 6.4).
Sponge ball squeezed in hand.
Another child collects persimmon.
A dad offers a plastic pear to Aikito.

"Last time I came, I lay in the bath and he scrubbed me from head to toe with every object in there," Grandmother shares.
Child blows into mouth of light blue velveteen-covered plastic bottle fish, it expands.
Adults read children's picture books together – no child with them.
Staff, parents and children wear self-made paper plate masks.
Dharma (9 months) crawling around, looks at boy with small wooden turtle toy.
He gives it to her.
She mouths it then offers it back.
He looks hesitantly.
She drops it and crawls on.
A few minutes later when no one is near the turtle, he takes the turtle back.

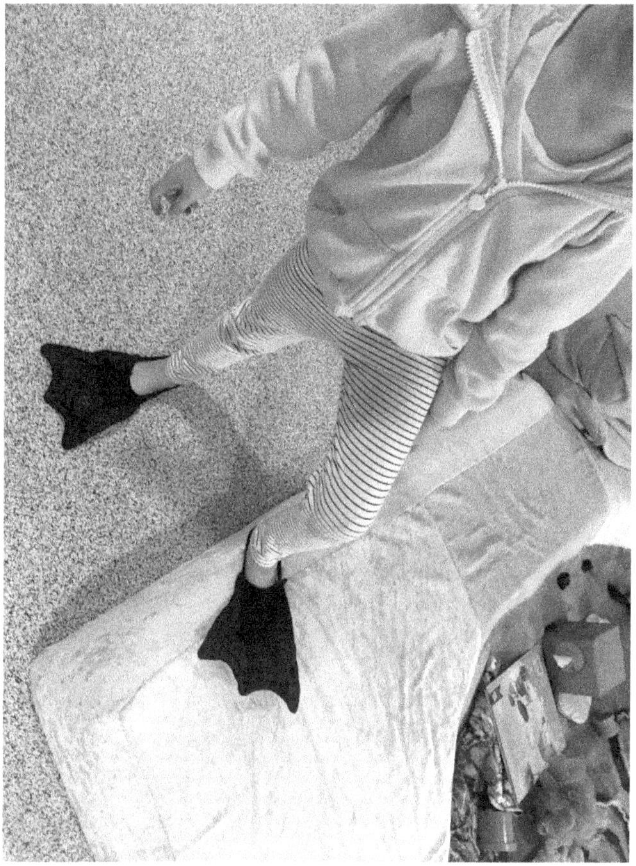

FIGURE 6.3 Flipper feet.

"One more thing on TV is the baby show."
Tim brings dad holding baby onto TV set.
One child in each egg carton hold of egg carton boat.
Plastic tomato flies past dad with eye patch and pirate t-shirt.
Tim shreds up strip of paper bag then tapes together at one end –
"Eye brows … Dragon fire … a hula skirt … in fact it is the tentacles of a jelly fish."
Colander worn on head as hat.
Torn piece of paper becomes "Big nose" (see Figure 6.5).

Jelly fish earrings.
Doll spins on floor.
Literacy brochure transformed into three-dimensional Tower of London.

My staccato verbal and pictorial offering of short bursts of The Corner's energy and rhythm – to sense the relational and material phenomena of The

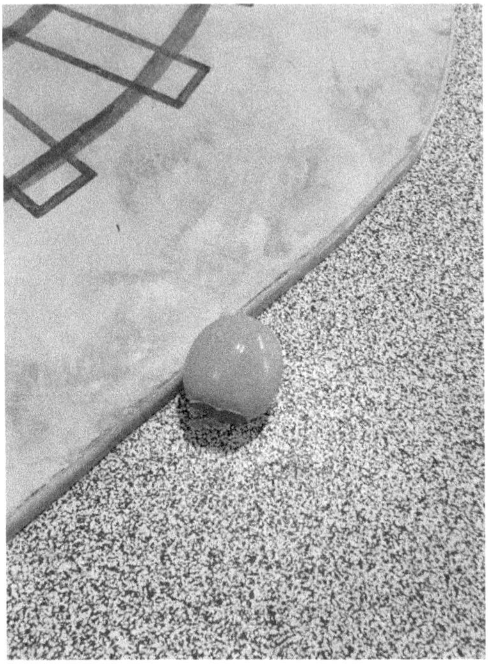

FIGURE 6.4 Persimmon.

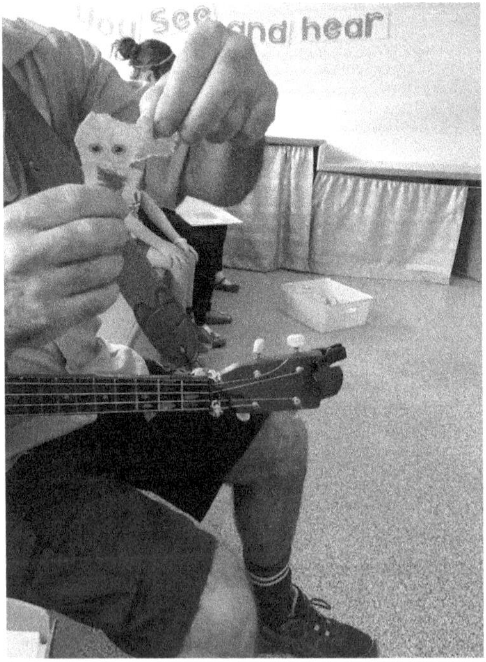

FIGURE 6.5 Paper big nose.

Corner. Things are constantly moving and being (re)configured in sporadic bursts across the various locales within The Corner. Random acts are welcomed and celebrated, privileging the diverse agential and sometimes foolish elements of "thing-power" (see Bennett, 2010). Things and actions don't have to have meaning. There is joy in being and doing. "Scenes never rest, but are reconfigured within, dispersed across, and threaded through one another … the hauntological nature of quantum entanglements" (Barad, 2010, p. 240). Each object in The Corner has been many different things, had many adventures in many different locales of The Corner (traces of The Corner even creep into other parts of the State library, such as bubbles in the air conditioner, feathers in the stairwells); each happening (scene) draws from those that have come before and spurs further happenings with differing configurations in different locales both in and beyond The Corner.

Noticing what emerges in the actions between entities, relata become visible. The relations define responsibility as the ability to respond, that is, a matter of inviting, welcoming and enabling the response of the Other (Barad, 2010). The Corner is a place where responsibility "is an iterative (re)opening up to, an enabling of responsiveness" (p. 265); body responds to can, fingers to sticky tape, bottle fish to blown air and so on. To sit and watch the happenings of The Corner is to witness responsiveness as constant quantum leaps sporadically all over the space with varying intensity and quantity and reappearances in other locales without recognition of it being anywhere in between (likened to ghostly matters in electron leaps in quantum theory). Ethicality was also present in the responsiveness through support for other's actions with objects (e.g., the plastic pear offered to Aikito to replace the persimmon; the turtle shared between a boy and Dharma). A political conception of democracy enacted through the initiatives of others being supported (Biesta, 2007), embedded in a culture of the communality of things, as Roxanne next stories.

The dynamic transaction of playfulness

Roxanne stories

In ecological psychology, perception is direct and "action possibilities" as the dynamic and situated relationality of person and place are named affordances (Gibson, 1979/2015). Examining the "affordances of place" reads the synergism of embodied action and material agency as affordances.

Looking to Yindi (3 years) plonking down in front of me and throwing off her shoes, I recalled a parent valuing the space because "there's not many places they can take off their shoes." I also remembered the sensorial depth I experienced yesterday taking my shoes off in the giant soft sculpture bathtub, allowing my feet to inform me, giving eyes and hands a rest. So, I too ripped off my sandals. I turned to Jaiben (Yindi's father) who tells me serendipitously: "It's nice how the space is communal. It's organic. It's amazing what a space can do. The artist is the big difference." My attention moved with the constant flux of body-object-mattering and when eventually I returned for my shoes, they were gone. Detached from body, shoes had become part of the communal belongings. My immersion in the space illuminates the *efforts* of the curators to create a safe and communal place via the playfulness *afforded* (Gibson, 1979/2015) by loose parts and multi-sensorial objects.

A child bumps my leg and surprises me as she emerges from underneath the curtained void below the bench I am seated on, followed by another child. "I'm playing with my friend!" she happily calls out to her grandmother. Tim (artsworker) jumps up and joins in the play, spontaneously grabbing one of the household objects animated by Vanessa (artsworker). He pokes the feather duster into the void behind the curtain and then he leaves and returns with a pan and brush similarly adorned for animation. He lets out a loud, sudden "GROWL" that catches the attention of the room for a brief immense moment. Then the grin. He leaves the children to carry on their play a little better equipped, having cemented the idea in all nearby that excited play in this hiding space is to be celebrated. Exploration and discovery are critical to the perception of affordances and attunement to affordances is part of our socialisation process (Heft, 2001). In this example we see Tim attuning participants in The Corner to playfulness. Rączaszek-Leonardi et al. (2018) refer to this as "social physics," where actions and objects become intentional, not through belief systems but as imbued in projects where cultural conventions ordinarily convey behavioural constraints. Tim's legitimising gesture contributes more than a permissiveness to play but perhaps a celebration of play as healing modality for the "frustrated child" in the adult body. Here playfulness reigns, pushing back against both the ordinarily powerful constraints for children in public spaces (such as libraries, galleries and museums) to restrain their ordinarily playful bodies and the constraints on adults to convey rules and limits in such spaces themselves. Objects enable. Spaces permit. People legitimise.

The affordances of The Corner are the dynamic transactions of playfulness.

Final thoughts and implications for practice

The Corner easily achieves what Birch (2018) describes as the "unpackaging" of the adult:child binary via a shift from child as learner to child as "experiencer," through an invitation for all to play. Attention to material agency (agential realism) and dynamic transactions (as affordances) in the design and curatorial elements of museum spaces offer a means to see what emerges in being with entities in The Corner and to offer explanations of the dynamism of transactions – the rhythms, culture and energy.

By being with The Corner, we came to know and feel the playfulness of random acts, the myriad of adventures loose parts have in their lifetimes in The Corner and the support for ethicality and communality in child/adult, artsworker, space, matter actions. We see that The Corner offers what Birch (2018) wondered if children's and adults' museum experiences could have: "embedded playfulness and openness of interpretation" (p. 10), in particular – curatorial playfulness with literacy. And so we invite museum workers to:

- notice what emerges in person and object actions (agential realism);
- examine the dynamic transactions of people and place as affordances (ecological psychology); and
- cultivate spaces where object-child/adult-space-mattering is playful and open through emplaced artsworkers in action in artsworker-curated installations of inviting objects.

Note

1 The themed installation changes every four months and is designed by SLQ Young People and Families Team Leader Stella Read and created by a team of artsworkers, many of whom work in The Corner as artsworkers.

References

Barab, S.A., & Roth, W.M. (2006). Curriculum-based ecosystems: supporting knowing from an ecological perspective. *Educational Researcher*, 35(5), 3–13, doi: 10.3102/0013189X035005003.

Barad, K. (2007). *Meeting the Universe Halfway: Quantum Physics and the Entanglement of Matter and Meaning*. Durham: Duke University Press.

Barad, K. (2010). Quantum entanglements and hauntological relations of inheritance: dis/continuities, spacetime enfoldings, and justice-to-come. *Derrida Today*, *3*(2), 240–268.

Bennett, J. (2010). *Vibrant Matter: A Political Ecology of Things*. Durham, NC: Duke University Press.

Biesta, G. (2007). Education and the democratic person: towards a political conception of democratic education [electronic version]. *Teachers College Record*, *109*, 740–769. Retrieved March 29, 2009, from www.tcrecord.org.

Birch, J. (2018). Museum spaces and experiences for children: ambiguity and uncertainty in defining the space, the child and the experience. *Children's Geographies*, doi: 10.1080/14733285.2018.1447088.

Gibson, E.J., & Pick, A.D. (2000). *An Ecological Approach to Perceptual Learning and Development*. Melbourne: Oxford University Press.

Gibson, J. (1979/1986/2015). *The Ecological Approach to Visual Perception*. New Jersey: Lawrence Erlbaum Associates, Inc.

Heft, H. (2001). *Ecological Psychology in Context: James Gibson, Roger Barker, and the Legacy of William James' Radical Empiricism*. London: Lawrence Erlbaum Associates.

Rączaszek-Leonardi, J., Nomikou, I., Rohlfing, K.T., & Deacon, T.W. (2018). Language development from an ecological perspective: ecologically valid ways to abstract symbols. *Ecological Psychology*, *30*(1), 39–73, doi: 10.1080/10407413.2017.1410387.

The State of Queensland (State Library of Queensland) (2018). Corporate information: our enduring values. Retrieved from www.slq.qld.gov.au/about-us/corporate.

7

FOR THE LOVE OF SMALL STUFF

Materialising theory in an early years artist residency

Lucy Hill and Aisling O'Gorman

Introduction: the residency context

The Ark is Ireland's only dedicated cultural centre for children and the first of its kind in Europe. Opening in 1995 as part of a city centre cultural regeneration project for the Temple Bar area, The Ark embodies a vision for children's right to art as equal citizens. As a cultural centre and arts venue The Ark, unlike other examples given in this book, is not a museum and does not have a permanent collection. However, visual art has always been a core discipline in the programming of the organisation. Within the five levels of the building there is one dedicated gallery space and a large workshop space with north-facing windows designed to support visual art practice. All of the spaces in the building are, however, designed to be adaptable and are used for different art disciplines depending on the programme being presented. As a result, past exhibition-based programmes, as well as workshop programmes, have utilised numerous spaces in the building, not just the gallery area.

The model of The Ark is unusual: a multi-disciplinary organisation producing year-round arts programmes for children aged 2 to 12 across all art forms including visual art, music and theatre as well as dance, film, literature and other cultural areas such as science. The programme includes both participatory work as well as, and often alongside, performance and exhibition programmes. The Ark commissions artists of all disciplines to create work specifically for children as well as producing and curating programmes for this audience.

Originally built for children aged 4 to 14, The Ark's age remit changed to children aged 2 to 12 in 2007 reflecting societal changes. Since this time, Early Years as a developing area of arts practice has become an important concern and area of programming for The Ark. In 2018 The Ark initiated its first Early Years Artist in Residence opportunity via an open call to artists of all disciplines. Visual artist Lucy Hill has been selected for 2018–2019, with a new artist being selected via open call for subsequent years. Lucy's work as part of her residency at The Ark is the subject for discussion in this case study.

The choice by The Ark to set up an Early Years Residency as a year-long opportunity came about in recognition of the growth of both interest and understanding of the importance of beginning a child's relationship with art from the earliest stages. The residency is named in honour of John Coolahan who was a longstanding member of The Ark board and a leading figure in arts education in Ireland. Sadly, John passed away in 2018.

Through its Early Years work since 2007 The Ark has come to understand that art and artistic provision in the Early Years in particular remains a developing area of professional arts practice with and for children. Artists working in this field need longer-term opportunities and specific supports to develop their practice, thinking and experience over a period of time. This is embedded in the residency in the form of travel and training support and the provision of a mentor for the artist. This aims to expand and enrich not only the artist's own practice but also add to the growing body of thoughtful and effective Early Years arts practice generally. As the only organisation of its kind in Ireland, The Ark wishes to use its position to advocate strongly for the importance of this area of work and one of the ways it will signal this over the coming years is through the establishment of this annual Early Years Artist in Residence opportunity.

By strategically focussing on facilitating 2–4 year olds, this residency carries the additional benefit of creating opportunities for developing meaningful connections with accompanying adults, supporting their confidence with art and creativity as they support the very young in their experiences of art programmes at The Ark.

Spinoza, the philosophical base

The residency has comprised a series of monthly materials-led visual art workshops. Lucy's approach of taking materials seriously as the starting point for play and artistry is theoretically informed by Spinozist posthuman philosophy, which offers new possibilities for ethics-centred education practices. At its core is the rationale for re-imagining subjectivity and agency where all body/minds (child/adult, human/non-human, living/non-living, organic/technological) are considered not as equal, but certainly as equally "capable of constituting unique ecological relations irreducible to qualities them in advance" (Snaza et al., 2014: 47). In *The Ethics* (1667, 1996) Spinoza does not privilege humanity but rather considers all entities (living and non-living) as existing in relation (Atkinson, 2018: 41). Enabling the emergence of strategies that foreground materiality rather than "mastery" (Singh 2018) has important implications for pedagogy. Crucially, however, it radically diverts those assumptions and exclusions which enact normative, complexity-reducing notions of childhood (Kennedy, 2006; Murris, 2016).

For this publicly accessed project, where none of the participants are known to the artist in advance, materials are curated with specific openings in mind. Ideas for materials may arise unexpectedly, through previous aesthetic experiences or perhaps reading. Lucy frequently relies on Jane Bennett's concept of thing-power as

> a good starting point for thinking beyond the life-matter binary, the dominant organisational principle of adult experience.
>
> *(Bennett, 2010: 20)*

Thing power becomes activated for adults and children alike through aesthetic attraction to objects in artistic events, where norms can be overridden. In the context of a workshop where the adult to child ratio is an undistracted phone-free one to one, it is possible to explore the intense desirability of tiny things and even to extend their possibilities beyond the potentially forbidden (as too precious, dirty or dangerous maybe). For example, smallness can temporarily become enormity through use of the overhead projector. Singular things can rapidly multiply by creating negative impressions in clay before casting multiple plaster positives. Things can be reimagined through new relational compositions using the children's digital camera. They can move about the room, roll across floors, hide in pockets or escape down plugholes. While attention to multidirectional experimental movement and play is key to opening creative possibilities, it is the aesthetic quality of play itself, as an affective state for both human and non-human, that is foundational:

> Such a view seeks to apprehend a notion of play as existing at least partially outside of the human experience of it and instead understands it as a fundamental force that drives not only the emergence of human culture and history but also of the natural and physical world in which humans find themselves.
>
> *(Shields, 2015: 300)*

"Thing power" in action

Deeply loved small things joined the workshops when children were invited to bring objects from home to create "sun print" cyanotypes on the roof garden during the summer heatwave. The capacity for love of seemingly random (often cheap plastic) things is immensely pleasant to experience in the company of young children. In the Photogram Cyanotype workshop (Figure 7.1) using the light sensitive paper is a fascinating process for adults and children alike, which dates back to the eighteenth century. Objects are selected and composed on the paper and are left in direct sunlight for a few minutes (untouched!) until the pale blue paper turns white. The objects are then removed, the paper is rinsed with water and left to dry again in the sunshine. After a few minutes, an intense cyan blue colour emerges where the paper has been exposed to the light, with the objects creating their own images in white "shadow" areas, which can be exquisitely detailed.

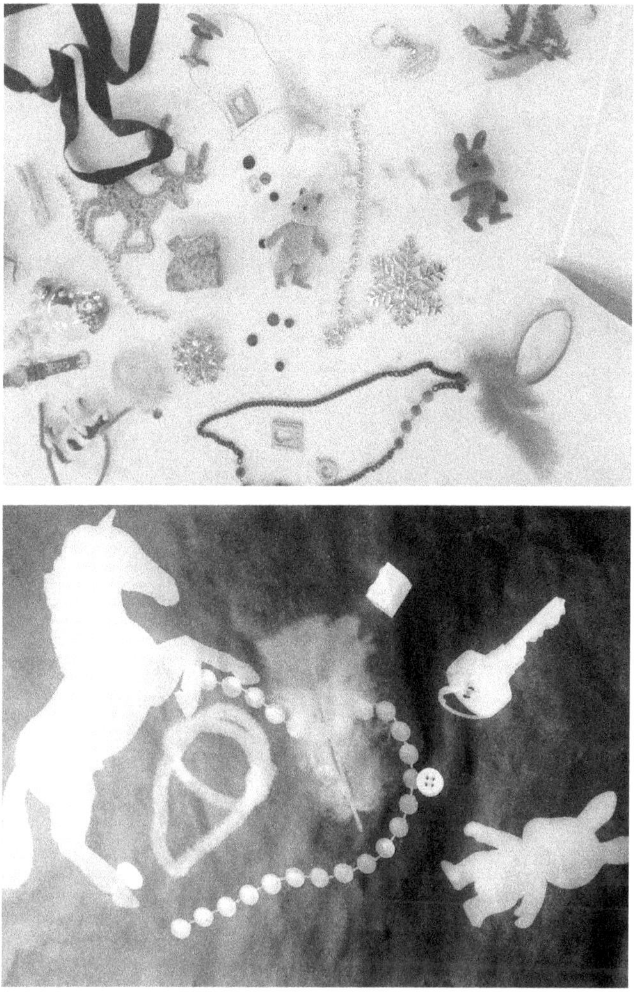

FIGURE 7.1 "Cyanotypes – for the love of small stuff." Photos by Lucy Hill.

For the Bealtaine festival at The Ark, an annual national festival celebrating ageing through the arts, workshops were programmed for children accompanied by an older family member, potentially a grandparent. The influence of this programming on the materials generated a combination that would connect known or expected processes with elements of newness that would be accessible enough to recreate at home (see Figure 7.2). The processes used were painting, collage and making doughs, where the novelty included painting on turnip slices and cabbage leaves (both surfaces accept paint beautifully), making coloured glues, grating chalk into "glitter" using sieves and using other kitchen cupboard materials and tools in new ways. The aesthetic of the presentation was like a buffet, encouraging self-service feasting, allowing the sensual particularities

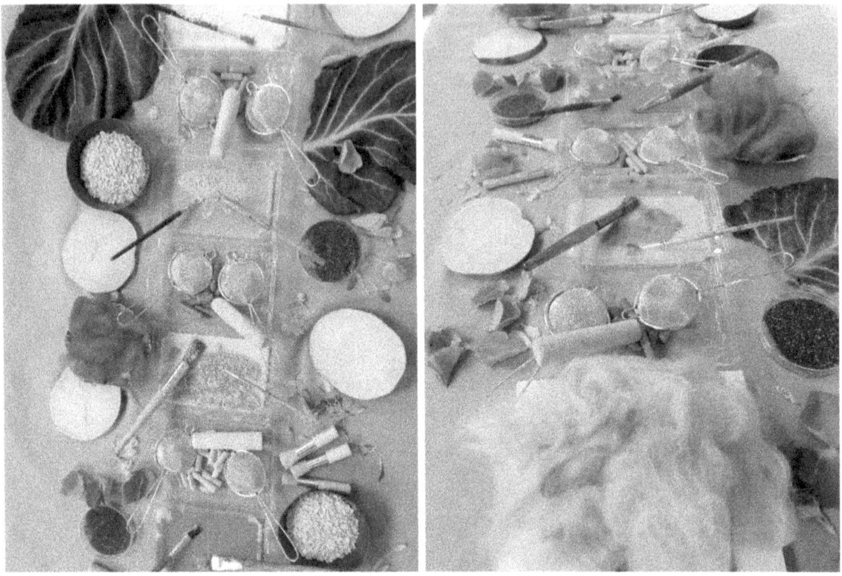

FIGURES 7.2 Seedlings Bealtaine Workshop. Photos by Lucy Hill.

and familiarity of the materials and their ease of access to invite the activity. The presentation played with Bennett's understanding of Nietzsche's writing on the innate potency of food:

> edible matter appears a powerful agent, as stuff that modifies the human matter with which it comes into contact.
>
> *(Bennett, 2010: 44)*

The material agency of food in this case is generated through aesthetic affect rather than consumption and yet is retained as a powerful force for instigating diverse and unexpected actions. In the workshop, different processes were allocated specific zones which helped to clarify their purpose through the tools and material combinations available in each area, however the mixing up of the original organisation was very much welcomed. These materials invite positive contaminations through stirring, pouring and sprinkling to create entirely new concoctions to work with. Materials and tools were given opportunities to surprise, their adaptability and potential for irregular compliance, which may be overlooked in their everyday roles, in this artistic context could be noticed anew and admired.

The materiality of space

Another approach of Lucy's residency is to explore and maximise the capabilities of a single material. Direct engagement with the materiality of the event space is crucial here. Examples can be seen in Figure 7.3 of "The Paperplayground" and in Figure 7.4 "Tangle/Wrap/Knot/Wriggle." The unique materiality of The Ark building itself is unavoidable. The interior wall surfaces are largely of untreated grey concrete, an unusual choice for a children's cultural centre. Yet, the soft pencil-grey surface is also playful, responsive to clammy hands, it darkens in tone with dampness and pressure, transforming points of contact into momentary mono-prints.

The Paperplayground was designed around The Ark theatre space while "Tangle" was designed for the gallery. The theatre space is at the core of the building on the ground floor. It has the wonderful option of converting into an outdoor theatre by opening out onto the market square at the rear of the building. In this instance, however, the monochromatic circular indoor space was used, experimenting with lighting and sound effects, creating a dramatically playful container for our explorations with paper. Lucy prepared for this workshop by making hundreds of different paper forms, such as paper string, pancakes, twists and snowflakes, a speculative alphabet of forms. The aim was for playfulness to open expectations beyond domesticated understandings of the functions of paper toward a wilder, more feral experience of its capabilities or,

> what Deleuze and Guattari called a certain 'vagabond' quality to materiality, a propensity for continuous variation.
>
> *(Bennett, 2010: 50)*

Participants were invited to play with combinations of paper forms, leading to new creations with the help of tools such as tape, scissors, elastic bands, lightboxes and projectors. A Kevin Volans soundtrack enhanced the flow of invention where the children's creations included paper capes, road sweepers, giraffes, robotic arms, treasure maps, circus penguins, giant hats and pencils.

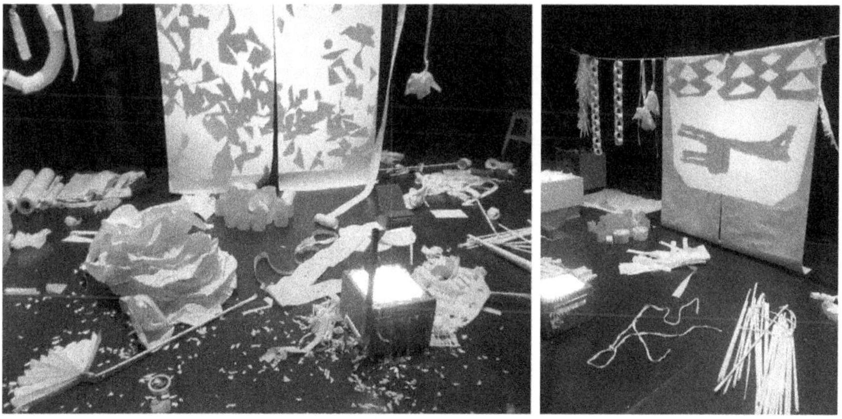

FIGURE 7.3 The Paperplayground. Photos by Lucy Hill.

For "Tangle/Wrap/Knot/Wriggle" (Figures 7.7 and 7.8), the physicality and materiality of the gallery space itself was also conceived as "vital." The material used was strips of reused cotton fabric that we named "string," which were initially rolled into multi-coloured balls by tying different coloured strips together. Small cup hooks and curtain rings were attached to the walls and ceiling in imprecise positions. Beginning with an empty gallery space, the string balls were explored playfully through choosing and sharing, tossing and catching and drawing circles and other shapes with small linear extensions. Gradually, intuitive thinking with string moved us mercurially throughout the space, where it defined boundary areas of islands and became skipping ropes, it encouraged

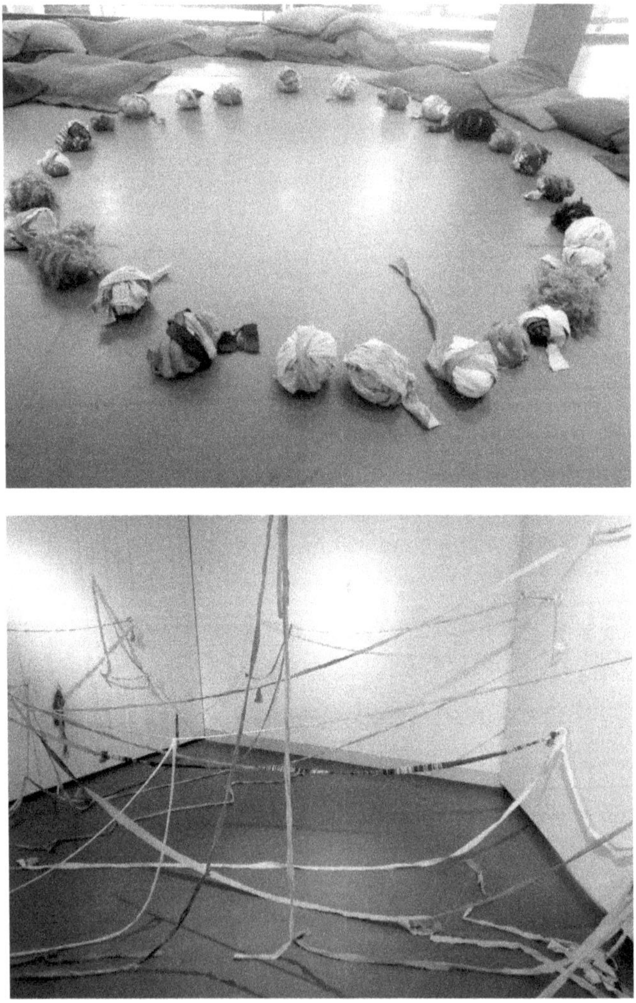

FIGURE 7.4 "Tangle/Wrap/Knot/Wriggle" – before and after. Photos by Lucy Hill.

jumping, crawling and inventing, for example, some adults became pets on leads while other children went "crab fishing" with theirs. Concrete pillars were bandaged lovingly. Attachments were formed with particular balls of string. Representational play also became non-representational and decorative. The string took us into parts of the space we would never have spent time in. At the end, together we had created a whole room tangle, mapping our movements with looping, tying, weaving and wrapping. We sat together to "twang" a piece of string so that the entire gallery space came alive with jumping as if by itself. Children were invited to choose a ball of string to take home while the gallery was untangled in preparation for the next workshop. In designing the workshops, the storylines of the materials are closely considered. The balls of cotton "string" for this workshop were rolled up again for re-use (it is very satisfying to create a huge mess that actually isn't one).

Final thoughts and implications for practice

For each workshop experience, a gentle introduction is inbuilt by way of sitting together, informally chatting and holding materials or sometimes demonstrating their unique capabilities. Here, "demonstrating" means an introduction to the materials' possible "unknowns" by exposing some of their particular properties in advance. This can be helpful, particularly for those materials which transform, or are transformed by others, or that may require a counterintuitive lack of human intervention. For example, in its powder state, plaster of Paris may be used to sprinkle or draw with like flour or chalk, however when mixed with water, its remarkable heat-generating, shape-shifting capabilities become activated. Exposing those "hidden" material properties in advance can engender new realisations and relationships with the materials. The introduction aims to avoid reducing the materials' potential by reverting to or being restricted by prior human experience of other seemingly similar materials.

The novel technicalities of different material combinations can be equally intriguing for both adults and children in the workshop. During the workshops there is a deep reliance on the accompanying adult–child relationship, a reassurance which fundamentally enables the creative activity, and so it feels important to also be inclusive of adult curiosities about materials, which can be piqued by the introduction. For everyone present, the irresistible attraction to the materials themselves becomes a powerfully unifying and cohesive force that can override any language-related barriers that may exist or arise.

Each of the workshops is designed to be repeated monthly, over four iterations (two per day). This repetition offers opportunities to respond to any elements that may be perceived as impeding the "event-ness" of the experience, deepening the understanding that response-ability (Barad, 2007; Haraway, 2016) is a fundamentally ethical attunement in improvisational artistic material engagements. Slime, seaweeds and plastic await our attention in future workshops.

Take home messages:

- Materials are enough.
- Accompanying adults are integral to the ecology of the event.
- Starting with materials dilutes perceived necessities for segregations (by age or ability for example).
- Materials are endlessly open to adapting and so warrant revisiting with new conditions and combinations.

References

Atkinson, D., 2018. *Art, Disobedience, and Ethics: The Adventure of Pedagogy*, 1st edition. Nature America Ltd, New York, NY.

Barad, K.M., 2007. *Meeting the Universe Halfway: Quantum Physics and the Entanglement of Matter and Meaning*. Duke University Press, Durham.

Bennett, J., 2010. *Vibrant Matter: A Political Ecology of Things*. Duke University Press, Durham.

Haraway, D.J., 2016. *Staying with the Trouble: Making Kin in the Chthulucene, Experimental Futures: Technological Lives, Scientific Arts, Anthropological Voices*. Duke University Press, Durham.

Kennedy, D., 2006. *Changing Conceptions of the Child from the Renaissance to Post-Modernity: A Philosophy of Childhood*. Edwin Mellen, New York.

Murris, K., 2016. *The Posthuman Child: Educational Transformation Through Philosophy with Picture Books*. Routledge, Taylor & Francis Group, London; New York, NY.

Singh J, 2018. Unthinking Mastery: Dehumanism and Decolonial Entanglements, Duke University Press, Durham.

Shields, R., 2015. Ludic Ontology : Plays Relationship to Language, Cultural Forms, and Transformative Politics. *Am. J. Play*. 7 (3), 298–321.

Snaza, N., Applebaum, P., Bayne, S., Carlson, D., Morris, M., Rotas, N., Sandlin, J., Wallin, J., Weaver, J., 2014. Toward a Posthumanist Education. *J. Curric. Theor.* 30, 17.

Spinoza, B., 1667, 1996. *The Ethics*. Penguin, London.

8

COMMENTARY ON PART I

On fire

Helen Whitty

This commentary uses fire as its motif to expose the manifold connections between people, technologies, entities, times and places that gives an object its *thing-ness* (Holmes et al., this volume, Chapter 2). Object meaning is expressed through a panoply of relationships and fire is one. This fire is an imp, an entity, an assemblage and a restless form of space (Mol and Law, 1994; Law and Singleton, 2005). It burns into the intermezzo world where things are at once "familiar and strange" (Wallis, this volume, Chapter 3). Fires gather the real, the imaginary, the practical, the poetic. And in their own way so can museums.

Within one socio material spirit museums (and their objects) are conceptualised as existing in a Euclidian space within a regional network. Each museum has a fixed address, a scripted brand and extensive connections into the known world. You know this or that museum even when it's seen in its online guise or in a box. It holds its shape and, so it is believed, its authority. This grip is never loosened within the networks and indeed it is the relations that perform agency (Latour, 2005) even when we are unaware of the performance.

Fire is a starting point to think differently about the agency of objects through their relationships. Children can lead us there. Children are spontaneously physical (a Degas dancer in Cambridge), reverential and dynamic (viewing artworks in Queensland), surprising (wood chips in North Lincolnshire), competent and responsive (The Ark in Ireland), but they do not act alone. On a prosaic level they can't – in a museum they are always accompanied, yet are expert navigators through these associations, pulling in or discarding resources including objects and (as so beautifully described by Hill and O'Gorman) the hidden potential of materials. These groupings are less prey to the *thick* routinised museum space (Sheehy, 2004; Leander et al., 2010) even when adults are trying to keep children "on task." They lean into the *thin* liminal space which can be fluid or fire.

Fluid spaces blend with another or flow around an obstacle. Change is gradual (Law and Mol, 2001). Take this co-constructed exchange about the nature of reality.

> One of the children in the group gasped, "a real horse!" The adults smiled to each other, before trying to explain to the child: "It's not really real, but I know what you mean: it's really a horse and it really is there!"
>
> *(Chapter 3, page 31)*

The fire space on the other hand is sudden and transformative. Fire suggests the creative powers: it has passion and spirit as well as destruction such as "in diverting from the intended purpose and distributing the wood chips more widely than intended around the room" (this volume, page 32). Fire burns as a flickering relationship between presence and absence, the single now and the alterity of multiple absent *others* (Law and Mol, 2001).

> He spoke with excitement – calling out "hot head, hot head" as he clambered across the room. The toddler became distracted by the flashing light of the nearby fire engine light interactive and stopped to push the button a few times before lifting his head again, catching sight of the artwork and calling out, "hot head" … He patted the cabinet and gazed at the work, then exclaimed "hot head" again to the nearby adults.
>
> *(Chapter 5, page 47)*

Fire co-exists and disrupts fixed and fluid spaces. Fire ignites a "dance of agency" between humans and non-humans (Pickering 1993 cited in Griswold et al., 2013: 348) and is where the museum object becomes assertive in its meaning making (Hetherington 1999). In opining in the name of change whether museums are object centred or visitor champions or child focussed we fail to recognise these boundless assemblages. An object is always a subject to be acted upon and indeed the child remains the essentialised child. If "focus on what is produced as they enter into a process of encountering each other that changes both child and thing" (Chapter 2, page 17), exploring meaning through materiality necessitates breaking more than the subject–object divide. It results in the re-formation of relationships, the re-evaluation of the material and (im)material within the Euclidian territory of a museum and closer consideration of the co-existence of fluid and fire spaces. We don't dispense with our solidity but we recognise that upon this rock water flows and fire burns and so we regenerate.

References

Griswold, W., Mangione, G. & McDonnell, T. (2013). Objects, words, and bodies in space: bringing materiality into cultural analysis. *Qualitative Sociology* 36(4): 343–364.

Hetherington, K. (1999). From blindness to bindness: museums, heterogenity and the subject. *In Actor network theory and after.* J. Law and J. Hassard (Eds). United Kingdom: Blackwell Publishers.

Latour, B. (2005). *Reassembling the Social: An Introduction to Actor-Network-Theory.* Oxford: Oxford University Press.

Law, J. and A. Mol. (2001). Situating technoscience: an inquiry into spatialities. *Society and Space* 19: 609–621.

Law, J. and V. Singleton. (2005). Object lessons. *Organization* 12(3): 331–355.

Leander, K., Phillips, N. & Taylor, K. (2010). The changing social spaces of learning: mapping new mobilities. *Review of Research in Education* 34(1): 329–394.

Mol, A. and J. Law (1994). Regions, networks and fluids: anaemia and social topology. *Social Studies of Science* 24(4): 641–671.

Sheehy, M. (2004). Between a think and thin place: changing literacy practices. In *Spatializing Literacy Research and Practice.* K.M. Leander and M. Sheehy (Eds), vol. 15: 91–142. Bern: Peter Lang.

PART II

Museum spaces

9

INTRODUCTION TO PART II

Abigail Hackett, Christina MacRae and Rachel Holmes

This Part starts with the premise that people experience the world through their bodies and these bodies are inseparable from the place in which they are located. Places are not fixed but are constantly changing and in flux. As Ingold writes,

> buildings are part of the world, and the world will not stop still but ceaselessly unfolds along its innumerable paths of growth, decay and regeneration.
>
> *(Ingold, 2013: 48)*

An understanding of the museum as a physical, material, conceptual *place* should be an important starting point for considering the experience of children in museums. Young children experience a museum through their bodies. A notion of the museum as a *place* experienced through a *body* points to the need to attend to what children's bodies do in places, paying attention to what happens beyond words. In particular, movement through and in place is the foremost way children experience museums.

When we talk about place, we are talking first about the museum as a physical building and, as Ingold states above, a physical building is never fixed, set, determined, it is constantly changing, evolving, surprising us, and means different things to different people. In addition, place can be understood beyond the physical building; a museum place is a combination of material things (building, objects, interpretation, facilities and so on) and ideas, discourses, aspirations, assumptions, emotions. There is never one version of museum-as-place; instead, each and every person, including young children and their families, will have different experiences and these experiences will also change over time.

Place has long been understood, within an interdisciplinary literature, as much more than a blank canvas on which human action can unfold. Rather, place shapes experience. Places are lively, animate, they can create different kinds of atmospheres, movements, ideas; what it is possible to think and know in one place is not the same as what it is possible to think and know in a different place. How can this be a starting point for understanding the importance of young children experiencing museum places? As a uniquely different kind of space, museums offer uniquely different forms of experience, thought, action. *What could happen between young children and museum spaces that could not happen anywhere else?*

Museums as places

In museums studies research, how visitors experience the physical spaces in museums has received much less attention compared with how visitors understand concepts and make meanings in exhibitions (Jones and MacLeod, 2016). Similarly, research and practice regarding children in museums often seems to start with words, concepts and social interactions, which, whilst important, have a tendency to imagine space only as a passive backdrop to human-led action. This is unfortunate as, whilst movement, place and knowing through the body are important for everyone, young children can be thought of as particularly spatial, as particularly interested in or open to this kind of experience. A rich literature on children's spatialities indicates the importance of sensory experience, movement and bodily memory in how children experience place (Bartos, 2013; Christensen, 2003; Tuan, 1977). Christensen (2003) describes this difference by arguing that children foreground emplaced knowledge that arises through being in a place, whilst adults tend to rely on both emplaced knowledge and abstract, generalisable spatial knowledge. Emplaced knowledge is not necessarily easy to articulate in words, but rather can be held within the body as "physical know-how" (Rasmussen and Smidt, 2003). Certainly, young children in museums move differently, occupy and experience spaces differently, compared with older children or adults (Hackett, 2016; Kirk and Buckingham, 2018). In museums, children do not just look at the exhibits, they jump on uplighters, climb stairs and move differently in gallery spaces according to size, layout and lighting. How can an appreciation of the importance of place help when considering the unique ways in which museums might be meaningful for young children in particular?

Movement and lines

We cannot think of place without thinking of movement. Movement of the body always happens in relation to place. In addition, place is always in flux, everything is moving and shifting, as the quote by Ingold which opens this chapter indicates. Some of this movement happens slowly, perhaps too slowly for the human eye to observe (Springgay and Truman, 2016), yet that does not mean it is not there. We recently ran a session with a group of Early Years practitioners at the museum. A display case usually filled with taxidermy animals was empty, with a note saying they had been taken for a "spring clean." A member of staff told us the animals had an infestation of insects and had to be frozen to destroy the insects. A timely reminder that there is always more-than-human movement in the museum (even when it is unwelcome!).

Whilst museum ground plans can be useful for adults accompanying young children, young children always experience the museum as an unfolding line of movement, as they walk, run, wander or are carried around the space (Hackett, 2014). For Ingold (2007), place is conceptualised not as dots or circles on a map, but as points where many lines of movement come together. Ingold's notion of wayfaring (2007), which he describes as a combination of moving through and perceiving place, is a theory we have used in our work to describe young children moving through museums as wayfarers (Hackett, 2016; MacRae et al., 2018). These lines of movement always exist within and beyond the museum walls. In fact, Ingold writes that a wayfaring line begins at birth and continues on through life. Movement that occurs in the museum place should, therefore, always be understood in relation to wider knots and lines of movement and wayfaring. Bates' case study in this Part offers a timely reminder of this as she discusses children walking, running, hand holding, singing and travelling with friends to and around the museum and the importance of this in both exploring newness and remembering past experiences. Drawing on the work of Kirk and Buckingham (2018) Bates shows how movement through the museum is related to moments of "lighting up" as young children connect with objects and ideas and begin to make meaning.

This understanding of place as dynamic and shifting is shared by geographers including Massey (2005), who critiques the conflation of space with representations of space, such as maps. Such fixed representations, argues Massey, deprive space of its dynamism and "supresses narrative, stories and trajectories." For example, in drawing a historical journey as a line on a map "a movement is turned into a static line" (p. 108). Instead, Massey understands space and time as intrinsically connected. As anything (human or non-human) makes a journey, time moves on and space continually changes. Thus, similar to Ingold's (2007) notion of wayfaring, Massey (2005) insists a traveller is "a participant in its [space's] continual construction."

A diversity of possibilities for moving seem particularly valuable to children in our research in museums, as well as possibilities for moving in ways that were different to what they had at home (such as big staircases or large rooms). Spaces shape possibilities for movement. For example, open, light spaces offer a possibility for bigger movements, seeming to encourage children to move quickly around, such as running with friends (Hackett et al., 2018). As Vergeront (2002) writes, "Long halls whisper Run!" (p. 8).

Mapping

Christensen (2003) spent much of her ethnographic study of children's experiences of living in cities and villages walking through places with the children.

Drawing on her own memories of childhood, she remembers lying in bed recalling the routes and paths she took during the day around her own local area. Christensen stresses, for children, the significance of "the understanding that emerges from embodied movement through place" (p. 16). The importance of movement for how children remember routes and create "mental maps" (Lynch, 1960) of their world has been noted by researchers looking at how children experience places including kindergartens (Myrstad et al., 2018), museums (Hackett, 2016; Kirk and Buckingham, 2018), housing estates (Horton et al., 2014) and local communities (Rasmussen and Smidt, 2003).

Just as children learn routes round their local neighbourhood (Christensen, 2003), learning their way around the museum is often important for children, particularly when they first visit a new space (Hackett, 2016). Parents, too, want a clear sense of the route, including where they are and are not allowed to go. Children's increasing confidence in and knowledge of museum spaces can be an important influence in how they experience these spaces and the extent to which they feel able to experiment with different ways of being in and playing with place.

Sometimes children's movement in place is conceived as the opposite of learning ("why won't they slow down, focus, concentrate?"). This is why notions such as scoping the joint (Hackett, 2016) and negotiating and navigating (Kirk and Buckingham, 2018) are very important because they show that fast movement is a typical way in which children deeply engage with and learn about new places, including museums. Additionally, although children often tend to talk less when they are moving fast (for example, because adults are following them behind rather than right next to them), notions such as emplaced knowing show that just because children are not talking does not mean deep, meaningful and important engagement is not taking place.

Emplaced knowledge and imagination

As Mackey (2010) points out, early experiences of place shape how children imagine other places. For example, Mackey describes her own childhood memories of "reading from the feet up," drawing on her emplaced knowledge of familiar places in order to imagine places described in books. Malouf describes knowing a first home "from my body outwards" (Malouf, in Mackey, 2010: 328) and Rasmussen and Smidt (2003) have described how the feel and sensations of a neighbourhood become part of children, just as much as children's presence becomes part of a neighbourhood. Embodied experiences of homes, streets or community places act as a starting point, a frame of reference for imagining and experiencing the rest of the world. Familiar places in children's everyday lives therefore have an important role to play in the possibilities for knowing or imagining. What might it mean for a museum to be a part of that familiar constellation of everyday places young children know so well?

What does it mean for a child to know a museum "from the body outwards?" How can we imagine the museum as a space that has a role to play in this bank of embodied knowing or experiencing that young children gather in the early years of their life? When young children first visit a museum, it can seem an unusual, mysterious or unfamiliar space. This is so different from the familiar experience of everyday spaces, such as homes, nurseries and communities in which young children tend to spend most of their time. We have written elsewhere (Hackett et al., 2018) about the importance of offering a combination of both familiar spaces and objects and unfamiliar new experiences for young children and their families visiting museums. The familiar provides confidence and respite, enabling children to encounter, investigate and begin to make sense of the less familiar. Carr et al. (2012) describe this movement between familiar and unfamiliar as boundary crossing, writing "Exploring at a boundary, with one foot in a place of belonging and familiarity and another foot in uncertain terrain, requires courage and curiosity" (p. 56). Clayton and Shuttleworth, in this Part, offer the metaphor of climate and landscape to describe how both ethos, relationships and physical design of museum spaces can come together to create conditions for young children and families to feel relaxed, confident and able to explore the spaces. In this way, encounters with different kinds of spaces, objects, atmospheres, architecture, can play a role in how children are able to imagine new possibilities or different versions of reality.

Spaces within the museum where parents and children can relax, that are clearly child friendly, perhaps familiar in terms of layout or resources, and where parents do not need to be so alert to whether their children's behaviour was safe/compliant with the rules, are important. Beyond a common courtesy (providing spaces that accommodate the basic needs of audiences we might hope to engage), spaces to pause and feel safe do so much more. Hoare and Kelland (this Part, Chapter 11) provide a powerful account of the impact of creating different kinds of spaces at the British Museum, a simple drop-in area, some fabric and soft toys, a rug; families begin to gather, young children begin to shape space, a makeshift buggy park is established by parents at one side, something is changing. For Hoare and Kelland, there is a balance to be created in these spaces between "'This is just what I expected to do in a museum' and moments of 'I never imagined we could do this in a museum!'."

The mundane

Whilst Schorch (2013) has shown that the architecture of the museum and the concepts (adult) visitors remember from a visit are very much intertwined, architectural features seem to have a particular significance for young children. Examples that frequently occur in research on young children in museums include children's interest in going up and down stairs, in operating automatic doors or buttons that made doors swing open, in moving through, up and down long narrow corridors, running or lying on the floor in wide open spaces and in crossing "thresholds" in the museum, for example through doorways or where the flooring changed (Birch, 2018; Hackett et al., 2018). For example,

Noble and Wallis' chapter in this Part provides a fine-grained analysis of children's experience of a revolving door at Fitzwilliam Museum. They describe the urgency with which children were determined to experience the character and feel of this door with their bodies. Drawing on Malaguzzi, they advocate for "leaving room" in order to take notice of these seemingly small incidents, these "critical moments" that could so easily be overlooked.

Mundane aspects of space are discussed by several case study contributors in this part of the book. For example, Cooke's case study in this section describes the significance of the sweeping staircase at Sewerby Hall in her research with young children. Features of the hall, such as the staircase and the polished wooden floors, seemed to exist somewhere between familiarity (children often encounter staircases and floors) and extraordinary (because of the scale, design and feel of these features in a stately home). With growing confidence and familiarity, the children wondered and experimented with their bodies to explore; what can this space do? What can I do in this space? What can I and this space do together? Children can play in and with spaces and their bodies, generating new possibilities and embodied ways of knowing the museum space. The space is not a blank canvas or an inanimate backdrop to this play, it has an important role to play in shaping what happens, in opening up or closing down possibilities for bodies and experience. Viewed from this point of view, it is not surprising that seemingly mundane aspects of museum architecture come up repeatedly in research on children in museums.

Being entangled with place

Across an inter-disciplinary literature there is an increasing recognition that humans are never separate from place. The boundaries we imagine between a human body and the rest of the world – a layer of impermeable skin and a brain locked safely away from harm inside a skull – are just that, imaginary. Instead, bodies of humans and non-humans are leaky, porous; we take in experiences, ideas, feelings and physical substances and, simultaneously, all these things leak out of us. This leakiness, writes Ingold (2013), is essential to the ongoingness of life; everything must leak (e.g., breath, metabolise, decompose) in order to carry on.

As people and place leak into each other, place can be viewed as lively, dynamic, part of the action. This is what we are alluding to when we describe children and place as playing together (Procter and Hackett, 2017). A child is not a bounded thing *in* a museum space, *acting on* a museum space; rather, in this scenario, child and place and so many other things (other people, objects, ideas, feelings) are tangled up together, making something new. This is entanglement in the museum.

Children make place

Ingold describes the entanglement between people and place as a meshwork, through which we "make our way through a world-in-formation rather than across its preformed surface" (2008: 1802). Ingold likens this entanglement to weaving. "A world that is inhabited is woven from the strands of [things] continually coming-into-being" (2008: 1797). Thus, for Ingold, being in and moving through the world is "place-making" (2007: 101), that is, we – adults and children – play a role in shaping the world as it continually comes into being.

The concept of place-making highlights the agency of children and their moving bodies to shape place (Myrstad et al., 2018). Describing a walk with two young girls down to a river, Somerville (2015) describes how "a different configuration of time and space" was created by walking with the girls. As a dip in the path led to the girls wanting to make mud sculptures, or as the children stopped to pick up each stone scattered along the path to the river, Somerville realised "the spaces and places of our walk are shaped by their stoppings." In these examples, children's entanglement with things and places lies at the heart of what places mean to children and how children shape places. Young children's paths of movement through the museum shape place in particular ways, foregrounding and highlighting some aspects of experience and connecting parts of the social and material together (Hackett, 2016). When children foreground mundane aspects of a museum space ("why won't they look in the glass case? All they seem to want to do is jump on the uplighters in the floor!"), it is powerful because these movements, these actions, recreate the museum anew, they make a new form of museum place.

Disrupting assumptions; places for children, children's places

Rasmussen (2004) wrote about the distinction between places for children (assigned by adults for children) and children's places, places that children themselves find meaningful or significant. As adults, as museum professionals, as researchers, we might have ideas already about what museum spaces are like, or are for. The key message about place is that it is always multiple; there is never only one way of understanding, experiencing, or playing in place (Hackett et al., 2018). Different conceptualisations of place reveal the imposition of one person's line, or map, or way of seeing the world, over another, for example, adults' views of the world imposed over those of children (Christensen, 2003; Hackett and Yamada-Rice, 2015), or Western conceptualisations of the world imposed over indigenous ways of knowing (Ingold, 2007). If adult-designated places for children are different from children's own perspectives about how places can become meaningful to them, it is important to attend to the power differentials at play here and to ensure that children's own experiences and modes of engaging do not become marginalised within the debate.

When we accept that children make place (as we have described above), this theory disrupts assumptions about the way in which children have been placed (Fog Olwin and Gullov, 2003) or categorised within the world. Understanding place as being created through movement and entanglement, and valuing forms of embodied knowledge that might emerge as a result of this, means understanding all people, including children, as participants in the emergence of the world. In this way, perhaps by attending to what happens between children and place in the museum, might enable us to attune to "something more, uncontrollable, indescribable, in excess, something we can taste yet always beyond whatever we might know, perceive, or ever hope to imagine" (Holmes and Jones, 2013: 358).

Concluding thoughts: beyond rationality

Sometimes, museum visits with young children can be dominated by a seemingly urgent and irresistible need to run through the many corridors and interconnecting rooms in the building. This is the sort of behaviour that seems deeply important to the children, whilst defying adult explanation. For example, if we were to ask "why do you like to run through the museum?" – an answer would be unlikely to be forthcoming. Perhaps there is no rational or objective "purpose"; something else seems to be going on here (MacRae et al., 2018).

The search for a rational explanation, or for intentionality in these scenarios, comes from an assumption that thoughts exist first in the mind, then are actioned by the body. In other words, this thinking assumes a sharp division between body and mind. Sheets-Johnstone (1981) makes a distinction between thinking *through* movement and thoughts *about* movement. Thoughts about movement might be along the lines of "what if I raise my leg up here?" However, thinking in movement is thinking that begins in the body and emerges through the body's exploration of its possibilities for moving, being and sensing. This kind of thinking takes place in the moment, in the movement, and between the body and its experience of place.

Paying attention to and valuing things such as children running down corridors, their fascination with a revolving door or their insistence of rolling around on a polished wooden floor, is radical and political. This is because in attending to these things, rather than dismissing them as irrelevant (or unfortunate), we are recognising children as people. Starting with how children experience place through their bodies, as a meaningful and important part of museum visiting in its own right, rejects rational, developmental explanations of children in museums (MacRae et al., 2018). In short, children are not just learners (Kirk and Buckingham, 2018), they are not developmental projects, and the value of young children being in museums exists far in excess of "an activity whose purpose is to deliver children with the desired characteristics" (Clarke, 2006: 717).

References

Bartos, A. (2013) Children sensing place. *Emotion, Space and Society*, 9, 89–98.

Birch, J. (2018) Museum spaces and experiences for children: ambiguity and uncertainty in defining the space, the child and the experience. *Children's Geographies*, 16 (5), 516–528.

Carr, M., Clarkin-Phillips, J., Beer, A., Thomas, R., and Waitai, M. (2012) Young children developing meaning-making practices in a museum: the role of boundary objects. *Museum Management and Curatorship*, 27 (1), 53–56.

Christensen, P. (2003) Place, space and knowledge: children in the village and the city. In Christensen, P. and O'Brien, M. (Eds) *Children in the City. Home, Neighborhood and Community*, London: Routledge, pp. 13–28.

Clarke, K. (2006) Childhood, parenting and early intervention: a critical examination of the Sure Start national programme. *Critical Social Policy*, 26, 699.

Fog Olwin, K. and Gullov, E. (2003) Towards an anthropology of children and place. In Fog Olwin, K. and Gullov, E. (Eds) *Children's Places. Cross-Cultural Perspectives*. New York: Routledge, pp. 1–19.

Hackett, A. (2014) Zigging and zooming all over the place: young children's meaning making and moving in the museum. *Journal of Early Childhood Literacy*, 14 (1), 5–27.

Hackett, A. (2016) Young children as wayfarers: learning about place by moving through it. *Children and Society*, 30, 169–179.

Hackett, A., Procter, L., and Kummerfeld, R. (2018) Exploring abstract, physical, social and embodied space: developing an approach for analysing museum spaces for young children. *Children's Geographies*, 16 (5), 489–502.

Hackett, A. and Yamada-Rice, D. (2015) Producing visual records of movement: making meaning of young children's interactions with place. In Stirling, E. and Yamada-Rice, D. (Eds) *Visual Methods with Children and Young People. Academics and Visual Industries in Dialogue*, London: Palgrave Macmillan, pp. 29–49.

Holmes, R. and Jones, L. (2013) Flesh, wax, horse skin, and hair: the many intensities of data. *Cultural Studies ↔ Critical Methodologies*, 13 (4), 357–372.

Horton, J., Christensen, P., Kraftl, P., and Hadfield-Hill, S. (2014) 'Walking … just walking': how children and young people's everyday pedestrian practices matter. *Social & Cultural Geography*, 15 (1), 94–115.

Ingold, T. (2007) *Lines. A Brief History*. London: Routledge.

Ingold, T. (2008) Bindings against boundaries: entanglement of life in an open world. *Environment and Planning*, 40, 1796–1810.

Ingold, T. (2013) *Making. Anthropology, Archaeology, Art and Architecture*. London: Routledge.

Jones, P. and MacLeod, S. (2016) Museum architecture matters. *Museums and Society*, 14 (1), 207–219.

Kirk, E. and Buckingham, W. (2018) *Snapshots of Museum Experience: Understanding Child Visitors Through Photography*. London: Routledge.

Lynch, K. (1960) *The Image of the City*. Cambridge, MA: MIT Press.

Mackey, M. (2010) Reading from the feet up: the local work of literacy. *Children's Literature in Education: An International Quarterly*, 41 (4), 323–339.

MacRae, C., Hackett, A., Holmes, R., and Jones, L. (2018) Vibrancy, repetition, movement: posthuman theories for reconceptualising young children in museums. *Children's Geographies*, 16 (5), 503–515.

Massey, D. (2005) *For Space*. London: Sage.

Myrstad, A., Sverdrup, T. and Helgesen, M. (2018) *Barn skaper sted – sted skaper barn. (Children create place – place creates children)*. Bergen: Fagbokforlaget.

Procter, L. and Hackett, A. (2017) Playing with place in early childhood: an analysis of emotion, agency and materiality in children's 'dark' play. *Contemporary Issues in Early Childhood*, *18* (2), 213–226.

Rasmussen, K. (2004) Places for children. Children's places. *Childhood*, 11, 155.

Rasmussen, K. and Smidt, S. (2003) Children in the neighborhood: the neighborhood in the children. In P. Christensen and M. O'Brien (Eds) *Children in the City. Home, Neighborhood and Community*, London: Routledge, pp. 82–100.

Schorch, P. (2013) The experience of a museum space. *Museum Management and Curatorship*, 28 (2), 193–208.

Sheets-Johnstone, M. (1981) Thinking in Movement, *The Journal of Aesthetics and Art Criticism* 39 (4): 399–407.

Somerville, M. (2015) Emergent literacies in 'the land of do anything you want'. In Somerville, M. and Green, M. (Eds) *Children, Place and Sustainability*. Melbourne: Palgrave, pp. 106–125.

Springgay, S. and Truman, S. (2016) Stone walks: inhuman animacies and queer archives of feeling. *Discourse: Studies in the Cultural Politics of Education*, 38 (6), 851–863.

Tuan, Y.-F. (1977) *Space and Place: the Perspective of Experience*. Minneapolis, MN: University of Minnesota Press.

Vergeront, J. (2002) Shaping spaces for learners and learning. *Journal of Museum Education*, 27 (1), 8–13.

10

LEAVING ROOM FOR LEARNING

University of Cambridge Museums' nursery in residence

Kate Noble and Nicola Wallis

In October 2017, nine children from a Cambridge city nursery spent five consecutive mornings "in residence" at the Fitzwilliam Museum (FM) and Cambridge University Botanic Garden (CUBG). The residency formed the basis of a multi-disciplinary action research project led by a team of museum, garden and nursery practitioners. This exploratory project gave us the opportunity to, "stand aside for a while and leave room for learning, observe what children do" in the hope that "if you have understood it well, perhaps teaching will be different from before" (Malaguzzi 1992: 82). This experience helped us to better understand what the museum and garden spaces offer to young learners. This case study describes the approach that we took and shares some of our findings.

Introducing the project partners

In the last ten years the Fitzwilliam Museum and CUBG have developed programmes specifically targeted at children under five years old and both sites offer opportunities to groups who may not routinely access their public programmes. These include preschools, nurseries, our local children's hospice (EACH) and Children's Centres in targeted locations in Cambridge. As this was a collaborative project, it was important that all the practitioners involved had a shared pedagogical approach and so we approached a local nursery school that had been bringing groups of children to the Fitzwilliam Museum for a number of years. The nursery is run as a parent co-operative and the community of parents, teachers and children encourage individual development within a context of co-operation, mutual responsibility and respect. The practitioners at the FM and CUBG also had experience of planning and running sessions together as part of their main public programme and during University of Cambridge Public Engagement Events. Both venues contain rich and varied collections for the young children to take inspiration from and offer a wide variety of different types of spaces for children to explore. The Fitzwilliam Museum collections come from all over the world and the galleries contain paintings, drawings, coins, armour, ceramics, textiles, musical instruments, sculpture and artefacts from Ancient Egypt, Greece, Rome, Africa and Asia. The CUBG is one of the largest University-owned botanic gardens in the world and offers 40 acres of garden to investigate with an unparalleled living collection of over 8,000 species housed in glasshouses and experimental plots. Both venues have a learning studio which served as our base on the days we visited.

Why did we develop the residency?

Although both sites have well-established Early Years programmes, the nursery residency provided the opportunity to create a rich and meaningful experience of extended engagement for the children involved. The project was inspired by "My Primary School is at the Museum" (Kings College London, 2017), which tested the benefits of co-locating primary and nursery school classes for extended periods of time within a museum. DeWitt et al. (2018) analysed evaluation data gathered from two of the partnerships within the project and found increased confidence in the children over the course of the residency and practitioners and parents reporting positive developments in the children's communication skills. They also found that the museums involved developed a deeper understanding of younger audiences, which in turn enabled the design of more relevant and engaging programmes. The project and resulting research drew attention to the fact that extended cultural residencies are a new way of engaging children with cultural spaces and that there is currently a lack of previous studies on which to build. Much of the research on the experiences of children under five in similar spaces has focussed on children's museums or science museums rather than art, history or botanical collections (Munley, 2012) and so we identified a need to develop work in this area. We were interested in observing the learning and play that takes place in museums and gardens and exploring the differences and similarities between the outdoor and indoor spaces. We also hoped that the residency would help better understand the intersection between arts- and science-based creative learning and problem solving within the UCM consortium.

Action research and practitioner as researcher

Our project adds a unique perspective as a piece of action research. As practitioners, we hope to give a fine-grained insight into the experience of the residency, through our own critical perspectives as well as through reflective observations of the individual children and the group as a learning community. Our research was influenced by the work of Pringle (2018), Pascal and Bertram (2012), Oliveira-Formosinho and Formosinho (2012), Barker and Weller (2003) and is based on the principles of praxeological action research and a cycle of planning–action–observation–reflection. Rather than seeing this in terms of traditional action research, which focusses on self-reflection and how to evolve our own personal practice, praxeology requires a focus on and a commitment to learning together as a community. It was important that we enabled equal and democratic relationships to form through the research process and that the findings and resulting developments to practice were made with shared outcomes in mind. In keeping with our theoretical standpoint, we aimed to ensure that spoken, written, drawn and embodied interpretations and contributions from adults and from children were all valued equally.

How did we document the project?

We collected a wide variety of different types of data in order to capture some of the richness and detail of the interactions and conversations which took place during the residency and to enable the qualitative analysis of the participant and practitioner experiences (see Table 10.1). We used this data to compile a series of detailed case studies exploring individual themes which we developed and reflected upon through the careful analysis of the data. We then wrote a project report[1] reviewing existing research in this area, explaining our approach and containing a selection of key case studies. The report enabled us to share and reflect on what we observed and to consider implications for future practice.

We collected far more data than we had time to analyse in depth. However, the time we spent reviewing our field notes, the project journals and watching

TABLE 10.1 Data collection chart.

	Pre-project	*During project*	*After project*		
			+1 day	*+2 weeks*	*+3 months*
All practitioners	Pre-project questionnaires	Structured field notes	Post-project questionnaires	Follow up interviews & questionnaires	
Museum/garden practitioners	Nursery visit field notes	Video and audio recordings/photography			Nursery visit field notes
Children		Children's journals			Children's photograph choices
Nursery practitioners		Project journal & blog posts		Project journal	Project journal

the videos enabled us to see afresh little moments and interactions which otherwise would have been missed. These moments might initially appear too mundane or inconsequential to pay attention to (Millei and Rautio, 2017: 246) but they have the possibility to reveal something which is usually hidden or overlooked, something potentially new and important. This case study explores an interaction which on first appearance seems rather every-day and ordinary. On reviewing the video footage, this episode challenged us as practitioners and made us feel uneasy. What we saw didn't match what we thought we were doing. In this way, it could also be described as what MacRae et al (2018: 1) call "sticky" data, something which "stands out, sticks to and often gets stuck in our thoughts, feelings, in our throat." It may also be that our evaluation of museum learning programmes is so often focussed on finding evidence of the positive impact of a museum visit, that we are in danger of deliberately overlooking these kinds of interaction. We were interested to interrogate our preconceptions and look at what the episode revealed about our understanding of the needs and interests of young children in our museum.

The revolving door: the conflict between freedom and control

It is Day 3 of the residency and the second visit to the museum. The group has spent around 40 minutes in the galleries and is in the process of moving back to the Education Studio for a snack break. They travel through the main entrance to the museum, which leads to an outside portico via a large circular revolving door. Jo, Alanna and Barney stand in one of the door's compartments and look up at Museum Educator 2 (ME2).

ME2: (points to the edges of the door) It's got these finger-trappers and is really heavy so it's a bit tricky. Look somebody's coming in! Let's go to the side because this lady's going to show us how the door works. She'll be very surprised to see all us waiting here, won't she!

ME2 moves backwards, taking Jo by the hand, and the other children all move back from the door too.

ME2: Let's come over here so she can get in … Here she comes! Lucky lady! She's got a welcoming committee!

The adults smile and the three children now move to stand just inside the door in a long row, watching silently and waiting for the visitor to arrive. The visitor pushes on the door and enters, Nursery Practitioner 3 (NP3): It moves!

GARDEN EDUCATOR 2 (GE2): It spins around!

ME2 explains that this is the way in for people who visit the museum. Jo gets back into the door and pulls on the handle.

ME2: You have to be very strong.

Another visitor approaches who wants to leave the museum. She stands to one side while Jo is experimenting with the door.

ME2: Someone wants to go out (takes Jo's hand to bring her out of the doorway). Sorry, are you trying to get out?
VISITOR (SMILING): I'm alright. [To the children] Shall I show you?
ME2: Would you like to see the door work?

The visitor pushes the door very slowly and the children watch it move and spin. The woman waves to them through the glass as she leaves. Another visitor follows after her and the children continue to watch. ME2 crouches near the children to explain how part of the door is always shut to keep out bugs that are not allowed in the museum.

CHARLIE: Is fishes allowed in the museum?
ME2: Only the pretend kind. (Brushing the floor tiles with her fingers) Have you seen this floor is made out of little bits?

Jo has made her way back into the revolving door and begins to push it round to return back to where she started. NP2 quickly follows her in. One by one, all the children take a turn moving the door around.

This case study represents a significant learning moment for us as museum practitioners. Having worked in the Fitzwilliam Museum for many years, we know that groups are not permitted to use the revolving door for reasons of safety but also due to the practicalities of working with large groups. Although she doesn't explicitly say that the children can't use the door, ME2 tries a number of different verbal and non-verbal strategies to keep the children away from the door, which include moving them back, suggesting that they watch other visitors use it and finally trying to distract them by pointing to the mosaic floor. The Garden and Nursery Practitioners look to the Museum Practitioner for guidance and follow her lead as she is in the role of "expert" within this setting. The children remain silent throughout this encounter, standing back and observing. The children are discouraged from using the door, then are asked to stand back and watch adult visitors passing freely through it. The physical weight, size and presence of the door are powerful – which the adults try to communicate to the children with their verbal descriptions (*it moves, it spins, you have to be strong*). However, the children know that they will only understand the door as object by interacting with it and experiencing it first hand and so, despite the tacit warnings from the Museum Practitioner, Jo steps back into the door and finally succeeds in moving it round. Although her initial attempts to use the door were thwarted she still perseveres – drawn in by the power of the object.

This example highlights some of the contradictions and challenges with regards to the amount of freedom and control we allow children within our spaces. Rather than a blanket "no," it was possible to find a way to use the door safely and not to cause a problem for other visitors. To think in new ways, we needed input from those with more diverse experiences and from those who have a different and more embodied response to these spaces. Young children can offer us new perspectives on our spaces and objects so that we can re-see what is familiar. The physical, embodied experience of being in museums for young children has been examined by Hackett (2016), Piscitelli and Penfold (2015) and was a key aspect of Dockett et al.'s (2011) study on co-designing a museum space with young children. The relationship between the messages that educators give children verbally about freedom and exploration, however, are sometimes at odds with the ways in which we seek to control their bodies in spaces which we understand as carrying an element of risk.

Final thoughts and implications for practice

Our research revealed how children made sense of the different spaces they encountered and that this knowledge was constructed in a multitude of ways. Children's meaning making is both active and multimodal, "both in the things they use, the objects they make; and in their engagement of their bodies: there is no separation of body and mind" (Kress, 1997: 97). MacRae et al. (2018: 11) argue that a large part of the value of visiting museums with children is in allowing the possibilities for becoming "entangled with different and unique kinds of objects, spaces, sensations, architectures." The residency project enabled us to spend time with a small group of children and to record and reflect upon the variety of different types of "entanglements," responses and interactions which took place within our spaces.

The data we collected contained numerous examples of embodied, non-verbal responses where the children used their bodies, feet and hands – stamping, rolling, splashing, running, climbing, sculpting, prodding, wiping, twisting, swirling and drawing. Not all of these actions are encouraged in the formal settings of a museum and botanic garden and so this project helped us to find the space and the time to "stand aside for a while" and allow this to happen. These findings demonstrate a need to make use of detailed empirical research of this kind to both highlight and acknowledge our blind spots as museum practitioners.

The revolving door incident can be described as what Albon and Rosen (2014) term a "critical moment" in our research, where we were forced to reconsider what we had previously taken for granted. The project has exposed some of our preconceptions, our prejudices and habitual ways of working, which can now be questioned and improved. It also highlighted to us how children can receive contradictory messages from us about the environments to which we introduce them. It is useful for us to acknowledge the inherent tensions between the adult's desire to teach, to shape and to control and the young child's need for the freedom to explore with their whole being, body and mind. As museum educators it is important that we consider how we might support and enable this process. The Nursery Residency has highlighted the benefits of enabling practitioners to stand back and take time to carefully observe and reflect. In so doing, we have a unique opportunity to learn from and alongside the young children we work with. Yet we must also be brave and embrace those moments which feel uncomfortable or difficult in order that we better understand the extraordinary potential of museum spaces for young children.

Note

1 www.fitzmuseum.cam.ac.uk/university-cambridge-museums-nursery-residence.

References

Albon, D. and Rosen, R. (2014) *Negotiating Adult-Child Relationships in Early Childhood Research*, London: Routledge.

Barker, J. and Weller, S. (2003) Is it fun? Developing children centred research methods. *International Journal of Sociology and Social Policy*, 23 (112), 33–58.

DeWitt, J., King, H., Wright, D., and Measures, K. (2018) The potential of extended cultural residencies for young children in museums. *Management and Curatorship*, 33 (2), 158–177.

Dockett, S., Main, S., and Kelly, L. (2011) Consulting young children: experiences from a museum. *Visitor Studies*, 14 (1), 13–33.

Hackett, A. (2016) Young children as wayfarers: learning about place by moving through it. *Children and Society*, 30 (3), 169–179.

Kings College London (2017) *My Primary School is at the Museum* [online] [accessed on 13 December 2018], http://myschoolatthemuseum.site.

Kress, G. (1997) *Before Writing: Rethinking the Paths to Literacy*, London: Routledge.

MacRae, C., Hackett, A., Holmes, R., and Jones, L (2018) Vibrancy, repetition and movement: posthuman theories for reconceptualising young children in museums. *Children's Geographies*, 16 (5), 503–515, [online] [accessed on 13 December 2018], https://e-space.mmu.ac.uk/619417/8/Vibrancy%20repetition%20and%20movement%20posthuman%20theories%20for%20reconceptualising%20young%20children%20in%20museums.pdf.

Malaguzzi, L. (1992) History, ideas and basic philosophy: an interview with Lella Gandini. In Edwards, C., Gandini, L., and Forman, G. (Eds) (1998) *The Hundred Languages of Children: The Reggio Emilia Approach: Advanced Reflections*. Greenwich: Ablex, pp. 49–97.

Munley, M. (2012) *Early Learning in Museums: A Review of the Literature*, Chicago: MEM and Associates.

Oliveira-Formosinho, J. and Formosinho, J. (2012) *Pedagogy-in-Participation: Childhood Association Educational Perspective. Porto: Porto Editora*, [online] [accessed on 13 December 2018], www.researchgate.net/publication/281094984_Pedagogy-in-Participation_Childhood_Association_Educational_Perspective.

Pascal, C. and Bertram, T. (2012) Praxis, ethics and power: developing praxeology as a participatory paradigm for early childhood research, *European Early Childhood Research Journal*, 20 (4), 477–492.

Piscitelli, B. and Penfold, L. (2015) Child-centred practice in museums: experiential learning through creative play at the Ipswich Art Gallery. *Curator: The Museum Journal*, 58 (3), 263–280.

Pringle, E. (2018) *Practitioner Research in the Art Museum* [online] [accessed on 13 December 2018], https://practitionerresearchintheartmuseum.com.

Wallis, N. and Noble, K. (2018) *UCM Nursery in Residence Project, End of Project Report* [online] [accessed on 13 December 2018], www.museums.cam.ac.uk/system/files/ucm_nursery_in_residence_report.pdf.

Zsuzsa Millei & Pauliina Rautio (2017) 'Overspills' of research with children: an argument for slow research, Children's Geographies, 15:4, 466–477, DOI: 10.1080/14733285.2016.1277182

11

THE SOUND OF LITTLE FEET AT THE BRITISH MUSEUM

Katharine Hoare and Kate Kelland

The British Museum is an iconic space housing objects from across time and around the world. As part of the public programme the Schools and Young Audiences Team run under-5s provision using different spaces and objects as inspiration for activities which encourage participation, exploration and enjoyment. In this chapter we discuss how this programme, known as Little Feet, developed and the type of activities offered to our young learners aged 6 weeks to 4 years old. We consider the opportunities and challenges of running a programme for under 5s in a large public building, dating from the Victorian era to the present day, full of diverse spaces (including over 50 galleries, a central atrium space and a modern learning centre) and filled with objects chosen to represent a myriad of historical and contemporary cultures.

The British Museum and under 5s

The British Museum's collection spans two million years of human history and culture including world-famous objects such as the Rosetta Stone, Parthenon sculptures and Egyptian mummies alongside less well known but equally important artefacts. Founded in 1753, visitor numbers have grown from around 5,000 a year in the eighteenth century to over 6 million today. Children were allowed to visit from 1850 although "babes in arms" had to wait until 1879. Nowadays, the Museum welcomes all children; in the company of teachers on school trips or as members of a family/care giver group. Our development plan aimed to extend the existing family offer to encompass under 5s and their accompanying adults, thereby raising the profile of the Museum, internally and externally, as a place for under 5s.

The starting point for Little Feet was the diverse and inspiring spaces of the Museum, which include over 50 galleries, the central Great Court and a learning centre with seminar rooms (including an art room) and lecture theatres with accompanying foyers. Each space offers a unique sensory experience with varied light levels, acoustics, air flow/temperature, route ways and style of object display. A key consideration during development was testing the ways in which under 5s experienced and used each space, and trialling activities which would best support their exploration of a particular area. For example, it is often assumed that a gallery full of glass display cases does not lend itself to young learners. However, one of the most successful spaces is the Enlightenment Gallery (Room 1) where the wall cases start at floor level, making them ideal for a small child or crawling toddler to see objects without having to be lifted up (Figure 11.1). This allows children to scan and self-select what they want to look at. An added bonus is that we never have to say don't touch and the adults never have to worry about objects being damaged. If we want textures to feel, or objects to touch, we simply bring them with us. Little Feet is shaped by the Museum building and the objects on display. Using the Museum as the context positioned the programme within the heritage learning landscape and encouraged our young visitors to develop a sense of place.

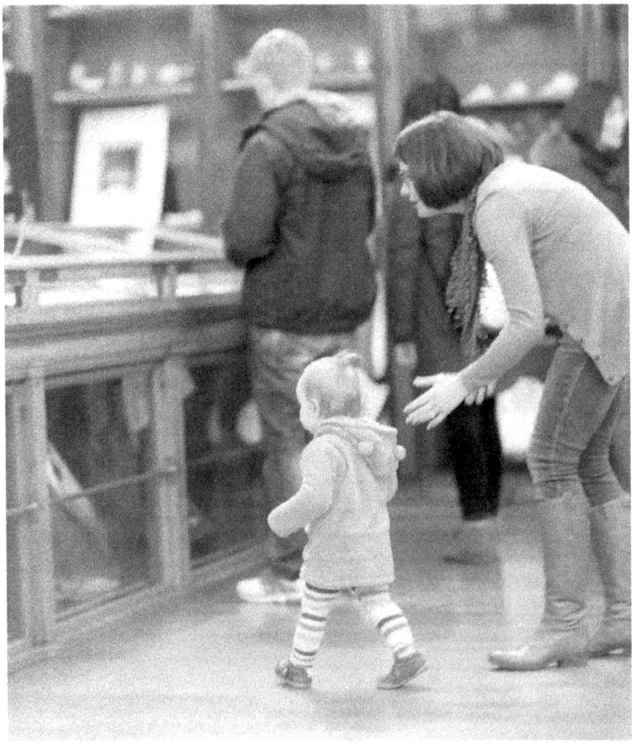

FIGURE 11.1 Space to move and easy-to-see objects support independent exploration.

How did we get going?

Our start-up phase explored what under 5s provision in the Museum might look like and how we could best deliver it. We wanted to test out some simple models in order to consider the potential audience, the opportunities to use museum spaces to help children make meaning and the best resources and session logistics (i.e., time of day and length of session). To evaluate this stage of the development we followed a grounded theory approach – develop and deliver an activity, observe what happens with no expectation of outcomes, and then use this observation to reflect on successes and future development.

We began by using our existing family programming infrastructure to create a supervised, but unfacilitated, under 5s drop-in area during holiday activities in the Great Court (Figures 11.2 and 11.3). Sessions were hosted within the surrounding programming and it did not matter if one, ten or fifty under 5s turned up. In effect it was fail-safe. The sessions were deliberately light touch and were used by families with a mixture of ages in their group. For example, during a family event about Ice Age art we set up an area entitled "Baby Tundra," with large pieces of white and silver fabric, some hand-cut paper snowflakes, soft toy woolly mammoths and hand-held jingle bells.

This gave us a chance to see how adults and children responded to the types of resources on offer. It also enabled us to have conversations with the adults; asking them what they liked to do in an under 5s session, where they found out about such provision and how often they used it. Older children enjoyed using the resources to re-create real life. For example, one child used the fabric to put the mammoths to bed. Younger children enjoyed experimenting – feeling the different resources (with hands and mouths), moving things through the air (especially the light fabric), creating noise

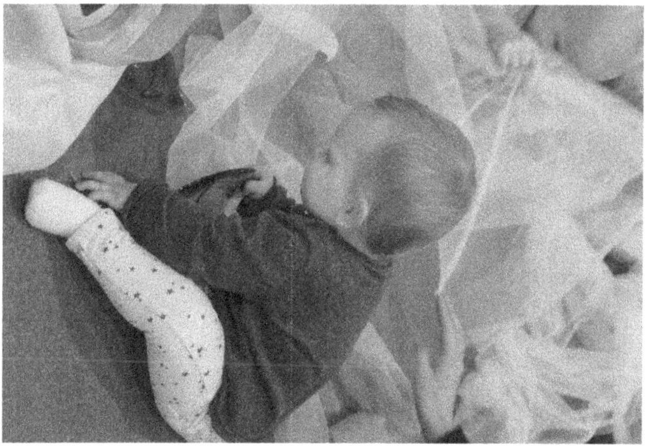

FIGURE 11.2 Exploring different textures during a drop-in Little Feet session. © Trustees of the British Museum.

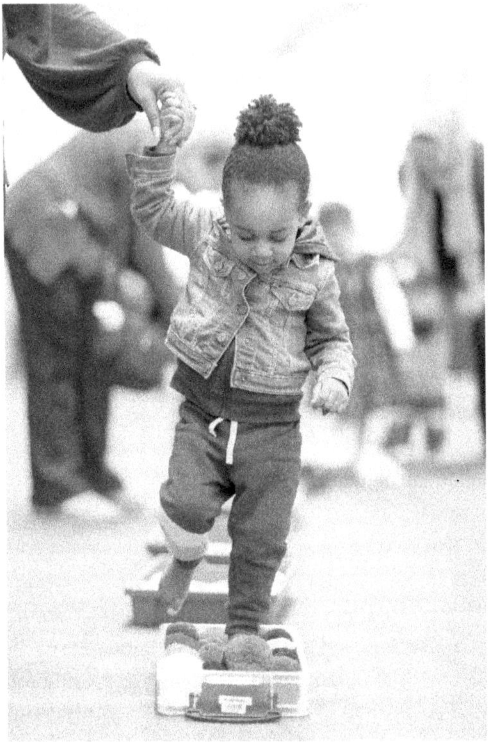

FIGURE 11.3 Using feet to explore different textures.

(using the bells or vocalising in response to the resources) and testing the materials (lots of scrunched up snowflakes). We were also able to observe visitor flow through the area, noting the most popular times for children to be out of buggies, and also the potential dwell time we could expect from this audience. The combination of observing participation and talking to adults led us to conclude that there was a hunger for this type of provision and offered some solid starting points for the next phase.

Pilot phase: stage 1

The success of the start-up phase led to a formal pilot phase. During this we planned, delivered and evaluated facilitated provision as part of wider family events. Sessions ran in a designated space near the other family activities and included explorative play resources together with facilitated moments such as a story or a song. For example, during Chinese New Year celebrations we told the story of the Chinese zodiac, with the children helping to move each animal across a blue fabric river as the narrative unfolded. After each session we generated an action point which fed directly into the delivery of the next session.

There is no formal buggy space at the Museum, although folded-up buggies can be left in the cloakroom. However, we noticed that adults started to create an informal buggy park on one side of the under 5s area so that they could access food and drink while keeping an eye on their buggy and belongings. This worked well for us since we could inform security staff that the buggy park was in sight of staff facilitating the session and only in place for the duration of the session. It also supported the children; repurposing a gallery corner as a buggy park changed an unfamiliar space into a space where a familiar activity was taking place as they got out of the buggy, parked it up and moved away from it into a new space. Adults were often accompanied by a walking toddler and a baby in a buggy. This prompted us to consider how we could support adults to move children out of buggies. We purchased some fabric baby mats and laid them out next to the activity area and several babies came out of buggies to lie on a mat while older siblings were engaged nearby. This encouraged other adults to bring children out of their buggy into the creative play zone so that, instead of adults taking resources to buggy-based babies, they were bringing the babies to the resources (Figure 11.4).

The majority of the adults did not need intervention/support from staff to engage their child with the resources. However, it was also clear that some adults were listening to what staff were saying to other adults/children and then building that into how they interacted with their child. Some people stayed for the whole time while others came for 20 minutes and then left. We noticed a drop around lunch time with the greatest number of people attending 11.00–12 noon and 1.00–2.00 pm. The combination of drop-in creative play

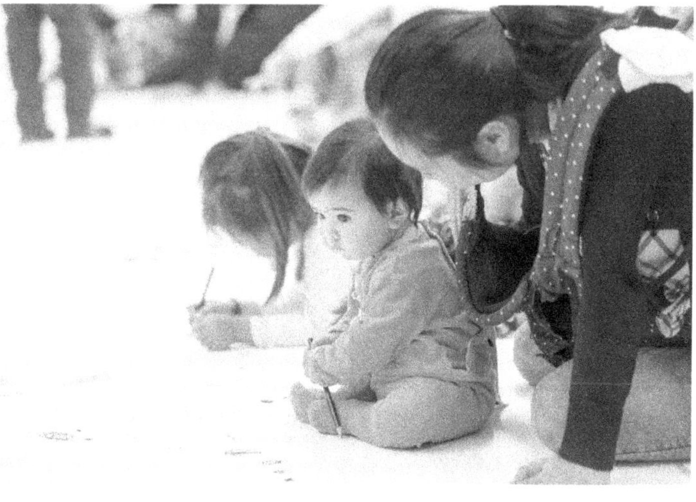

FIGURE 11.4 Children and adults creating a Little Feet collaborative artwork.
© Trustees of the British Museum.

with short bursts of song or storytelling facilitated this movement as people were able to self-select how long they stayed without feeling they had to do a certain number of activities. This led us to consider the blend of open-ended and time-bonded activities offered in a session and how the overall structure could help adults make the most of the activities.

These were the first sessions to be advertised as Little Feet sessions using existing Museum marketing platforms. In response to feedback indicating that this audience did not see themselves as part of the general family programme and wanted under 5s activities clearly signposted, we requested a separate tab on the Museum online calendar so that this audience could filter for the events most relevant to them. Consequently, we were keen to find out how people knew about the sessions. When asked, the majority said they had been before, others said that they had heard about it from a friend and some people were using the under 5s tab on the website.

As the numbers attending increased, with up to 100 adults and children at some sessions, it became clear that hosting Little Feet during family activities in the Great Court was reaching capacity. We had successfully created an audience for these sessions and we had the marketing tools in place to promote the events, so now we wanted to look at how we could deliver Little Feet in different areas of the Museum and widen the types of activities offered.

Pilot phase: stage 2

The second part of the pilot phase saw us trial standalone under 5s sessions on term time weekdays in spaces beyond the Great Court (Figure 11.5). We were particularly interested in quieter galleries where we could set up activities between cases or in a corner while other visitors circulated through the rest of the room. On hard, cold stone floors we used large rugs while warm wooden floors worked without a carpet. Most materials used in the galleries were soft and left no residue and where we used glue we set up papered areas for the children to work on.

For our first gallery-based Little Feet we invited local partners to attend and give feedback. A local adult education centre brought a group of parents and toddlers from a parenting class and a nearby charitable Early Years setting brought a nursery group. The sessions took place in the recently re-displayed Korean gallery which had a small public programming budget. We used this to pay a freelancer to develop and lead two 90-minute sessions a day: one for the public and one for a partner organisation. Objects on display acted as starting points for the activities. For example, wooden boxes inspired a set of small cardboard boxes full of hidden objects. We had invested in some teddy bears for earlier sessions and a display of Korean footwear meant the teddies came out with a pile of socks which the children put on paws, and occasionally heads. The adults said they enjoyed being in a new gallery with unfamiliar objects and felt inspired to try some of the activities at home, particularly those which linked to home learning, e.g., putting on your socks.

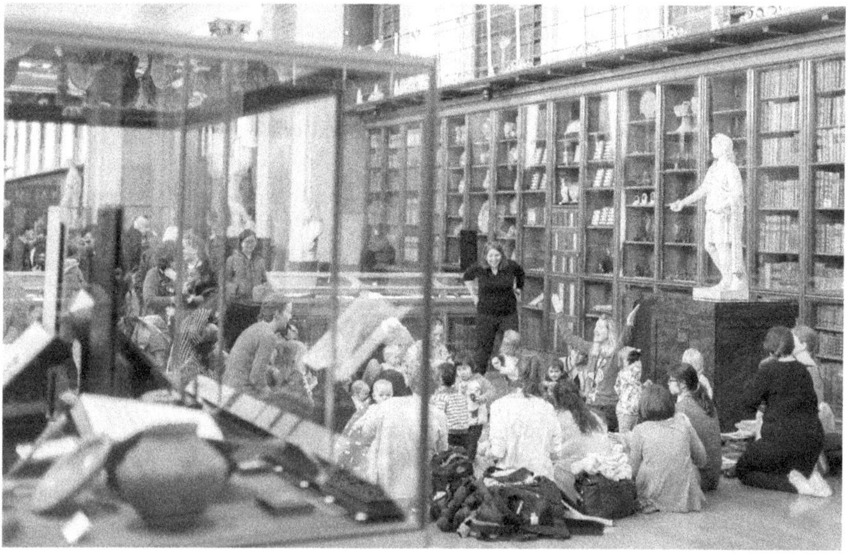

FIGURE 11.5 Little Feet session in the Enlightenment Gallery (room 1).
© Trustees of the British Museum.

The art room in the Clore Centre for Education provided a chance to trial some wet art sessions. We started outside the room, saying hello to everybody, singing a couple of songs and practising our colours. In the art room itself we had taped paper on the floor and walls so that the children could explore mark marking with chalks and paint to create a giant mural. Some adults really enjoyed the open nature of the activity and stayed for over an hour, with one excited adult commenting that they did not realise that you could do messy things at museums. In contrast, a number of adults enjoyed the staff-led introduction in the foyer but were less comfortable with the art session. One commented that they liked sessions with structure (i.e., directed by staff) but was reluctant to engage in the immersive art activity. We realised that adults themselves bring different expectations of what they, and their child, want to do and that we needed to allow for a range of ways into an activity. For the next art session we set up additional dry play activities in the foyer. Being able to move between the two spaces helped to spread numbers and meant that adults and children could dwell in the place where they felt most comfortable. Logistically, the larger delivery area necessitated additional facilitators to staff the different spaces, with increased set-up and close-down time.

We also trialled Little Feet sessions in paid exhibitions, funded by the sponsored learning programme. We began by running sessions on school exclusive morning when we knew we could introduce more movement and sound than usual into an exhibition space. The Little Feet teddies joined us as the focus for some activities and, during the Celts exhibition, we admired the gold torcs before practising our twisting skills to make pipe cleaner torcs for the teddies to wear. These proved popular and we now have exclusive Little Feet sessions in most exhibitions. Sometimes we set up activity stations throughout the exhibition, guiding the under 5s as they journey through the space and encouraging them to respond through an explorative or craft activity. Alternatively, we set up a single activity hub which draws on themes from across the whole exhibition. For example, in a sculpture exhibition a central activity hub focussed on faces, hands and feet, and from here adults and children could then independently move around the exhibition spotting these parts of the body on the sculptures.

Little Feet becomes part of core programming

The final part of our development plan was establishing Little Feet within the ongoing public programme (Figure 11.6). We continued to run 90-minute drop-in sessions and experimented with free, but pre-booked, shorter slots with a set capacity. During these we ran more structured art sessions based around a higher value material, such as clay or textile, with greater opportunity for the artist to interact with adults and children as they experienced specific crafting skills. Soft branding started to emerge around the name itself and in relation to activities common to all sessions. The Little Feet teddies grew in number and became a popular part of every session; featuring in marketing, waiting to greet the children on arrival, cuddled during the introduction and acting as companions in the creative play zones. The start of each session became an opportunity to welcome people to the Little Feet experience, singing a song or playing a game as people settled in a circle. The under 2s were fascinated by hearing other voices, seeing other children and watching facial expressions. Meanwhile the older children confidently copied song actions and joined in the game. For us it became a way to demonstrate that Little Feet is welcoming of all, available to be enjoyed at whatever cognitive level your child has reached and aspirational in the diverse activities it offers (Figure 11.6).

Final thoughts and implications for practice

The development of Little Feet has been an inspiring, joyful and professionally satisfying experience. We have watched it grow from small beginnings during the start-up phase, where we gave ourselves the opportunity to dip our toes in the water and reflect on what we saw, through a pilot phase where the inherent nature of under 5s provision at the British Museum started to take shape and evolved through the tandem stimuli of museum practice and participants' feedback, to becoming a full-fledged strand of the Museum's public programme. Our path will not necessarily be the path taken by others and so, in summary, we would like to propose three top tips to help shape the process for anybody considering under 5s programming within a heritage space.

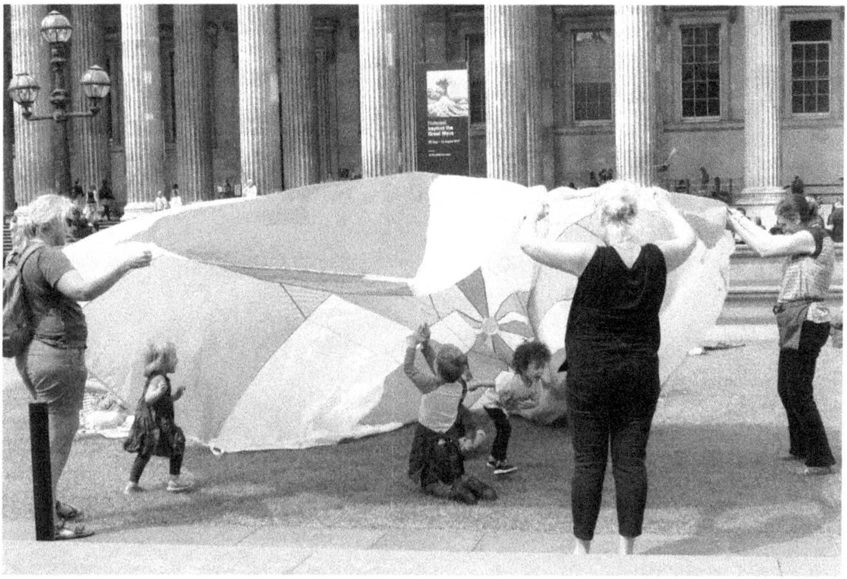

FIGURE 11.6 Creating waves for a Little Feet session on the forecourt lawn.

1. *Start with safe areas and then, as practice and procedures firm up, move into more challenging areas.* If you have areas on site which already host family events, use these for trialling under 5s activities. As you move into a new space, you will need to set-up the usual programming protocols expected by your organisation, but once established for one area you can then roll them out to other spaces. Remember it is not necessarily the age of the audience that is the barrier, but the guidelines galleries may have around materials being brought into a space (i.e., fabric brought into an organics gallery) or art materials (glue or felt pens) that have to be negotiated first. The more you can show it works in one space, the easier it is to approach the guardians of a new space. The nature of a space can also be changed by something as simple as adjusting the light level or introducing sound. Collect evidence about how your young learners are using the space to develop a sense of themselves and a sense of place. Make it work successfully in one space and you could find yourself invited into others.
2. *Use feedback to create action points to improve the sessions.* Feedback is often seen as an evaluation form at the end of the activity, but don't overlook the power of an informal chat. Talk to the users about what is working for them and what would make it even better, then create achievable action points which feed into the very next session. Use feedback to keep testing in the early stages, and access hard-to-reach audiences through invitation events so that you can find out from them directly about the support/information they need to attend.

3 *Experiment so there is a balance between people thinking "This is just what I expected to do in a museum" and moments of "I never imagined we could do this in a museum!"* Under 5s love to touch. They look, then they grab, they hold, they drop. Think about how you can use this behaviour to create activities which use the context of a museum to explore different object textures, colours, shapes and stories. At the same time be creative in thinking about how spaces can inspire unexpected activities. Challenge the idea of what it means to be in a museum while holding true to the idea of museums as environments for curious minds to explore, investigate, experience and enjoy.

12

YOUNG CHILDREN EXPLORE SEWERBY HALL

Lucy Cooke

Introduction

Sewerby Hall is a Grade I listed country house set in 55 acres of parkland and gardens on the outskirts of Bridlington (a small seaside town situated on the east coast of Yorkshire in England). The area is predominantly rural and noted for the chalk uplands of the Yorkshire Wolds. Dating back to the 18th century and formerly the home of the Lloyd Greame family, the hall came into public ownership in 1934. Today it is owned and managed by the East Riding of Yorkshire Council. The house is displayed to reflect the appearance it would have had as a private home in 1910 and the council's Museum Service (ERYMS) is responsible for its collections and exhibitions.

In 2012 the Museum Service obtained funding through the National Lottery to restore the house to the appearance it had in 1910. To accompany the restoration it was envisaged that the Museum would develop an ambitious public offer using extensive handling collections, costumed interpretation, interactives and open display.

Demographic research into the locality showed that Bridlington had a higher than average number of low-income families and single parents. This group was identified as a key target audience. However, we were also aware that people in this demographic are not traditional museum visitors. It was therefore agreed that the house, as redisplayed, would be consciously family friendly through specifically targeted interventions. Additionally, we appealed to family audiences through our marketing and signed up to the Kids in Museums Manifesto.

Since 2013, ERYMS has worked in collaboration with Hull Museums and North Lincolnshire Museum Service to carry out joint initiatives for exhibitions, learning and outreach. What started out as Joining Up The Humber, aided by Arts Council England's Strategic Fund, became the Humber Museums Partnership (HMP), a Major Partner Museum; and in 2018 the HMP was awarded National Portfolio Organisation status. During 2015–2018 the HMP received funding from Arts Council England in order to develop, increase and improve its offer for under 5s. Each service employed a learning officer to lead on this and I was appointed to the post of Under 5s Learning Co-ordinator for East Riding of Yorkshire Museum Service in June 2016.

As a dedicated Under 5s Learning Co-ordinator, I was based at Sewerby Hall and Gardens with the aim of developing a body of best practice at the hall that could then be rolled out amongst the other museums within our service (The Treasure House and Beverley Art Gallery, Beverley Guildhall, Skidby Windmill and Goole Museum). This included creating ways for very young children to interact and engage with museum collections and themes, improving physical accessibility, creating a programme of activities for under 5s, forming local partnerships and advocating for this age group to visit museums. It also involved working with learning colleagues across the Humber Museums Partnership on joint under 5s initiatives for the Humber region.

Developing under 5s access at Sewerby Hall and Gardens

At Sewerby Hall I developed a range of interventions in order to increase access to collections and exhibitions for under 5s and their families. They fall into the following categories:

Physical access:

- giving young children as many opportunities for hands-on exploration as possible, through the use of handling items and interactive areas;
- using low-level cases, and the bottom levels of full-sized cases, to exhibit objects that young children have some familiarity with;
- providing step stools where cases or displays can't be lowered.

Visible access:

- dressing objects within cases to provide a context and make it easier for under 5s to understand their purpose.

Conceptual access:

- sitting exhibition content within a broad theme that is accessible and understandable to under 5s (for example, creating activities around the theme of "flight" to link with a collection of Amy Johnson memorabilia);
- creating interpretative room cards that provide a way for children to interact with the themes and concepts of period rooms, through finding an object and a pattern, and singing a related song.

Empowering access;

- providing Explorer Kits to investigate exhibitions, objects and spaces;
- using signage to clearly signpost to adults that children's exploration is welcome.

The research project

In November 2016 the HMP partnered with Dr Abigail Hackett and her colleagues to research the way under 5s use our museum spaces. The nominated ERYMS venue was Sewerby Hall and Gardens, with a particular focus on the house itself. We were keen to observe the children's interactions with the house, museum objects and one another in the environment, and to discover how these interactions changed over the course of several repeat visits. Four families joined us for the research, each with one child and one or more adults.

The research visits took place over three Wednesday afternoons and one Saturday morning. On the Wednesdays there were costumed volunteers in the house, interacting with visitors. This reflects the usual offer during the summer season, whereby volunteers provide costumed interpretation on Wednesdays and Fridays. Each visit took a slightly different format, with different tools facilitating the children's interactions with the house, including cameras, Shape Finders and Explorer Kits (featuring a magnifying glass, kaleidoscope, colour paddles, torch and small soft toy). None of the families had been inside the house more than once, to their recollection, so this was a new experience for them.

The following sections summarise observations made by myself and Dr Lisa Procter, lead researcher for our site, some of which are drawn from the end-of-project report (Hackett et al., 2017).

The house: making sense of the space

Over time, we observed the children's confidence in the space and understanding of the space growing (and that of the accompanying adults too!). On the first visit, the children had no concept of the differences between period rooms with restricted access and those where they were free to roam, but they quickly became aware of the "rules" of the environment and learnt how to engage with the spaces differently. Parents and grandparents were initially anxious about their children being in such a "precious" environment and worried they would break things, with one parent saying it was "frightening being in a space like this with little children" (Field notes, Lisa Procter, 9/11/2016). However, as they explored together, becoming familiar with the interactive areas and learning where they could engage the children both physically and conceptually, they began to relax.

As the children became more familiar with the house and more confident in the environment, they began to experiment with movement, returning to favourite

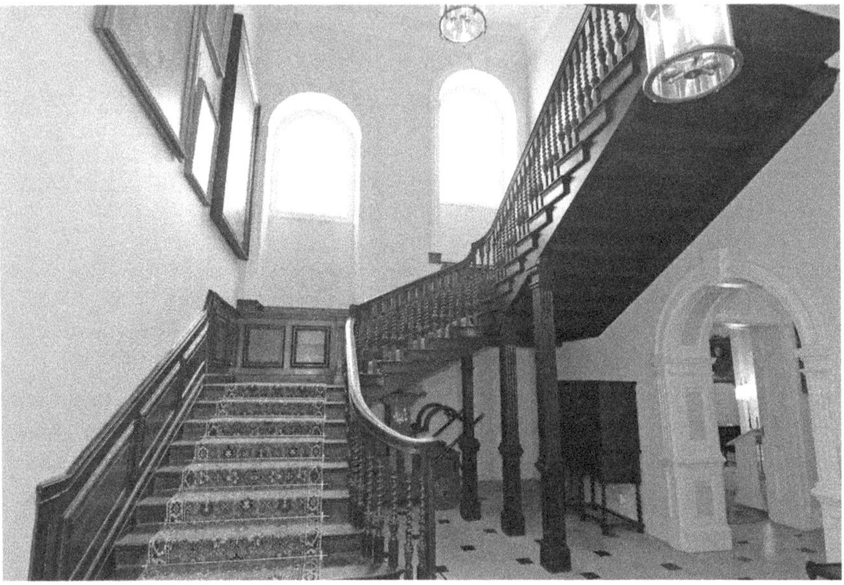

FIGURE 12.1 The staircase at Sewerby Hall.

rooms and engaging with the space differently. One child preferred the West Wing Gallery (which houses temporary exhibitions). Museum cases lined the walls and the central floor space was unoccupied. On one visit, she chose to lie down on the wooden floor and spin around, perhaps enjoying how different the flooring and space were to her home environment. Other children preferred the Dining Room, with its beautiful carpet, decorative ceiling and familiar objects (dining table, chairs and prop food). All the children returned time and time again to the Nursery, where there were many replica toys to play with as well as a child-sized bed and low-level window ledges.

The staircase (see Figure 12.1) fascinated the young visitors, perhaps because it is a familiar architectural feature but on a different scale to the stairs in their homes. It also has a low-level bannister, patterned carpet runner and shallow steps, making it more accessible to them. By the third visit, one of the children felt comfortable enough in the environment to "bump" down the stairs on her bottom, instead of walking down them.

Objects: finding familiarity and strangeness

From the very first visit, some children had clear favourite objects, which they returned to time and time again. One child fell in love with the wooden doll's house and spent a great deal of time playing with it by herself and with others, her grandma remarking that she didn't have anything like it at home. Another hunted

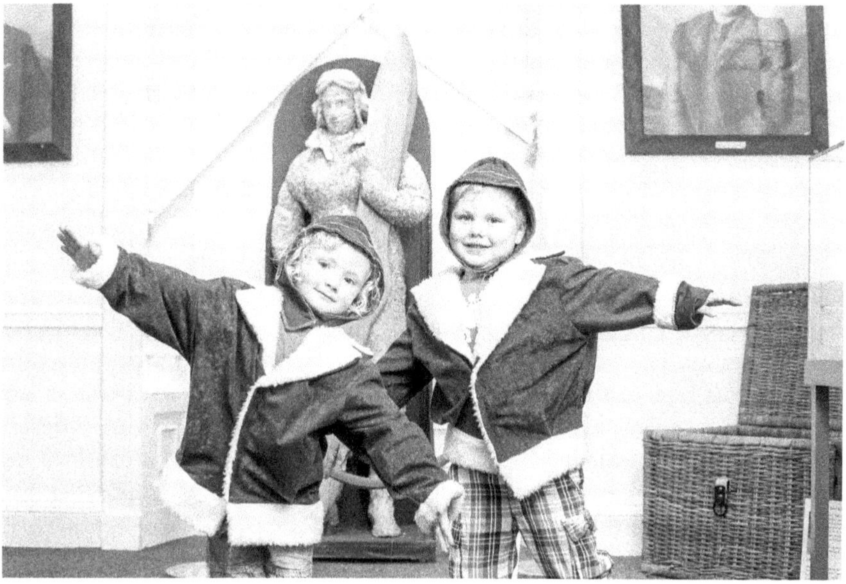

FIGURE 12.2 Dressing up as Amy Johnson in front of her sculpture.
© East Riding of Yorkshire Council.

high and low on the second visit to find a small wooden dog he had played with the previous week. A sculpture of Amy Johnson made from paper money (see Figure 12.2) also held a fascination for the children, who enjoyed touching it to experience the different textures (in spite of the fact that the sculpture stood behind a barrier and should not have been touched).

Initially the children were most interested in objects that had been deliberately placed for them to engage with (toys in the Nursery, handling items in the Kitchen and activities in exhibition spaces), perhaps because the objects and activities were presented in a familiar way or were familiar themselves. However, by the third visit, they began to interact more with, and be more interested in, museum collection items, such as a taxidermy stag head, a large chest used to collect donations and real period toys displayed in a case.

Within her observation notes, Lisa made the following comment: "It's interesting which objects the children want to show to their parents, indicates something of their significance to them – they are often different to the ones that the parents want to show to their children. Over time it seems like the children are showing their parents more objects than the other way round" (Field notes, Lisa Procter, 26/11/2016).

People: moving, talking and exploring together

Although the parents allowed their children to lead the visit, they followed closely during the first session, especially through the formal period rooms with restricted access. On subsequent visits and in rooms where everything could be touched (e.g., the Nursery), they were more relaxed and tended to talk to one another while the children interacted with the rooms and objects, demonstrating how important repeat visits and familiarity are. There was a slight difference in exploration when, for one of the sessions, a participant was accompanied by her grandparents instead of her mother. On this occasion, the grandparents took the lead and set the pace for the visit, showing their granddaughter round the house on the recommended route and leading conversation about the content of the rooms. This may be reflective of the relationship between grandparents and granddaughter, or perhaps it demonstrates their understanding and previous experience of visiting similar environments.

Conversation between participants varied from instruction regarding the rules (e.g., parents directing children not to go beyond the ropes and pointing out "please don't touch" signs) to children's interaction over play in the Nursery (joining in with one another's imaginative games and speaking on behalf of the toy characters) and intergenerational discussion about objects on display that had been in common use within living memory (e.g., dolly tub and stick). There was a natural element of conversation facilitated by the house itself, the museum objects, Explorer Kits and trails, as families progressed from one room to another.

On the first visit, all four families entered the house together and therefore explored much of the space as one group, with children playing together and adults conversing with one another; but on subsequent visits the families arrived separately and therefore spent more time exploring and conversing as family units. This highlighted the different dynamics when families visit together with friends or by themselves in a more intimate group.

Benefits and challenges

The timescale of the project meant we carried out the research during the winter season, when the house was open only on Wednesdays and weekends. This meant the house was much quieter than in summer months and the research participants almost had the space to themselves for three of the four sessions, although there were more visitors in the house during the Saturday visit. In addition, there were costumed volunteers in the house on each of the Wednesday sessions, which, though normal for Wednesdays, is not indicative of the experience on other days of the week. We wondered how the experience would have differed during the busier summer season and how extra visitors might have affected interactions or changed the atmosphere. However, it was beneficial to see the ways in which children interacted with the volunteers and the quieter environment had the added benefit of providing the families with greater freedom of movement around the space.

The repetition of visits by the same families meant we saw the change in ownership and autonomy for the children, as they became familiar with the house, the collections and the rules of the environment (i.e., in which rooms you could not go past ropes and couldn't touch objects and in which rooms you could roam around more freely and handle objects). This observation has reinforced our prior notion that repeat visits are worthwhile, for both the families and the museum; and as a result at least one of the families involved purchased an Annual Pass for the estate.

Reflections: what values and ideas might guide our future work in developing access for under 5s?

The incidental

Sewerby Hall is a rich environment for incidental discoveries as it is full of the "stuff of everyday life," but with a difference (e.g., the staircase). There are many objects that spark reminiscence, particularly from grandparents, and lots of ideas for children to relate to and explore; and these discoveries facilitate family conversation.

Diversity

Not only, as mentioned above, is there a contrast with their daily life, but there is diversity in the room layouts, light levels, themes and materials – even down to the floor tiles and wall colours. Lisa noticed how different flooring influenced the way children moved in the space – the sectioned tiles on the ground floor broke up a long stretch of corridor, whereas a carpet runner upstairs highlighted it and caused children to move much more quickly along the hallway.

Repetition

The pattern of children's dependence on their accompanying adults changed as the children became more familiar with the space, layout and location of their favourite experiences or objects. This meant that children re-visited their favourites from the first visit over and over again – but also felt more confident to discover new favourites as well.

Movement

As mentioned above, the flooring made a big difference for our young visitors, as did the room styles (more formal vs more physically accessible). Although on the first visit children passed underneath the ropes, on subsequent visits they stayed within the normal visitor space. Movement was also facilitated by the use of Explorer Kits (see Figure 12.3), which children could use to discover new things, highlight what they were interested in and take ownership of their visits.

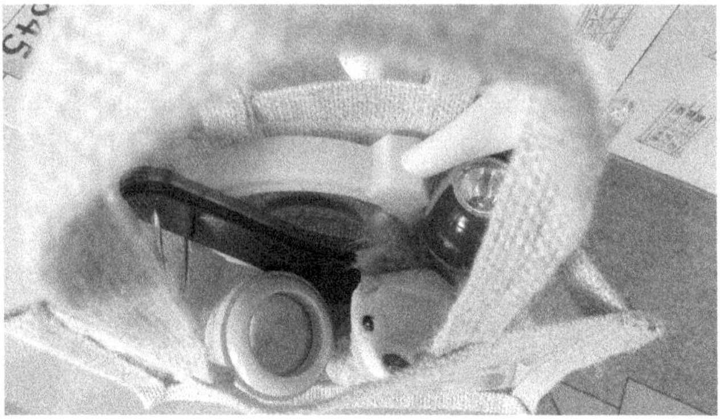

FIGURE 12.3 Explorer Kit containing a magnifying glass, torch, kaleidoscope, colour paddles and squirrel soft toy.

Final thoughts and implications for practice

We learnt so much from taking part in this research project and observing how this group of families interacted with Sewerby Hall over time. I highly recommend the following for heritage practitioners:

- Spend time observing how young children use your museum/heritage space – it will help you see how great your site is for them, highlight positive features and challenge you in unexpected ways too!
- Provide objects for them to physically touch if possible – but don't feel it has to be "hands on" everywhere – the diversity provides different opportunities and experiences.
- Provide tools to help them explore (e.g., Explorer Kits/interpretative cards).
- Give clear messages for parents/grandparents – e.g., through joining Kids in Museums and using their logo, through using "please touch" signs and letting them know noise is fine.

On a personal level, I can't stress how wonderful it has been, not only during this research but in the course of the whole HMP under 5s project, to see young children engaging in a meaningful way with our heritage settings and collections.

I know that Lisa valued seeing this interaction too and, in her absence, I would like to include her words from an email we sent to the participating families halfway through this research project:

> The visits have been really illuminating already, and it is great to see the enjoyment of exploring the museum spaces. Some children seem to have

their favourite spaces and objects. This week everyone seemed more confident about exploring the spaces, engaging with the volunteers and handling objects, showing that familiarity is an important part of how the spaces and objects become meaningful to young children.

Acknowledgement

With thanks to my colleague Robert Chester (Sewerby Hall Education Officer) for writing the introductory information regarding Sewerby Hall and its restoration.

References

Hackett, A. Procter, L. and MacRae, C. (2017) How do families with under fives experience museums? Research report for Humber Museum Partnership. Unpublished.

13

CLIMATE, LANDSCAPE AND LANDMARKS

Providing spaces for belonging

Elizabeth Clayton and Jack Shuttleworth

At the heart of our practice is an enthusiasm for families, space, welcome, belonging and chance. This ranges from the nature of the welcome of a space and practical issues of access to how meaning is made in a museum environment. Over the past 15 years, our engagement with exhibitions and museum spaces has led us to evolve an agenda of accessibility and engagement, with a focus on what we have called "Spaces In-between" (Clayton and Shuttleworth, 2018). Spaces In-between are the often-overlooked spaces beyond formal creative delivery and traditional museum provision, whether physical or intangible, planned or accidental, that can emerge during research and work with children and families.

We constructed a geographical metaphor to structure our thoughts, examining Climate, Landscape and Landmarks as a response to an invitation to write an article for *Children's Geographies* journal (Clayton and Shuttleworth, 2018). Climate as a metaphor can be employed to consider a set of conditions that go towards making a museum or gallery space truly welcoming to families with young children. Climate is in the air, in the atmosphere, ephemeral, intangible, difficult to describe and control, but impossible to ignore. The climate can encourage Spaces In-between by accepting each visitor's choices as to how they use the space. Climate in turn shapes the Landscape or terrain, the physical space manifesting the qualities that make people want to be there. From this starting point, we think about young children and families in museums in terms of encountering a terrain. The landscape has a rhythm, has obvious features and hidden corners, all of which can be appropriated as Spaces In-between when a visitor makes their own meaning of a feature. Finally, Landmarks are the way we discover and map a landscape and the surprises and lures that make us return.

By welcoming the unexpected and letting it influence our work in the moment and in our planning, our approach is inherently rhizomatic, where the hierarchy and linearity of planning and delivery can be productively disrupted.

Our language is often naturally rich and overly descriptive as we inspire and communicate with families. We rejoice in the new layers of meaning that children create and assimilate children's language into our own. We try to use this voice throughout this case study, where we will focus on "5 Nests," a museum installation we created in Wolverhampton Art Gallery, and interrogate the metaphors of climate, landscape and landmarks.

Climate: welcoming families and anticipating needs

The climate of a gallery is most clearly expressed through the welcome conveyed by the museum or gallery to its visitors. If a museum decides to welcome families with young children, it must offer them an experience they can enjoy in their own way. The welcome incorporates subtle but important considerations and can include recognising families' realities, valuing diverse styles of play/learning, promoting well-being and planning spaces and provision with welcome in mind.

This is not always easy; young children in museums present a challenge because of their less predictable behaviour. They move a lot, are attracted to the unexpected and use space in surprising ways. In addition, parents are often anxious about attending the venue, are unsure how to act, are concerned by how their child may behave or feel that museums are just not for them. Here the challenge is slowing families down, removing as much stress, anxiety and perceived barriers as possible and being aware of families' realities, needs and likely actions when visiting a museum or gallery.

Informal interaction with our audience, chatting and spending time with them, has built enduring relationships and enables us to gather a broader range of knowledge about the realities of visiting museums. These informal encounters break down barriers and enable us to move away from traditional forms of audience engagement that are often ineffective and can distance museums from their audience. As researchers, we listen and observe, building our experience and knowledge of the practical, lumpy bumpy, hands-on doing in galleries. By exploring multiple, informal ways of knowing (Pink, 2009) we do not narrow our approach or thinking, (by already formulating answers or only looking for results we want or need); instead, we build true encounters, engagement and research with families, materials, objects and space (Figure 13.1).

This changes our role, putting our work with families on an equal footing rather than from a position of privilege. We believe families visiting museums can play an important role in the designing of family provision and we value parents becoming co-researchers (Hackett, 2016) and children knowledge makers (Dodd-Nufrio, 2011). This co-production encourages active engagement and establishes a bigger picture of children's lives, again to better understand families' realities and needs. We gain knowledge through our whole experiencing body (Pink, 2009: 25) just as young children do. As children undertake their own research through their senses and body, we argue that museum professionals should do so too. We play alongside families, providing opportunities for chatting, a purpose for spending time in an exhibit and

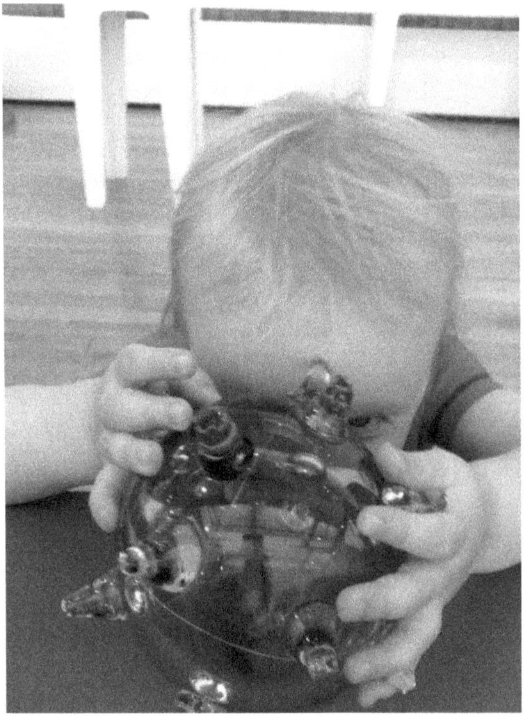

FIGURE 13.1 Allowing for deeper engagement.

experiencing our curated space first hand by talking the talk and walking the walk (DeWalt and DeWalt, 2011). This way of experiencing our own spaces, provision, exhibit content and visitor interaction enables us to continually rethink our understanding alongside families. We can therefore distinguish how they are likely to use space and provision and are able to react effectively to change, whether that involves change in families' needs, exhibit content or museum policies, funding and priorities.

We use social media and photography as valuable tools of communication and an extension of our Reggio-inspired documentation. We also use Facebook to ask questions, to increase engagement and show our work behind the scenes. This allows visitors a sense of ownership and control over the process, responding in greater detail and depth and understanding and appreciating our process and motivations.

Landscape: exploring space and families realities

In planning spaces such as exhibitions, play environments, spaces we consciously leave unfilled, or social spaces, we are aiming to embody an unpredictable, welcoming and practical approach. Spaces such as these form a landscape, sitting within and shaped by the wider climate of the museum.

5 Nests was an interactive installation we delivered and developed for 0–2 year olds at Wolverhampton Art Gallery over the summer months. Designed and made with babies and young children in mind, it is a specific example of how we have experimented with landscapes of surprise and welcome. Seen in Figure 13.2, the sensory exhibition consisted of five immersive nests beneath a white life-sized tree. Each nest embodied a different bird, environment and sensory play experience, a heron high up, a colony of swallow's nests, robin's nests in found objects and game birds nesting on the floor. The space was lit dramatically and occasional birdsong played to enhance the woodland theme and create interest.

Our overall aim was for a calm, cool space, where carers could relax and enjoy their children's company. Calm is often a core expectation of a contemporary art gallery – and the installation had a strong overall aesthetic and visual centrepiece. A messy space might have worked just as well for most parents, but further conflict with gallery norms would have undermined the work, given that the intended audience already challenged gallery traditions.

Working in this new space, we brought our knowledge of children's play and family's needs with us, making a controversial decision not to entirely fill the space or present a finished piece. We created opportunities for encounters and experience, with multiple trajectories of play and opportunities for children to immerse themselves and choose the nature of their interaction. The sensory nests provided whole bodily experiences, with the smaller spaces enabling children to explore materials and objects, crawl in or curl up, role play, use their

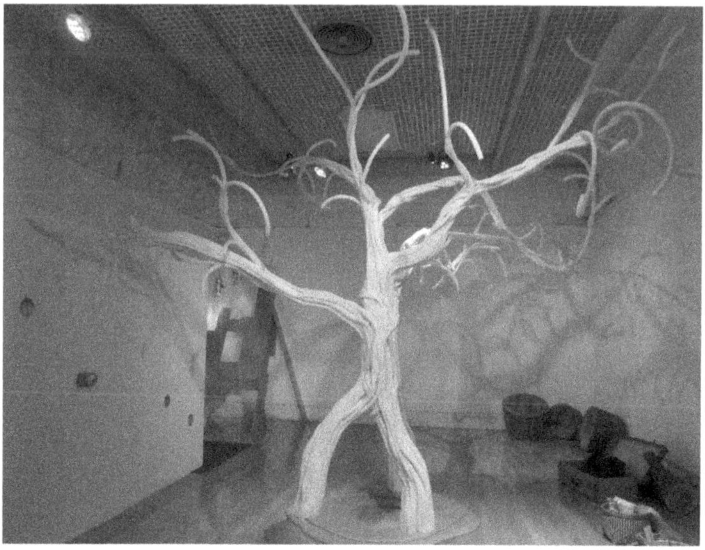

FIGURE 13.2 The landscape of 5 Nests.

imagination or just hang out. Additional space was left empty for the children to fill with their play, which often took the form of baby birds or animals being nurtured by their parents.

Sensory play for babies was additionally supported through durable discovery baskets (available at reception) which were loosely inspired by levels of the woodland – the tree canopy, amongst the branches and the forest floor. These combined sound, scent, movement, light and texture and supported those parents that needed a little guidance or felt the need to "do" something, as well as allowing non-mobile babies to have additional experiences as fully-fledged cultural participants.

Traditional expectations of a museum visit were discarded in favour of the realities of a family's visit, which included the nature of welcome in the space, practicalities, issues of access and how meaning is made in a museum environment (Clayton and Shuttleworth, 2018). To encourage parents to spend time in the space and know they belong, we addressed practical realities of a family's visit. From the entrance, children and carers could survey the whole landscape of the space, so they could make decisions about what they wanted to do from the moment of arrival and feel comfortable about young children running ahead.

We appropriated a raised platform to allow children to see the whole space, observe, hide and, unusually, to play off the ground. This gave a bird's eye view of the space, a hidey hole when a calm refuge was needed, a little removed but still connected. It was ideal for those children who needed to observe before they interact, have a slower rate of interaction or want to be hidden. To improve observation and parent sightlines we created view-holes in the side which supported "can't see me" play and more anxious children who wanted to keep eye contact with carers. We recognised that the platform would be an attractive running route and deliberately prevented this by creating a barrier halfway. As well as re-directing high-energy play away from stairs, this also created "baby backwaters," dead-ends where calmer play isn't put in conflict with older children's need to run.

How visitors negotiate their way through gallery spaces and museums can have considerable implications for how they relate and interact (Macdonald, 2007: 157). 5 Nests avoided any linear curation or unfolding narrative and carefully considered practical considerations such as moving around objects freely with prams/buggies, sharing experiences and allowing families to spread out with the numerous bags that go hand-in-hand with babies' visits.

Realistically we need to plan for movement and the physicality in museum spaces. We should celebrate children's need to run, climb, investigate and discover their bodies. Museums should understand that young children's movement and physicality is a way of learning and appreciating the museum's spaces, not a challenge to their ethos or traditional use of their spaces. In 5 Nests we planned generous routes for anticipated transportation and play, allowing margins for activities to spread. We knew some children would not

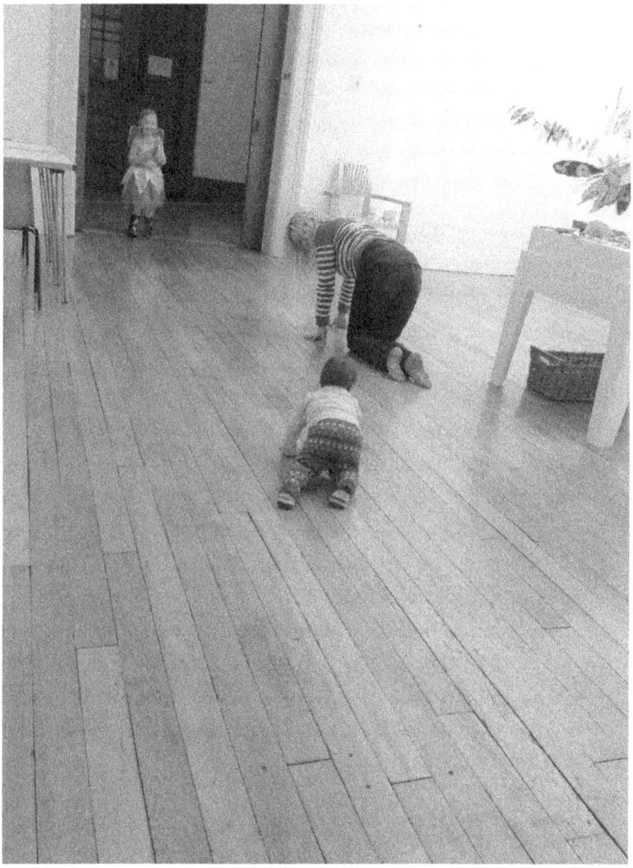

FIGURE 13.3 Exploring and appreciating gallery spaces.

have seen a gallery space before and a large expanse of polished floor might be a new experience for many, so we left much of the floor blank and, sure enough, the prime activity for many children was toddling, wandering or bum shuffling (Figure 13.3).

Controversially, we provided a bin, dustpan and brush. The bin was often full and we realised that if we hadn't put it out we would have been forcing parents into the role of litterers, creating a negative relationship between families and the museum. We also provided pram parking to encourage parents to get children out of the pram and, alongside social spaces, encourage parents to relax and enjoy, break-out and "be." In practice, many carers made repeated visits, often as informal groups or extended families, both popping in and spending considerable time in the space. The informality and no-charge entry meant that, as well as being a haven from the busy city centre bustle, it was a place to be social, perhaps breastfeed or just spend time with their child. By creating and allowing for these calm fluid spaces, we have found they are appropriated or used in a different way without the pressures of a formal café or seating. Indeed, sometimes just the addition of a simple rug is all that's needed to indicate permission or purpose.

When an exhibition is open or a project "finished" it is tempting to move on to the next thing, for your sanity if nothing else. However, we view spaces as an ongoing production; 5 Nests was trialled to ensure the physical, environmental and social spaces thrived whilst open-ended resources and objects enriched these and the children's "encounters of the terrain" (Debord, 2011: 176). We explored alongside families and observed them using the space, evolving provocations, making and remaking to expand our understanding of the space and accommodate the way the exhibit was used by families at different times. This was a springboard to dissect and scrutinise our practice and, importantly, to begin to connect instinct and practice with contemporary theory and methodologies. We now approach planning with social interaction in mind, making choices about location, balancing ways to enrich the space that contribute to making families' visits easier. We have refined our approach, thinking in terms of fluid zones, with mutual relationships, sitting within the geography of our terrain. Breaking down the hierarchy of space and putting elements such as sightlines, floor hygiene, breastfeeding, well-being and socialising on par with theme, museological narrative and intended learning outcomes. We tend to find objects, exhibitions and spaces are given meaning when repurposed by visitors and may have no relation to the curated intentions of the space. In this way, they become "landscapes of surprise and welcome" (Clayton and Shuttleworth, 2018: 3).

Landmarks: encounters, connections and chance

Museums are places of "chance encounters and of the imagination" (Glancey and Brandolini, 1999: 16). Landmarks are the embodiment of this and can take infinite forms, both physical and abstract. Within a museum, Landmarks can be a way to negotiate buildings and travel through Landscapes. They are important for everyone, especially for children that are strongly, inexplicably drawn to them and make unexpected connections, repetitions, rituals and language that provides comfort, confidence, imagination and expression. For museums, Landmarks can be an effective and even humorous way to engage with their audience.

Landmarks can also be serendipitous, a chance find, an unexpected detail. A ray of light, an echo, a shadow. The lighting of 5 Nests gave us unexpected reflections on the floor and cast shadows on the wall and the air conditioning provided movement, gently blowing the foam branches of the tree. There is a delight in spotting, valuing, reinterpreting and sharing new details that enrich a familiar space and practice. Children feel proud to have discovered some landmark off the beaten track, an unexpected detail such as a reflective metal plate on a door or a plug hatch in the floor. These accidental happy happenings and many more are appreciated by us, made important and amalgamated into our provision and language. A museum gathers these Landmarks into their midst, becoming more than they are (Massey in Pink, Massey, 2005). The handle inlaid in the floor, the reflective plating on the door, the moving tree all have vital vigour that is returned to again and again. They have "the curious ability of inanimate things to animate, to act, to produce effects dramatic and subtle" (Bennett, 2010: 6).

Final thoughts and implications for practice

Each museum has a culture of its own, with inherent rules and expectations. We appreciate this and the strangeness of young children or a play environment in a gallery space for some, with our practical provision not always thought fitting. The move away from curatorial traditions, allowing for chance, the addition of the bin and leaving empty floor space, for example, were very popular with visitors but not with some gallery staff who did not perceive the space to be in use. Often the challenge is mediating between the culture of the museum and the contrasting expectations of family and traditional visitors. This can be a genuine tension that needs a meeting of minds. It was therefore essential to communicate purpose and value for both families and their provision and the museum's own customs and rituals. We were often in the space, inviting families, traditional users and staff into 5 Nests (during and after the installation), and ensured the content was visually consistent with the rest of the venue to build connections between the exhibit and the wider landscape.

For us, children's Spaces In-between and the Climate, Landscape and Landmarks we create are as important as more traditional concerns for museum provision. This is what often attracts families and young children to museum spaces and, crucially, encourages them to dwell.

We have found these goals helpful in overcoming challenges in our practice:

- Be present, in the space and with your audience.
- Plan for possibilities but embrace the things you can't plan for.
- Be brave, leave room for children's own interpretation and use.
- Be inspired by children, chance and imagination.
- Be kind to yourself, fail usefully.

References

Bennett, J. 2010. *Vibrant Matter: A Political Ecology of Things*. Durham, NC: Duke University Press.

Clayton, E., and Shuttleworth, J. (2018) Spaces in-between. *Children's Geographies 16*, 5.

Debord, G. (2011) The theory of dérive. In *The Improvisation Studies Reader: Spontaneous Arts*, eds R. Cains and A. Heble, vol. 176. Abingdon: Routledge, p. 176.

DeWalt, K., and DeWalt, B. (2011) *Participant Observation: A Guide for Fieldworkers*. Second Lanham: Rowman AltaMira Press, pp. 56–60.
Dodd-Nufrio, A.T. (2011) Reggio Emilia, Maria Montessori, and John Dewey: dispelling teachers' misconceptions and understanding theoretical foundations. *Early Childhood Education Journal 39*(4), 235–237.
Glancey, J., and Brandolini, S. (1999) Aldo Van Eyck: the urban space man. *Guardian*, Thursday 28 January.
Hackett, A. (2016) Young children as wayfarers: learning about place by moving through it. *Children and Society: The International Journal of Childhood and Children's Services 30*(3), 169–179.
Macdonald, S. (2007) Interconnecting: museum visiting and exhibition design. *CoDesign 3*(1) pp. 149–162.
Massey, D. 2005. *For Space*. London: SAGE Publications Ltd.
Pink, S. 2009. *Doing Sensory Ethnography*. London: SAGE Publications Ltd.

14

NAVIGATING, NEGOTIATING AND LIGHTING UP IN A NATURE GALLERY FOR UNDER 5S

Elaine Bates

Introduction

Manchester Museum is home to 4.8 million objects, spanning both human cultures and the natural world. Our strategic aims are to use these collections to provoke debate and understanding between cultures and to promote a sustainable world. Children under 5 have always been an important audience for the museum which has run a core family programme, Magic Carpet, for approximately 15 years. The Early Years offer for schools and families began to expand with the investment in a city-wide Early Years post in 2006 (with Renaissance in the Regions funding).

As Early Years coordinator at the museum, I was asked, in 2014, to lead on the redevelopment of an existing gallery, Nature Discovery, for children under 5 (and their parents and carers), which would act as a gateway to the rest of the museum and would use the collections to support a connection to nature in an urban setting. The context for this was prompted by research studies indicating that contact with nature is important for children's development, as it supports creativity, well-being, problem solving and could potentially support empathy with nature in adulthood. Whilst studies raise concerns that children's experiences of playing outdoors and their contact with nature are being eroded by a decline in green spaces (especially in cities) and an increasingly risk-averse society (Bragg et al., 2013; Louv, 2005; Moss, 2012; Pretty et al., 2009), Kellert (2005) has suggested that "vicarious" and "indirect" experience of nature, including within museums, may be able to compensate for this loss of "direct" experience.

Drawing on existing studies of young children's experiences in museums (Dockett et al., 2011; Dunn, 2012; Kirk, 2013; Piscitelli and Anderson, 2000; Tunnicliffe and Reiss, 2000) and nature connection measures (Cheng and Monroe, 2012; Ernst and Theimer, 2011), I undertook an initial research study, orientated around natural history objects, family interactions and children's affective, cognitive and physical experiences, to underpin the development of the new gallery as part of a Masters study (Bates, 2014). A follow-up study (with different families) focussed on evaluating the new gallery (Bates, 2015) and a third study documented a series of supported visits by families with 2-year-old children and practitioners from a local children's centre who had not previously visited the museum (Bates, 2016).

Research methods used to document young children's verbal and non-verbal responses during their museum visits included written observations, audio-recorded interactions between parents and children and informal interviews with parents and practitioners. In the third study, parents and children were invited to take photographs and given a photo album in which to display them. These were really valued by families as a record of their individual visits and supported family voice in sharing museum experiences with their wider family, as well as with myself, practitioners and other visiting families.

Reflections on research themes

As a museum practitioner I had a wealth of experience of observing and facilitating visits for young children, but undertaking my own research gave me the opportunity to reflect on the wider literature documenting young children visiting museums and to develop the gallery and subsequent activities within this context. It is interesting to note that very young children display a particular range of characteristic behaviours which reflect the way they make sense of their museum visits. Their interactions with gallery spaces, objects, peers and adults are communicated through physical movement, nonverbal actions and repeated behaviours or rituals (Hackett, 2012, 2016). Kirk and Buckingham (2018) describe these behaviours as overlapping and interconnecting "phases" of "navigating and negotiating," "lighting up" and "making sense" (of their experiences) and I will use these as a model to reflect on findings from my own studies.

Navigating and negotiating

This phase includes children exploring the "physical, social, cognitive and affective dimensions of the space of the museum" (Kirk and Buckingham, 2018: 72).

Although each child will have a unique visit, as they come to the museum with a set of different experiences and expectations, there are some characteristic behaviours that I frequently noticed. For example, in each of my studies, I observed young children moving quickly and seemingly randomly through the gallery spaces, including the Nature Discovery gallery. Hackett refers to this behaviour as "scoping the joint" (2016: 174) and Kirk and Buckingham describe this as "a kind of foraging reconnaissance" (2018: 67). However, it becomes clearer, especially through repeated visits, that this behaviour is partly about physically exploring spaces which are very different in terms of size, architectural features and materials, as well as making connections with objects they may choose to engage with at a deeper level.

Physical exploration of museum spaces

Running, jumping, chasing, crawling and climbing are important nonverbal characteristics of young children making meaning of and communicating about their museum experiences (Hackett, 2016). For example, an 18-month-old child repeatedly climbed up and down the stairs in the Natural History gallery (Bates, 2014). One child was walking across a bridging corridor connecting the two museum buildings, one side of which is glass and looks out over the museum entrance space. One of the practitioners observed that the child, "was putting her hands out and testing if it was open – outside or inside?" (Bates, 2016). On another visit, two children enjoyed playing a chasing game in a hidden space at the back of some exhibits in the Fossils gallery. These behaviours suggest that museum spaces can both invite and afford young children the opportunity to explore at this physical level and communicate their experiences in a nonverbal way that is suited to their level of development.

Although Nature Discovery is not a large gallery, we tried to create four distinct areas which reflect the real-life natural environments of the chosen natural history objects and these are named: The Den, The TreeTops, The Meadow and The Forest. Within these areas we also tried to create spaces within spaces and to place objects at different heights which would appeal to this aspect of children's development.

"Lighting up" and "making sense of" (their museum experiences)

The phase of "lighting up" is used to describe how the physical spaces and objects "become more or less salient to the children" (Kirk and Buckingham, 2018: 68). In study 1 some of the most visited natural history objects were mainly those which children were familiar with, through "vicarious means" (stories, films, images), through their own experiences and which they had an affective response to or empathy with. For example, these included apes, birds, animal and human skeletons, a fox, a lion, a tiger and a hedgehog. Children's affective responses to the natural history objects were mostly positive, but some of the most visited objects also elicited a negative or fearful response. For example, children visiting the orangutan or reticulated python in The Living Worlds gallery would hide behind their carer or move away from the cases. One child, although cautiously keeping a distance between herself and some of the insect exhibits in The Meadow area of Nature Discovery gallery, kept returning to them. Kirk and Buckingham describe this fear of and fascination with living things as "biophobophilia" (2018: 113). Kellert (2005) asserts that this response is a normal aspect of young children's affective development and

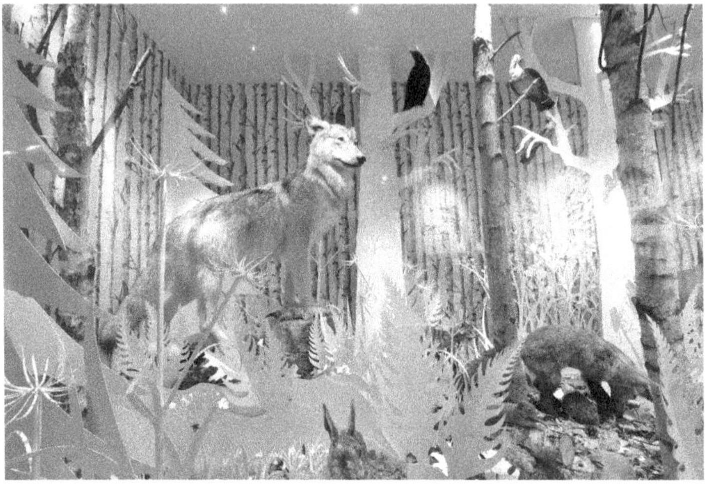

FIGURE 14.1 View of "The Forest" case in the Nature Discovery gallery.
Credit: Joe Gardner Photography.

that the museum is a safe space to experience these fears. We tried to incorporate these aspects of young children's experience and development into the design of the gallery. For example, the objects in The Treetops and The Meadow areas of the gallery include aspects of nature that children are familiar with, including birds, butterflies, insects, small mammals and plants. The Den area includes animals that are familiar to children from UK stories, for example a badger, a squirrel, an owl and a rabbit, and The Forest case contains some British wildlife animals (in a story-book setting) that children may be unfamiliar with or fearful of (for example, a wolf) in real life (see Figure 14.1).

As children become more familiar with and confident in the museum through regular visits, they may revisit objects and spaces they have a particular connection to, either cognitively, affectively or socially. For example, 2-year-old children visiting the museum with their caregivers (Bates, 2016) began to seek out objects that were both "highlights" of their museum visit and that acted as physical "waymarkers" (Hackett, 2016: 175) helping them to remember routes to other spaces and exhibits. The Forest case in Nature Discovery gallery (and particularly the wolf) became one of the most visited objects by the children on subsequent visits to the museum. Some other examples of "waymarkers" included large exhibits like the T Rex skeleton (in the Fossils gallery), the Tigon (Manchester gallery) and the polar bear (Temporary Exhibition gallery).

Social relationships

I also had the opportunity in the third study (Bates, 2016) to observe and document children's behaviours on their journeys to and from the museum each week. What particularly interested me was the way that the journeys and the growing significance of the museum as a familiar place supported the development of a friendship group between three girls (Christensen and Mikkelsen, 2013; Harju, 2013). As they entered and left through a small gate close to the museum, the girls developed the ritual of holding hands, jumping up and down and singing in anticipation and remembrance of their repeated visits. Hackett (2016: 178) describes this as an example of "shared embodied responses" to their experience. In other related studies, Harju (2013) suggests that children's social relationships can be rooted in place and Christensen and Mikkelsen (2013: 204) also specifically reference the importance of "companionship in movement" in the developing social relationships between girls. By extending my research to encompass the journey to and from the museum, it highlighted the importance of conceptually considering how museum visits for young children sit within their wider lives, local areas, relationships and daily experience.

Key strengths and benefits of project

As the gallery was underpinned by research with local families, we were able to tailor the space to include a range of objects which were of particular interest to our audience in a local context. The design of the gallery also reflects the ethos and strategic aims of the museum and the adjacent natural history galleries in using the collections to support a sustainable world. In keeping with the other natural history galleries at the museum, it is also an object-rich space and, as such, is popular with a range of visitors and not just families with young children. One of our volunteers commented, "Some adults and grandparents like to come in without children and sit and look because it is a pretty space … it's not like it's completely for children and full of children's stuff. So they don't feel like they need to leave" (Bates, 2015).

The redevelopment of the gallery was undertaken as an in-house project on a small budget by a cross-museum team, involving curatorial, conservation, visitor service and exhibition support staff. One of the challenges at the beginning of the project was finding an overarching theme for the design of the gallery as we did not have a design budget and there are also relatively few examples of children's galleries to visit in the United Kingdom. However, this did mean that we had to be more creative in terms of our time and resources. We used a Pinterest board to share ideas and develop design themes and recycled cases and objects from other exhibitions as far as possible. A small amount was spent on new British wildlife taxidermy specimens, for example a badger, squirrel and a variety of common birds which are used in other exhibition cases. The really valuable outcome of working in this way has been that the gallery has not only helped to raise the profile of the Early Years audience with our visitors but within the museum itself. This has helped to increase ownership of the space, which is now used for a variety of purposes including as a base for activities with young children visiting with their schools and families, to deliver researcher talks, musical and dance activities and as part of corporate events.

Manchester Museum is at the beginning of a capital redevelopment programme which will realise the building of a new South Asia gallery, Exhibition hall and China gallery by 2021. During this period, although some of the building will close, the natural history galleries will remain open and the Nature Discovery gallery will be used as an experimental space to develop new and innovative practice with a diverse range of families and schools bringing young children to the museum.

Final thoughts and implications for practice

Whilst a dedicated gallery for children under 5 is a great resource and asset for Manchester Museum, it is recognised that this will not be either possible or appropriate for other organisations. As each museum or gallery is unique and is funded differently, an Early Years offer will look different at each one, being integral to its strategic aims and appropriate for its collections and spaces. However, there are some key learning points from our experience of developing the gallery and engagement activities for young children which can be shared and used as a starting point for other organisations.

The gallery was developed at relatively low cost by undertaking research with local families and developing ideas in-house with a small museum team. For museums and galleries at the beginning of their journey in developing an Early Years offer, starting with a small idea and developing a sustainable and reciprocal relationship with a key local Early Years setting or group (within walking distance, if possible) to help you realise it, is a good starting point. Working in this way will support you to develop expertise in child development, pedagogy and best practice with young children. In return, the setting will have support from you to access the museum and to pilot and evaluate activities alongside you to develop an offer which is appropriate to the needs and experiences of young children in your locality. There is also an opportunity to support parental engagement and to encourage return family visits during weekend and holiday periods to access the wider museum or gallery offer. New activities can be marketed using a variety of platforms appropriate to your local audience and it is useful to ask them what works best. We have found that word of mouth and a Manchester-focussed Facebook page (culturekidsmanchester) work well for us. In order to ensure sustainable delivery, documenting and continuing to learn from practice is vital. Sharing experiences with other Early Years settings, local stakeholders and other museums and gallery professionals enables a wider conversation about the benefits of developing an offer for young children, in order to create gallery spaces that work for all audiences.

Acknowledgement

Parts of this case study have been previously published in the following journal article: Bates, E. (2018) Can natural history collections support a connection to nature for young children and families? *Museum & Society*, 16(3) 369–382 and are reproduced here with kind permission of the editors Gudrun D. Whitehead, Julia Petrov and Helen Saunderson.

References

Bates, E. (2014) Nature discovery: museums using natural history collections to support a connection to nature with young children and families. Unpublished report submitted as part of MA Education (Early Years), Birmingham City University.

Bates, E. (2015) Nature discovery: how can museums better support parent and child interactions? Unpublished report submitted as part of MA Education (Early Years), Birmingham City University.

Bates, E. (2016) An exploration of how museums can support the development of cultural capital in previously non-participating families with 2 year old children. Unpublished report submitted as part of MA Education (Early Years), Birmingham City University.

Bragg, R., Wood, C., Barton, J., and Pretty, J. (2013) *Measuring Connection to Nature in Children Aged 8–12: A Robust Methodology for the RSPB*. Royal Society for the Protection of Birds, visitwww.rspb.org.uk/Images/methodology-report_tcm9-354606.pdf.

Cheng, J. and Monroe, M. (2012) Connection to nature: children's affective attitude toward nature. *Environment and Behavior*, *44*(1), 31–49, doi:10.1177/0013916510385082.

Christensen, P. and Mikkelsen, M. (2013) There is nothing here for us ...! How girls create meaningful places of their own through movement. *Children & Society*, *27*(3), 197–207, doi:10.1111/j.1099-0860.2011.00413.x.

Dockett, S., Main, S., and Kelly, L. (2011) Consulting young children: experiences from a museum. *Visitor Studies*, *14*(1), 13–33, doi:10.1080/10645578.2011.557626.

Dunn, R. (2012) A vision of history: young children's perspective on a museum. In Peter Whiteman and Katey De Gioia (Eds) *Perspectives, Places and Practices* (1st edn), pp. 151–186. Newcastle upon Tyne: Cambridge Scholars.

Ernst, J. and Theimer, S. (2011) Evaluating the effects of environmental education programming on connectedness to nature. *Environmental Education Research*, *17*(5), 577–598, doi:10.1080/13504622.2011.565119.

Hackett, A. (2012) Zigging and zooming all over the place: young children's meaning making and movement in the museum. *Journal of Early Childhood Literacy*, *14*(1), 5–27, doi:10.1177/1468798412453730.

Hackett, A. (2016) Young children as wayfarers: learning about place by moving through it. *Children and Society*, *30*, 169–179.

Harju, A. (2013) 'Children's use of knowledge of place in understanding social relations. *Children and Society*, 27(2), 150–160, doi:10.1111/j.1099-0860.2011.00396.x.

Kellert, S. (2005) *Building for Life: Designing and Understanding the Human–Nature Connection*. Children and Nature.org, www.childrenandnature.org/uploads/Kellert_BuildingforLife.pdf.

Kirk, E. (2013) Gaining young children's perspectives on natural history collections. *Journal of Natural Science Collections*, 1, 138–143.

Kirk, E. and Buckingham, W. (2018) *Snapshots of Museum Experience Understanding Child Visitors Through Photography* (1st ed.). London: Routledge.

Louv, R. (2005) *Last Child in the Woods* (1st ed.) London: Atlantic.

Moss, S. (2012) *Natural Childhood*. Nationaltrust.org.uk, www.nationaltrust.org.uk/document–1355766991839.

Piscitelli, B. and Anderson, D. (2000) *Young Children's Learning in Museum Settings 2019*. Informal Science.org, http://archive.informalscience.org/researches/VSA-a0a6u6-a_5730.pdf.

Pretty, J., Angus, C., Bain, M., Gladwell, V., Hine, R., Pilgrim, S., Sandercock, G., and Sellens, M. (2009) *Nature, Childhood, Health and Life Pathways*. Healthy Parks, Healthy People Central, www.hphpcentral.com/wp-content/uploads/2010/10/Nature-Childhood-and-Health-iCES-Occ-Paper-2009-2-FINAL.pdf.

Tunnicliffe, S. and Reiss, M. (2000) What sense do children make of three-dimensional, life-sized "representations" of animals? *School Science and Mathematics*, *100*(3), 128–138, http://onlinelibrary.wiley.com/doi/10.1111/j.1949-8594.2000.tb17248.x/full.

15

COMMENTARY ON PART II

Places along lines of flight

Ricardo Nemirovsky and Molly L. Kelton

The chapters in this Part explore "what children's bodies do in places, paying attention to what happens beyond words. In particular, movement through and in place [which] is the foremost way children experience museums" (quote from the introduction). In this commentary we review how the case studies seem to engage Deleuze and Guattari's idea of "line of flight." First we outline the concept of line of flight and then we illustrate it with vignettes from the research reported by the contributors.

A place can be thought of as an *assemblage*. One way to describe a place, such as a museum, is by drawings displaying its layout as a whole. Another is by representing selected rooms or locations that can be found in it. As an assemblage, a place is neither an overall plan that can be stored on its own nor a collection of isolated locations, but a living sense of the place as a whole anchored in a set of interconnected and significant locations. A place-assemblage is a configuration of relations and noteworthy corners that is altered on an ongoing basis by, say, children hiding, currents of air, sunlight across windows, a family entering into the museum and so on. Some of these modifications can open up what Deleuze and Guattari called *lines of flight*. Lines of flight are prompted by local and circumstantial events sparking off the realization of possibilities outside the ones that had been ordinary or customary in that place-assemblage.

The vignette entitled "The revolving door" (Chapter 10) is the most developed example for the pursuit of a line of flight. As a commonplace, the revolving door at the main entrance of the museum is a routine presence. Nonetheless, during this episode it became a captivating mechanism filled with tensions and sparking possibilities that had been previously unnoticed and closed off. Its elements, such as the glass windows enclosing its inner compartments or the arduously turning surfaces came to be in-between adults and children, museum educators and visitors, the inside and the outside of the museum and so forth. The scene of the visitor coming out of the museum who decides to re-enter the revolving door and later waves her hand to the children, as the museum educators felt torn between concerns about safety and desires to nurture startling learning experiences, seem transformative of the place; in fact, the revolving door became a new place, traversed by pretend fish but not by live bugs. Sometimes budding lines of flight are not pursued because of risks, norm challenges or distractions, but in this case it was, as "one by one, all the children take a turn moving the door around."

Each chapter includes at least one example of a line of flight that opened, or could have opened, a transfigured place. In Chapter 11 we encounter an "informal buggy park" that had spontaneously been created by visitors allowing adults "to bring children out of their buggy to the creative play zone." Chapter 12 describes a staircase that "held a fascination for the young visitors" to the point that one of the children went down the stairs bumping on her bottom. Chapter 13 discusses the use of a raised platform that transformed the gallery. Two children played "a chasing game in the hidden space at the back of some exhibits in the Fossils gallery" (Chapter 14). These episodes lead us to think that a major methodological approach of the research conducted by the contributors of this Part is to create conditions for the emergence of lines of flight and their careful pursuit. This is a type of research focussed on the powers of place-creation, towards enabling a more inclusive capacity for who can be playful and at home at the museum.

PART III

Time, new experiences and repeat visits

16
INTRODUCTION TO PART III

Christina MacRae, Abigail Hackett and Rachel Holmes

In this final Part of the book, the case studies variously touch on ways that experience, duration, time and memory are an entangled aspect of ways that young children and their families visit museums. Most obviously a child's (or carer/parent's) first visit to the museum is a significant moment: they encounter an unfamiliar building and one that contains a wealth of unfamiliar objects. The sheer scale of the building, along with its strange sounds and sights, can be overwhelming. In the case studies in this Part, we hear stories of how, in very different ways, children and their families have made the strange space of the museum or gallery familiar through emerging patterns of behaviour, some of which have developed over repeat visits. All too often there is an anxiety on the part of adults that revisiting the same exhibits, coming back to the same place and repeating the same routines is not productive in terms of museum and gallery learning. However, these case studies demonstrate how, in different ways, attuned relationships and creative improvisations emerge through encounters that are both familiar and unfamiliar. It is these routines, traditions, as well as emerging small events that become anchoring threads in "now" time of the present moment. At this same time these encounters reverberate through and across time, transforming the "not now" time of past memories, as well as transforming our future times to come. Recurring routines can generate moments of deep connection-making and relationships built both with human others (for example, the comfort of friends at a playgroup session) as well as relationships formed with non-human others (for example where a routine coalesces around a particular location in the building, or around a particular object or exhibit). Traditions, routines and unique encounters that emerge through families' engagements with the museum (Hackett, 2016) can allow us to think more profoundly about how time, memory, movement and meaning-making are deeply interconnected. Further emphasising this theme of emergent routine and encountering the unfamiliar, two of the case studies in this Part (Thorp and Drum) describe off-site engagements with children and families, where curators and artists are themselves navigating less familiar territory as they feel their way into new approaches to engagement and address new questions. Often off-site engagements are seen in terms of future-oriented audience development, however in these case studies it becomes clear that the relationships and experiences created in and of themselves have their own value. When working beyond the museum or gallery building, and engaging on a regular basis with a local community, the museum can make an unconditional offer of time to the participants and accompanying this is an intense focus on the experiences and relationships that take place in the moment.

The introduction to this Part will explore some of the complex ways that time unfolds for families, both when they first encounter museum spaces as well as over regular and repeat visits. Regular visits might be in the form of play sessions or workshops, and here internal rituals and routines are co-created through the active participation of museum practitioners and families over time. Where families explore the museum space beyond the play sessions, more singular rituals and routines emerge that are particular to specific children and carers, but that also coalesce around encounters with objects and places. Threading through the temporal qualities at play during and across visits, key themes come to the fore: the unpredictability of how encounters with the museum unfold; the comfort and the joy of the anticipation of the familiar and the emergence of ritual; and, finally, the pleasures of losing oneself in time.

The emergence of communities through improvisation, routines, traditions and repetition

Throughout the case studies we see how, over the duration of repeat visits, patterns and routines are always in a dynamic process of emergence. This might be expressed in the immersive space of an art installation in the Manchester Art Gallery (McCall) where parents wait to see Health Visitors, or in the ways that children engage with the opening and closing routines of play-based sessions such as the ringing of a bell or a goodbye song. These routine signals offer the reassurance of anchor points, like familiar landmarks on a map, but they are also lively routines that are enacted dynamically. This allows for transformation and the emergence of the new forms, ideas and practices. The signatures of these routines seem almost to be impressed invisibly into the fabric of the museum or gallery space; spaces that await future visits where routines will be lived through once again. Following Orley (2012), this can help us to take seriously James Joyce's thought that perhaps not only do people remember events, but that also "places remember events." For example, when children re-encounter a place or objects that have triggered a running routine in a previous visit, they find themselves set in motion once again as the running is re-ignited: it is as if the place was waiting for the child.

In Hallberg's case study a data vignette describes a family tradition that has been produced by a child and a grandmother over weeks of attending a regular playgroup at the Streetlife Museum in Hull and where, after each session, they walk back through the gallery space. Child and grandmother make their way to a particular bench, located next to a stationary steam train. Sitting on the bench signals the start of them acting out a tradition where the two of them pretend to be going off on a holiday. This sophisticated routine was rehearsed over a period of visits and involved actions as well as a verbal narrative. At the same time as they repeat actions from previous visits, there is a sense of an improvisatory quality that continues to allow for new actions to be set into motion each time the family re-encounters the bench and the steam train. Perhaps it is possible to imagine that the bench remembers this routine, just as child and grandmother do? The bench that the two sat on became an animating force that, coupled with the sound of the steam train (activated by a nearby sensor), had a powerful force that propelled TH and his Grandma to act out the familiar routine. The bench could be seen as having a vitality that was productive in bringing the routine to life but, at the same time, both TH and his Grandma had their own dynamic parts to play in the ritual. The bench has become something they both look forward to: it is a site of "anticipation" (Manning, 2016: 72). As TH and his Grandma approach the bench they have a sense that they are about to enter a particular "shift in register" (Manning, 2016: 67) that takes place as soon as they sit on the bench and start to act out the holiday routine. While the bench is something that they can look forward to, at the same time it is a site of "memory" (ibid: 72). This ritual is something they share and "do" together. It is also something they can look back at in other times and in other places. Finally, the bench tradition expresses a material "attunement" (ibid) between the visitors and the space and stuff of the museum; this involves forming a kinship and attachment with the bench, the stacked suitcases and the soundtrack of the steam train. The impression that the bench makes on their bodies is lasting and extends through and across time. This collective and repeated set of responses to place, object and sound demonstrates a dynamic and deep level of engagement with both the architecture as well as the collections afforded by the gallery. As Ingold might say, "materials are not in time; they are the stuff of time itself" (2012: 43).

Museums and galleries as event-ful space: assemblages and lines of flight

Children's experiences in museum spaces, then, consist of movements back and forth between the familiar and the unfamiliar. Deleuze (1995) and Guattari's (1995) notion that minor events are always full of unpredictable possibility is something that can help us to think about this. The kind of events that they speak of are not the large-scale events that we plan in advance; the kind of events that galleries and museums organise through their programming. Here, we are talking about the small-scale events that unfold unpredictably through encounters with things and people. Sometimes these events are so small and seemingly inconsequential that we do not always even notice them taking place. Returning to the bench routine, we need to remember that it was at first initiated through an encounter with an unfamiliar space of the museum. What might the initial encounter with the full-size steam train on their first visit have been like? Perhaps it was overwhelming because of its scale and the first time they accidentally set off the sensor, activating the very loud sound of the steam train, would have been a startling event. This shock of the unfamiliar led to an in-the-moment response; over time this developed into a materially entangled story-action routine; one small event, leading to the production of repeated enactments of the event.

In Deleuze and Guattari's philosophy, events like the bench routine unfold when we respond to encounters with things or place. Events, as defined by Deleuze and Guattari, are sites of potential and possibility, as we are never entirely sure how they will unfold or what connections or directions they might lead us towards. These encounters stop us in our tracks and absorb us intensely. In doing so, they can trouble our common-sense understanding of time as necessarily linear. They remind us that time can also seem to move at different speeds and sometimes almost stand still when we are lost in experience. Deleuze and Guattari talk about two kinds of temporality: first "Chronos" as dominant institutional time, characterised as linear and measured. In contrast is "Aeon," which they describe as cyclical time: a kind of time that unfolds in events and encounters, moving at different speeds, with different intensities (2004: 289/290). Aeonic time is time that is associated with the unfolding of events that emerge out of encounters of bodies and things. The space of this encounter is something that Deleuze and Guattari would call an "assemblage." Assemblages express what Massey (2005: 151) describes as the "throwntogetherness" of space, a constellation of matter (the bench, the train, the steam train sound, the child, the grandmother and more). An assemblage has the capacity to set events into motion. These events are constituted in both space and time, but the way that time unfolds in a small, but intensely felt event bears the quality of Aeonic time. We do not know exactly where it will lead us and it moves at different speeds that respond in the moment to the dynamic and shifting assemblage in which micro-encounters set off connections or "lines of flight" (Deleuze and Guttari, 2004: 10) that set new things in motion.

> The construction of an assemblage does not take place in a rationally planned manner. It must be treated as a little machinery that sets itself going and that nobody really controls.
>
> *(Olsson, 2009: 150)*

Holding on to this notion of the event and encounter in relation to family visits in museum and gallery space, we can now look more closely at the ways that events unfold in time and space. A lovely example of ways that an event unfolds is described by Penfold and Turner when they tell the story of Oliver and the "big brother trap." Here we witness how cardboard, paint, colour, texture, baby brother (and so much more) all played their part in how Oliver and box acted on each other as the "big brother trap" event played out. And, as with many of the other case studies, Penfold and Turner invoke the educational philosophy of Reggio Emilia as influential in the way they plan their work. In particular they emphasise the environment as the third teacher and, along with this, they pay attention to both materials and the qualities of space, such as light and colour, as all playing a part in mobilising bodies in action.

Small events generate very singular meanings that have a life of their own and go beyond pre-defined learning outcomes. These moments have the effect of producing very close relationships between children and the museum and gallery space. It is clear that these kinds of engagements with both the materials and the fabric of the museum are not ones that can be sought in advance, but rather they will flourish when both the space of the museum, as well as the adults who accompany the child, maintain a quality of openness that is difficult to pin down. This openness demands an ability to anticipate where children's interests may lie, but at the same time to quickly respond to unexpected directions of thought, or "lines of flight," that emerge in the moment. It also requires that as adults we recognise that the body itself thinks-in-action, rather than our usual expectations that learning always needs to be expressed in language. Atkinson talks about the pedagogy of the event, saying that:

> We need pedagogies that are open to the irreducible singularity of what happens; pedagogies that can be fed and nourished by the surprise of the unexpected. Such pedagogies would then be pedagogies of the event.
>
> *(2011: 19)*

If we start to recognise the potential of these moments, we need to let go of our expectations of what *should* happen in the museum and instead respond to what *is* happening in the here and now.

The tyranny of chronological time: the importance of noticing and caring for small events

Iris Duhn draws our attention to how:

> The movement towards the event, towards the encounter and the desire for change and becoming may be cherished in theory, including educational research theory, but in practice, adult (and children's) lives are governed by risk-averse sensibilities and rationalities that deal cautiously with bodies and matter.
>
> *(2015: 928)*

What is so refreshing in the case studies presented here is the intuition that making spaces and environments that are open and supportive to the creation of small, local, but significant events requires thought, experimentation and an attention to the non-chronological lived times of many families. For example, one common theme emerging from all the session case studies is the need for flexibility in relation to the timings of the sessions or workshops. Drum's case study takes inspiration from the pedagogical approach of St Miniato, where the giving of time to participating families is a core principle. She describes sessions at the Irish National Gallery, aimed at families with babies, that were repeated twice in the day to provide the same sessions in the morning and afternoon as a way to respond to different family care routines. They also were able to offer sessions outside the museum in localities where the families lived, offering proximity when family-time is so often under pressure. In the case studies from the Whitworth (Penfold) and the Manchester Art Gallery (McCall), there has been a shift from pre-booked sessions to drop-in formats in order to better accommodate the more unpredictable and messy realities of young children and their families. We also hear about family-oriented galleries that are accessible to families at all times, like the London Docklands Museum Mudlarks Gallery (Smith) and the Transport Tots sessions in Hull (Hallberg) that are run on a flexible and drop-in basis. This flexible open-door policy adopts an approach to time that is less clock-bound and aligned to the chronological time of institutions and, instead, moves more in the direction of aeonic time with its variable speeds that might better reflect the everyday realities of families with really young children. For example, this reality might be where a family's plan for the day does not unfold as expected; somehow it is already mid-afternoon and the trip to the museum that was supposed to have taken place in the morning never materialised. Or equally it could reflect the reality of a child who has become absorbed in an intensive period of play in the gallery space and an atmosphere that gives adults permission to wait and let time stand still, without the pressure of finishing on time or moving onto the next thing.

Furthermore, having a safe-base, whether it is in the form of a dedicated gallery or a play-session in the gallery space, offers an anchoring point from which families can explore other rooms, spaces and collections, but always in relation to the more familiar space that they visit on a regular basis. The offer of safe-bases from which to venture from, of flexibility but, at the same time, of supple patterns and routines, all become political acts of inclusion, ensuring that time is allowed to flow at different speeds and intensities. As Peter Moss says, we need to give thought to time as it is under such pressure and in such short supply: he asks "how we might redistribute it across a range of activities and relationships, for example to enable parents to participate in democratic and experimental early childhood institutions" (Moss, 2012: 146). He goes on to point out that in both the St Miniato and the Reggio approaches to early childhood, a fundamental principle is that of the complementarity of care and education rather than them being opposed. And keeping care as a guiding principle helps to ground our practice in "now" time.

In the case study that took place across four Stockholm museums, Carter deliberately followed the paths forged by children's curiosity in order to embrace the unknowability of the visit experience as it unfolded. Following the lead of young children as they respond to the museum objects and spaces can be read as what Manning would call "a care for the event" (Manning, 2016: 192), which she also describes as a "dance of attention" (p. 193). This kind of attention is cultivated by slowing down, in tuning into the small moments that play out during encounters. Another way of expressing a care for the event is in the pedagogical practice of documentation (another practice borrowed from Reggio Emilia); a practice that Penfold and Turner's case study describes. Documenting can become a way to value the singularity and significance of events through making them visible. The act of documenting events (for example, filming or photographing), as well as discussing, sharing and reflecting on these, are ways to make visible the lines of flight and movement that unfolded during the event. This practice allows us to attend more to the activating qualities of materials and space that through the encounter "force us to think" (Deleuze, 1994: 139).

In the case of Penfold and Turner's study, Oliver's encounter with the slippery-ness of paint on a cardboard box, for instance, seems to temporarily cause him to change tack. The meeting of child and box offers the "potential to interrupt a pre-determined order of things, producing their own inventive and singular forms of knowing" (MacRae et al., 2018: 512). Pedagogical documentation offers a tool that allows us to think more deeply about time in that it "maps out a fraction of a learning event and makes it materialise before us in the documentation" (Lenz Taguchi, 2010: 60). Not only does the documentation make visible the singularity of the event as it unfolds, it also shifts our attention to the way that adults respond to these moments. In this instance, the documentation was put to work in order to reflect on the role of the atelierista to guide Oliver rather than to teach him and to "value uncertainty, contextuality and subjectivity in learning" (Penfold and Turner's case study this volume, Chapter 22), as well as the sheer potential of improvisatory practice (Hackett et al., 2018: 484).

Time and play: being in the middle

> A sense of wonder that causes children to "stop [in their] tracks, to convey an arresting sense of uniqueness, to evoke an exalted attention."
>
> *(Greenblatt, 1990: 20)*

> One never has a tabula rasa; one slips in, enters in the middle; one takes up or lays down rhythms.
>
> *(Deleuze, 1988: 123)*

The case studies in this Part remind us that we should take the play-time very seriously. In both the cases of the Whitworth (Penfold and Turner) and the Serpentine (Thorp), artists and curators engage families and Early Years practitioners in a process where research is part of the terms of engagement. At the Whitworth the process of documenting play as it unfolds demands adults (with children) think more deeply about the potential of play events. In the case study from the Serpentine Gallery, a partnership between curators, a designer and a local children's centre was deliberately staged as an experimental investigation into exploring the potential of the city as play-scape. In this case, the designer Bahbak began with a question to explore, asking "what are the conditions of play?" and, linked to this, what might adults do to best support the here-and-now of play? This question about the part played by adults acknowledges how important it is that we recognise that adults are part of any assemblage in which children play. Here the collaboration between artist, curator and children's centre resulted in repeat visits to the space around a nearby tower block. This urban landscape is unfamiliar as a sanctioned play space, however it also is familiar to the children who walk past it on their way to school. Recalling Peter Moss's earlier reminder that time is always a political matter, this case study helps us to think about time in relation to play and asks how do we open possibilities for play-time? The project took risks by exploring spaces not usually associated with children and play, dark, dirty and uncomfortable concrete urban spaces. It allowed children to encounter litter, a dead pigeon, puddles and locked spaces. As with other case studies, the repeat visits with the same group of children engendered a sense of community, which became stronger over time but also payed close attention to ways that children became part of a community of material things. Here sheets of industrial fabric, the activity and effort of carrying wooden planks to the tower block locale, the bridges created when planks were connected to wall and concrete ledges, were more than simply a community of people, but also a community of things.

In this Part, the mixture of experiences that are familiar, or almost mundane, and those that are unfamiliar, challenging or confusing, seemed to provide a rhythm to the families' and children's visit. This temporal back and forth between the familiar and the unfamiliar gives rise to the emergence of rhythms that connect with place; places in (and out) of the museum that feel both safe and unsafe. Familiar spaces and objects invite an engagement that is obvious and predictable, while unfamiliar places and strange things have the potential to set in motion wonder, "exploring" and ambiguous feelings. This is a constant and oscillating movement between the known and the not yet known. Perhaps, as Costa suggests, we should talk of *cyclical time* instead of *linear time*, "a sort of wheel of time rather than an arrow" Costa (1996: 64). During these rhythms, the roles of adults and children undergo transformation, as the linear time that so often governs the lives of adults is dislodged to make way for the slowness, the intensity and the circularity of the here-and-now.

References

Atkinson, D. (2011) *Art, Equality, and Learning. Pedagogies against the State*. Rotterdam: Sense.

Costa, C. (1996) Time doesn't exist for colours. In Filippini, T. and Vecchi, V (Eds) *The Hundred Languages of Children*. Reggio Children, Reggio Emilia, pp. 64–66.

Deleuze, G. (1988) *Spinoza: Practical Philosophy*. San Francisco: City Light Books.

Deleuze, G. (1994) *Difference and Repetition*. Trans. Paul Patton. London: Athlone.

Deleuze, G. (1995) *Negotiations, 1972–1990*. New York: Columbia University Press.

Deleuze, G. and Guttari, F. (2004) *A Thousand Plateaus: Capitalism and Schizophrenia*. London: Continuum.

Duhn, I. (2015. Making agency matter: rethinking infant and toddler agency in educational discourse, Discourse: Studies in the Cultural Politics of Education, 36:6, 920–931, DOI:10.1080/01596306.2014.918535

Greenblatt, S. (1990): Resonance and Wonder, *Bulletin of the American Academy of Arts and Sciences*. 43:4 11–34.

Guattari, F. (1995) *Chaosmosis: An Ethico-Aesthetic Paradigm*. Sydney: Power Publications.

Hackett, A. (2016): Young children as wayfarers: learning about place by moving through it. *Children and Society* 30: 169–179.

Hackett, A., Holmes, R., MacRae, C. and Procter, L. (2018) Young children's museum geographies: spatial, material and bodily ways of knowing. *Children's Geographies*, 16:5, 481–488, doi: 10.1080/14733285.2018.1497141.

Ingold, T. (2012) Toward an ecology of materials. *Annual Review of Anthropology*, 41.

Lenz Taguchi, H. (2010) *Going Beyond the Theory/Practice Divide in Early Childhood Education. Introducing an Intra Active Pedagogy*. Abingdon: Routledge.

MacRae, C. Hackett, A. Holmes, R. and Jones, L. (2018): Vibrancy, repetition, movement: Posthuman theories for reconceptualising young children in museums. *Children's Geographies*, 16:5, 503–515, doi: 10.1080/14733285.2017.1409884.

Manning, E. (2016) *The Minor Gesture*. London: Duke University Press.

Massey, Doreen. (2005) *For Space*. London: SAGE Publications.

Moss, P. (2012) Governed markets and democratic experimentalism: two possibilities for early childhood education and care, In Kjorholt, A. T. and Qvortrup, J. (Eds) *The Modern Child and the Flexible Labour Market*. Basingstoke: Palgrave Macmillan, pp. 128–149.

Olsson, L. (2009) *Movement and Experimentation in Young Children's Learning. Deleuze and Guattari in Early Childhood Education*. Abingdon: Routledge.

Orley, E. (2012). Places Remember Events: Towards an Ethics of Encounter. In H. Andrews and L. Roberts (eds) Liminal Landscapes: Travel, Experience and Spaces In-between, Routledge.

17

TRANSPORT TOTS AT STREETLIFE MUSEUM, HULL

A familiar and unfamiliar space

Esther Hallberg

Transport Tots is a weekly playgroup held in a central gallery in the Streetlife Museum in Hull. It started its life experimentally to explore ways to engage families with under 5s in Hull museums. Our starting point was to think about what would attract us, as parents, who also had children of that age. Our aim was to develop the sessions as we learned more about the audience and what they wanted to see and do at our museums. It has grown to become the flagship activity of our Under 5s programme in Hull. This case study explores how a weekly playgroup became a familiar space through repeated visits. As families became "at home" in the playgroup, this space operated as a launch pad for visits into the less familiar spaces of the wider museum. When families made these excursions into the Streetlife Museum, unfamiliar spaces were transformed through rituals and return visits. These sites then became familiar spaces that families would look forward to visiting as well as becoming places where memories were shared. This is a story of playgroup sessions that have taken place over a long period of time and developed through both improvising as well as through practice and research.

Background

In early 2016, we were in the beginning stages of our Arts-Council-funded Under 5s project and planning our activity programme. A survey had been undertaken in 2015 to establish how the Hull Museums sites were performing in terms of engagement with Under 5s and families. Streetlife (our transport-themed museum) had performed relatively well in the survey and had proved the most popular with Under 5s and families (DBA Consultancy, 2015: 11). In the survey (and our own preliminary consultation), a number of parents had said that they'd like to see interactive sessions happening for Under 5s at the museums. At the same time, we wanted to encourage independent exploration of the Streetlife Museum building and collections, as we felt strongly that its sounds, smells and collection of transport and vehicles (including some you can climb aboard or ride on) seemed a perfect match for a first venture. Importantly, it also had a community exhibition and event space which could host an Under-5s session.

In the first year of our Under 5s project we visited other museums, galleries and heritage sites to observe examples of best practice of working with Under 5s and families. We worked with the University of Sheffield to produce the APSE framework to gather our observations and draw conclusions about what could work for us at our sites (Hackett and Procter, 2015). Drawing from what we found to be engaging in these sessions, as well as observing play sessions at children's centres locally, we gave our own session a basic play group format based on: toys, sensory materials, stories and singing. To try and encourage visitors to engage with the collections, we also developed a series of "trails"; themed vehicles and items to spot around the museum. In April 2016, *Transport Tots*, advertised through the Hull Early Years Service and Social Media, was delivered for the first time. In the first full year we had 2,273 participants.

Research and development

We collected evaluation and qualitative data in a number of ways at Transport Tots, from scribbles on sign-in sheets to artwork produced by children in sessions, as well as through external evaluator interviews and academic research. This has helped us understand the impact of the sessions and also informed our planning. As part of the Humber Museums Partnership, we worked with researchers from Manchester Metropolitan University to gather data that would help us to gain deeper insights into how young children and their families experience our museums (Hackett et al., 2017). In 2017/2018 we also had the project formally evaluated, including interviews with parents, staff and partners. Combining this evidence has provided a comprehensive picture of participant engagement (especially when, for many families, an evaluation form or interview is not appropriate).

As facilitators, we had heard from families who attended the Transport Tots sessions that before, during and after the sessions they would visit other spaces in the museum and many of their children had particular places or vehicles that they liked to go back to every week. Some had particular routines that developed around these objects, from stepping on and off the tram, to "feeding the horses" or sitting on a particular seat in a bus. For others there were also areas that they would avoid; for one child this was a darker room with a laughing policeman arcade game. For some children the darkness, sounds and smells of the museum were overwhelming and frightening.

Because we were facilitating the sessions, we could not get a feel for the different ways that families interacted with the museum space during the play-sessions as we were either preparing, delivering or tidying up when families went off to see other parts of the museum. In order to get a deeper understanding of ways that families engaged with Streetlife over a duration of many sessions, we worked with researchers from Manchester Metropolitan University and ten families who attended regularly and were recruited from the Transport Tots session. The researcher attended a series of four weekly sessions, both observing Transport Tots sessions, collecting field notes and photos taken by the children themselves, talking to parents and children and (when invited) participating in the families' walks around the museum space after the sessions.

We discovered that some rituals were complex and had developed over time using a variety of physical, sensory and verbal cues. For example, a young boy (TH), who came to Transport Tots with his Grandma, would lead her to their special bench (see Figure 17.1):

> TH rushes ahead and knows when to turn off to find his special seat. By the time we get to the corner he is already sitting on the middle of a bench – he looks expectantly at us and he faces a large steam locomotive. Next to the bench are a pile of old leather suitcases. His grandma sits next him. Grandma says "look so here's our luggage, where are we going to go?" It is evident this has been done many times before. TH answered "don't know" and Grandma suggests a place where they have been on holiday and he nods his head. Grandma says, "shall I make it go, are you ready," and again he nods, and Grandma gets up and goes out of sight to where the motion-trigger is that sets off the sound of a moving steam train and its hoot.
>
> *(Hackett, Procter & MacRae, 2017)*

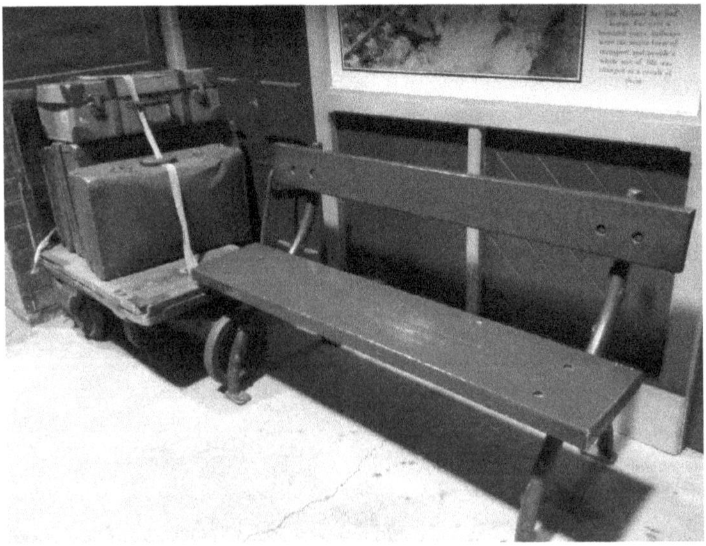

FIGURE 17.1 The bench by the steam train.
Credit: Christina MacRae.

Because these rituals had developed over time, they often had a greater significance for the participants than was obvious at first. This is partly because of the bonding during these shared family experiences and also because the memories of each visit offered children ways to make more connections and build on these past experiences.

> This collective and repeated set of responses to place, object, and sound demonstrates a dynamic and deep level of engagement with both the architecture and as well as the collections afforded by the gallery.
>
> *(Hackett et al., 2017)*

Reflections on playgroup rituals and attachments

A number of regularly attending children at Transport Tots just wanted to play with the same toys each week. For some it was cars, the train set, the construction and emergency services role play, while for others it was quite simply very familiar items like the jigsaws. In one case, a child and carer always arrived after the songs and story, and the child only ever played with cars. He would rarely talk to facilitators, however the two returned week-on-week for the predictable but eagerly anticipated special time spent together within the museum space. We also noticed that relationships between children that developed over time also grew out of repeat play rituals, for example two children who attended regularly and who initially played independently began to interact and play together as firemen and builders, carrying out familiar routines, but only in each other's presence.

Each week we put out objects linked to our chosen theme, but where possible with an awareness of their interactive and sensory qualities. This led to a sense of anticipation before arrival and excitement about the theme that week. The most popular of these objects was the pirate ship (especially if combined with sand), the foam rocket launcher and the bubble wrap road. One regular visitor asked nearly every week if the rocket launcher was coming out. On weeks when it was, they were occupied for much of the session with it, returning regularly to have another go. On other weeks they tended to move around and take part in everything. We also responded to adult and child suggestions, for example one parent requested a cardboard box to become a car and the following week we found one child completely engaged with the box, "fixing" it with tools from other areas. Similarly, we found that certain objects (like the pirate ship) entertained children for long periods and this was especially true of materials such as water, sand or lentils that absorbed children through sensory engagement.

Paths of activity, movement of things and safe-bases

Some children moved from one activity to another and others tended to stick with favourites. We tried to keep some consistency in the set up, so that the environment was mostly familiar and felt "safe," but at the same time we introduced a few different elements each week. This gave children both familiarity as well as freedom to move around and explore different things. We also noticed that it is not only children who move around, but things. The toys and materials offered in each session are appropriated and they also travel around the playgroup space. For example, tools from the construction area may be transported to "fix" the much smaller cars in the toy garage and pom-poms from the baby area are used as a car wash for a larger toy fire engine. At the same time as recognising the need to allow this dynamic of movement of people and resources, we recognise the importance of the playgroup space itself as a constant. For example, at first, when the temporary exhibitions in the space changed or we had to change rooms during an installation, this caused issues for the Transport Tots visitors, who felt lost. These disruptions to the sessions have made us value the regular and dependable safe base from which children and their families can explore: we now work around the exhibition and it works around us.

Personal relationships, group dynamics and conviviality

The atmosphere in the group depends very much on the visitors on that day. For example, when we have childminders or groups of friends visiting, the singing is louder and the story is more interactive because they are used to being in a larger group. Operating as a drop in, it is hard to strike a balance when there are new visitors, but the presence of a core group of regular visitors is key. Regulars would sometimes take on responsibility for helping with some aspects of the smooth running of the sessions. In one case, when the facilitator had lost track of time, parents stepped in to start the process. Parents commented that they love how informal, inclusive and welcoming the group is and that this is unusual for play groups which can often feel cliquey (Mair et al., 2018):

> I like seeing how she [under-five child] interacts with [the facilitator] and the other children and their parents. It's important to help her develop confidence.
>
> *(Parent of under-five child, Transport Tots feedback, Streetlife Museum)*

> It's a small number so you can talk to other people – not too loud. The group leader gets to spend time with the children which is really nice as a parent.
>
> *(Parent in Mair et al., 2018)*

For a period, two friends, who visited nearly every week with their daughters up until they went to school, took a degree of ownership over the group. Not only did they help out with tidying up and in busy periods but they also brought in cakes to one of our outdoor sessions, be-friended others and welcomed newcomers.

Improvising in space

Our sessions are held in a plain temporary exhibition space that does not have any of the architectural idiosyncrasies of older buildings. It does, however, have a long corridor that leads up to the room which is lined with mock shop fronts from the past. We've found that many of our younger walking visitors (aged 18 months–2 years) have a habit of using this as an opportunity to practice running and walking and they will do this throughout the session. When parents and carers run after and catch them, this is almost always met with giggles, because this is part of the game. At times we've witnessed how this can become contagious and other children join in. Older children tend to notice the contents of the shop fronts (particularly the old toys) and these become lingering and talking points on the way in or out. Some participants "take a break" from the session to explore the museum (sometimes following previous paths and journeys taken) and return later: we feel it is important to build in flexibility to the session for families to respond to the habits that they have developed slowly over their visits. Creating a space within the Streetlife Museum that children and parents come back to week after week has created an environment from which families can explore and create their own routines and rituals. As museum professionals we have come to value the improvisatory practices of children and their carers; these practices affirm that we have been successful in responsively creating the familiar playgroup space that allows families to venture securely from, into the less familiar spaces of the wider museum.

Final thoughts and implications for practice

- It is through investigating and researching families' experiences of provision that best shapes the ways to respond to how sessions should be structured; for example, we shortened our session after noticing that children became distracted as it was close to lunchtime.
- Regular playgroup attendance offers a safe-base and a springboard for families' self-led visits to the other galleries before, during and after the sessions. Initially we provided trails for participants to find items in the museum, but we quickly found that they were happy to find their own interesting vehicles and objects. By researching these self-initiated visits we were able to discover and celebrate the family traditions and rituals that developed over repeat visits in the wider gallery spaces.
- The regularity of the playgroup session has not only made parents feel at home in the museum, but has also resulted in front of house staff getting to know the participants and their needs and building relationships with them.

References

DBA Consultancy (2015) *Humber Museums Partnership Audiences Survey: Families with Children Under-Five*, Sheffield, unpublished.

Hackett, A. and Procter, L. (2015), *APSE: An Analytical Framework to Examine Young Children's Engagements with Space*, Sheffield: Centre for the Study of Childhood and Youth and School of Education.

Hackett, A., Procter, L., and MacRae, C. (2017) How do families with under fives experience museums? Research report for Humber Museum Partnership, unpublished report, Manchester Metropolitan University.

Mair, S., Mair, L., and Billson, A. (2018) *HMP Under 5s Evaluation*, unpublished.

18

WORKING OFF-SITE WITH FAMILIES WITH YOUNG CHILDREN AT THE NATIONAL GALLERY OF IRELAND

Joanne Drum

This chapter reflects on two off-site projects initiated by the National Gallery of Ireland that have both emerged from, and fed back into their Early Years programme. In both cases we found that we needed to attend to a careful balancing act between the rhythms and routines of families, and the rhythms and routines in the workshop sessions. We became aware of the need to be responsive to diverse family practices and to create a space that was flexible enough to allow relationships between participants as well as to enable the workshop space itself to flourish. Our off-site projects have, in different ways, demonstrated how time is precious and that it becomes a significant factor when planning family programmes.

Background

The National Gallery of Ireland (NGI) is located in Dublin's south city centre. The collection is comprised of about 16,000 paintings, drawings, watercolours, miniatures, prints, sculpture and decorative arts. It includes masterpieces by many of the most celebrated figures in the history of western European art, such as Caravaggio, Vermeer, Monet and Picasso. In addition, the Gallery houses the most comprehensive collection of historic Irish art. The Education Department of the NGI aims to provide a year-round public programme of participation, engagement and learning events connected to the public building, the national collection and temporary exhibitions. We aim to provide many access points for our diverse audiences and we value the transformative, complex and curious qualities inherent in art education. We believe that the learning process can be a rewarding experience with the power to inspire and engage diverse audiences. Following on from the very successful NGIBaby workshops (begun in 2013), provision for babies and under 3s has become part of our core programming. In this time, the NGI has tried to tackle the "invisible" perceived barrier to parents and carers of small children who might feel as if this place is not for them.

This chapter is an exploration of two off-site Early Years projects begun by the NGI in 2017. The first project, *Big Way, Little Ways*, was with an Early Years group in a local community centre in a disadvantaged area of the south inner city, close to the NGI. The second longer-term project is ongoing with young children and their families in a residential centre for homeless families. In 2013, we developed the first museum programmes for babies and toddlers in Ireland, NGIBaby and Tiny Tots. This was in response to the increasing numbers of families with very young children visiting the gallery. This consisted of a pilot phase followed by free monthly workshops. The age guideline for babies is babies from birth to not yet walking. The Tiny Tots workshops were for the under 3s. This expanded our existing programme of Parent and Baby tours, established in 2005, but shifted the focus more on to the experience of the babies and toddlers.

Through various feedback-led small changes and iterations, the workshops became cemented in our programme with two free baby workshops on one Monday per month, one at 12 pm and one at 2 pm. The workshops are delivered by the same facilitator and they are identical, but the times mean that they fit into the varying routines of young babies.

The Tiny Tots workshops developed into something different. In response to how real families function and visit the gallery, we created a new workshop offering in January 2017: free drop-in family workshops. These take place every Sunday and are suitable for families with children of all ages. The theme always takes inspiration from some element of the collection or exhibition. Tables of varying heights are set up and the children select the height that works best for them. The workshops run from 11.30 am to 1.30 pm and families are welcome to stay for as long (or as little) as they choose. We have found that this approach works very well. We don't have to turn anyone away and families are encouraged to create artwork together. During the two off-site projects, we recommended that families visit the gallery by themselves and attend these workshops.

The NGIBaby workshops were free but ticketed and such was the demand that the ten baby places per workshop would often book out (even with a small amount of planned overbooking) within half an hour of going on sale. In September 2017 we decided to charge a nominal fee of €5 for these workshops so that they would be almost cost-neutral. The allocated budget for them could then be re-directed to Early Years workshops for people in disadvantaged areas or situations, as these people were typically not attending the NGIBaby workshops on site.

Off-site activities

To give some insight into how we cater for babies and toddlers off-site, it is necessary to understand the current Early Years education scheme in Ireland. The Early Childhood Care and Education (ECCE) scheme was introduced in 2010. This entitled all children to a free year of preschool before entering

Junior Infants (Reception in the UK). This scheme was extended in September 2018 to include a second year of preschool for children aged 2 years 8 months and over. Currently, the majority of pre-school children are entitled to 15 hours a week, 38 weeks a year, of education for two years. The uptake is at approximately 95% of eligible children. The preschool must adhere to the principles of Síolta, the National Framework for Early Years care and education.[1] This scheme means that, effectively, when we go off-site to provide Early Years activities during the preschool and school day, we can now expect to encounter children from birth up to approximately 2 years, 8 months.

Project 1: *Big Way, Little Ways* at St Andrew's Resource Centre

The first off-site Early Years project was with a local community resource centre, St Andrew's. We had made initial contact with the centre's Family Support Social Worker, Dara Terry, and both sides expressed an interest in working together. The Early Years creative practitioner, Jackie Maguire, was invited to devise and deliver a course of workshops for service users. Jackie had previously run a baby course in the NGI, *The Moonlight Project* (2015), which had been a great success. Artist Beth O'Halloran also co-facilitated six of the sessions by creating participative visual art elements.

Focussing on babies and toddlers up to about age 3, Jackie created a course inspired by one of the NGI's newest works, *Magnus Modus* by Joseph Walsh. This is a wooden sculptural piece commissioned for the new NGI courtyard space, created during a recent refurbishment. To take a literal translation, *Magnus Modus* means "Big Way," which then engendered the project title of *Big Way, Little Ways*.

Taking the natural material and form of *Magnus Modus* as the initial inspiration, Jackie also used two key pedagogical approaches to influence the project plan:

1 The St Miniato approach, in particular one of their key principles, "Time." The artists were interested in exploring the idea of really giving children and their parents/carers the time to create, make and explore in each workshop.
2 The Reggio Emilia approach and their key principles. First, "The environment as third teacher": designing and using space to encourage encounters, communication and relationships. Second, "The child as collaborator": education that focusses on each child in relation to other children, the family, the teachers and the community rather than the child in isolation. Third, "The child as communicator": this approach fosters children's intellectual development through a focus on symbolic representation and expression, including words, movement, drawing, painting, sculpture, shadow play, collage, dramatic play and music (Figure 18.1).[2]

There were ten sessions in all. Eight of these took place in St Andrew's and two sessions took place at the gallery. A total of 13 children and parents signed up, with about 70% returning each week. While our target audience was disadvantaged families, the group who signed up reflected the cultural, social and racially diverse demography of the area.

The space was divided into distinct areas and the group began each session with a song, sung by Jackie, accompanied by shruti box, an accordion-like instrument. Then the children were invited to explore the other areas in the room, for example an area with a projection on the wall, or a corner with nest-like piles of shredded paper with birds hidden inside, waiting to be discovered. The materials used in each session focussed largely on natural objects, such as sycamore seeds, branches and leaves. Light boxes, coloured chalks, cellophane and paint were also offered. Each session ended with a song and the shruti box, followed by a picnic, usually of fruit, cheese, crackers and water. This gave the families time to chat and play and relax after the sessions.

The two NGI-based sessions followed a similar format, which offered the group a familiar routine. Most of the participants had not been to the gallery before and were excited to come to visit (Figure 18.2). On both occasions, however, attendance was not as high as in the off-site location.

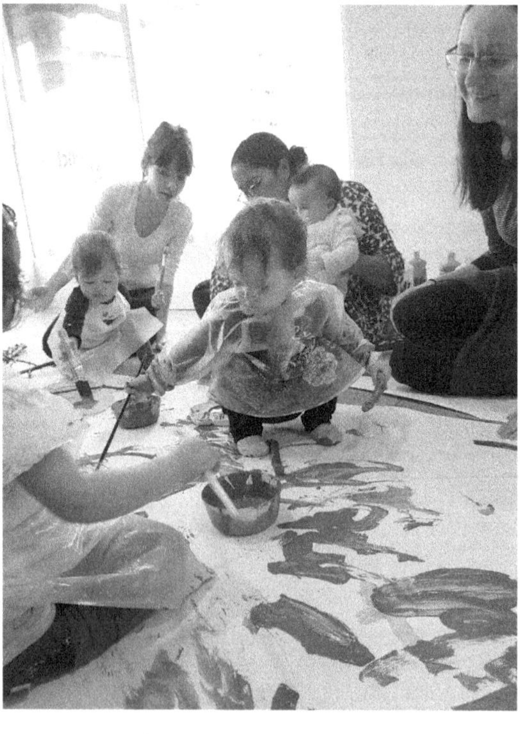

FIGURE 18.1 Painting at St Andrew's Resource Centre.
Photo © National Gallery of Ireland.

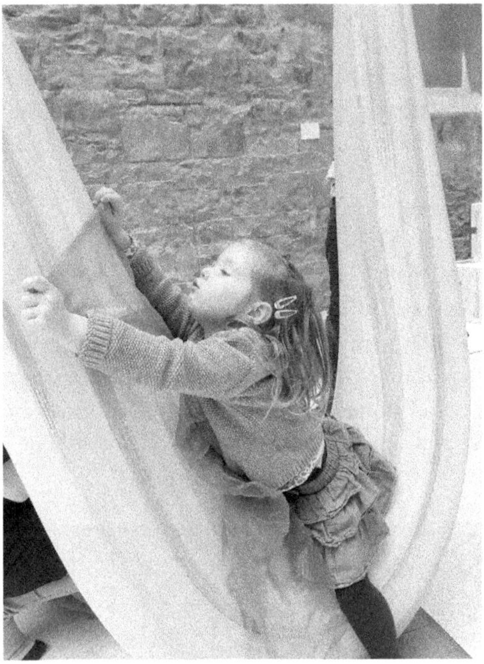

FIGURE 18.2 Getting to know Joseph Walsh's *Magnus Modus* at a Gallery-based session.
Photo © National Gallery of Ireland.

Project 2: Respond Family Hub

Ireland is in the midst of a severe housing crisis. By July 2018, 9,891 people (including 3,867 children) in Ireland were homeless.

"Family hubs" are a state-run interim response to this crisis. Families, usually with single parents, are placed in a communal accommodation facility, in this case a former Magdalene Laundry,[3] as a temporary measure before suitable housing is found. On average, families spend 5–9 months in a family hub. In February 2018, Emily Loughran, Childhood Development Project Leader at the Respond Hub for homeless families in High Park, Drumcondra (north Dublin city),[4] contacted the NGI. This hub can accommodate up to 27 families. She enquired as to whether it would be possible to book all places on one of our baby sessions so that she could bring her group. After discussing her situation with the team, we decided that we could provide more long-term support by putting this partnership under the remit of Early Years outreach.

Emily had begun a family group on Tuesday mornings in the hub. The majority of the families at the hub are single-parent families. This fledgling gathering was designed to encourage the parents to gather together and share knowledge about parenting. It was decided that we would lead one of these existing sessions, to test the water to see if there was interest from the parents. Artist Beth O'Halloran, who had by this time a good deal of experience of working with babies and toddlers in the NGI, was engaged to lead the workshop. Using images from the collection as inspiration, Beth encouraged the toddlers and their mums to explore the materials she had brought. These included light-up cubes, coloured Perspex and wood shapes, coloured noodles and rustling cellophane and tin foil (Figure 18.3).

The workshop lasted about 40 minutes and there was a small picnic at the end. Attendance was small, with just three children, but it was agreed that Beth would come again the following month. This has now developed into a monthly event, which happens as part of the weekly parent and child group sessions, and Beth is the artist who facilitates each workshop. Verbal feedback from participating families has been positive and all have expressed interest in visiting the Gallery and attending our events and workshops in the future. The

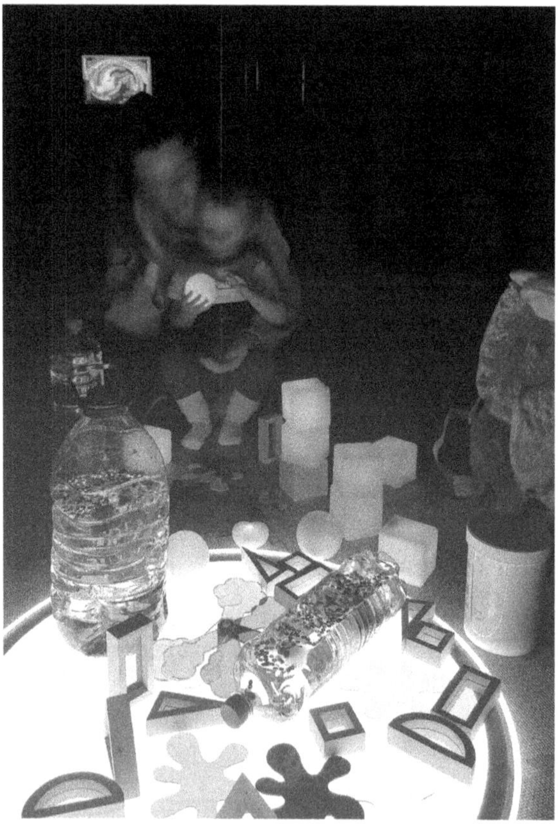

FIGURE 18.3 Exploring colour and light at Respond Family Hub (faces blurred to protect identity).

Photo © National Gallery of Ireland.

Family Hub staff are understanding about the need to create a comfortable, flexible space for us to engage with families who are living through extremely challenging times. The staff at Respond allow plenty of time for arrival, settling in, chatting, cups of tea and all that goes hand in hand with meaningful engagement. The feedback from parents has been overwhelmingly positive. Emily Loughran of Respond Family Hub has noted that living in emergency accommodation is very challenging for families and it has been really beneficial for the families to meet new people and have new experiences, as it reminds them of the positive opportunities available in the wider community. The workshops have been a fantastic introduction to the work of the Gallery and how accessible it is for children and families. Many of the families attending the workshops have made plans to visit the Gallery in their own time.

Final thoughts and implications for practice

While all NGIBaby workshops incorporate settling-in time, we recognized that this time, as well as relaxed time at the end of the workshop, has been particularly valuable with off-site events. Flexibility allowing for latecomers, or for children who need time to wake up from a nap, and creating familiar routines are key ingredients. In St Andrew's, the children responded to the shruti box being played without being called to gather around Jackie; the shruti-sound emerged as a ritual that signalled the beginning and end of each week's session. This created an atmosphere of anticipation about what would happen next and offered anchor-points of joint attention. The weekly picnics at the end of each session also added to the sense of community-building and this was very popular with the children and the adults.

The two Gallery-based sessions as part of the *Big Way, Little Ways* project were not as well attended as the St Andrew's-based workshops. We discussed this with the parents and carers and reasons ranged from not being available on that day to illness. However, one of the key learnings from this project was that meaningful engagement with participants was not dependent upon a Gallery visit and that the connections made during our time in each centre were valuable in themselves.

Some institutions, galleries in particular, might be deterred from holding off-site Early Years activities. Galleries are, by their nature, often without handling collections, but clever use of materials, projections and images can circumvent this problem. Budgets can also be challenging as materials can be expensive. We ensure that most workshops incorporate materials which are inexpensive and easy to access (recyclable household packaging, leaves, stones, shells, etc.). These ordinary items can be easily and simply transformed into objects of wonder through creative engagement (and this is a message we share with parents). Reiterating the St Miniato approach, these sessions have allowed us to really give children and their grown-ups the time they need to create, make and explore. For us, it's all about making the right place and time to light creative sparks.

Notes

1 http://siolta.ie.
2 Joanne Drum, Jackie Maguire and Dara Terry, National Gallery of Ireland *Big Way Little Ways* Report, 2018.
3 https://en.wikipedia.org/wiki/Magdalene_Laundries_in_Ireland.
4 www.respond.ie.

19

COME AGAIN! HOW FAMILIARITY LEADS TO REPEAT VISITS AND CONFIDENT LEARNERS

Victoria Smith

Introduction

In this case study we will explain why we believe familiarity supports young children and their families to feel safe to explore, to experiment and to take control of their own learning and, at the same time, to develop confidence in engaging with the unfamiliar space of the museum.

It is well-known that young children learn through repetition and, following Montessori, we want to work with the idea that "when the environment is predictable, a child feels safe and secure, which establishes the optimal environment for learning" (Montessori, 2017). This case study will examine the importance of repeat visits for young children, as well as for the wider family group that are visiting with them. It will also demonstrate how repetition and routines help families develop a sense of ownership and belonging in our museum space. We will do this by sharing examples of our programming for Early Years audiences and by showing how we have created dedicated spaces and gallery activities for young children at the Museum of London Docklands.

The Museum of London Docklands in Canary Wharf, East London, is housed in a beautiful Grade-I-listed Georgian warehouse which was used to store goods from all over the world such as tea, rum and sugar. The museum opened in 2003 and was then called Museum in Docklands, but it is now fully integrated with the Museum of London and the two museums operate as one. The museum charts the history of the River Thames and London's trade with the rest of the world and explores topics including: the Second World War, how the transatlantic slave trade shaped London, the decline of the Docks in the 1980s and the creation of one of the world's most influential financial districts. The museum also holds the Mudlarks children's gallery, an interactive and hands-on gallery for families and school groups with children aged 0–8.

Familiar starting points

As part of the Early Years programme at the museum we offer weekly baby (Mini Mudlarks) and toddler sessions (Little Mudlarks) (September 2018). This programme has been running for over nine years and, for regular families, it offers an adult-led session as part of their Monday morning routine. Our toddler and baby sessions always begin in exactly the same way, regardless of whether they are art workshops, musical or storytelling sessions. Families arrive at a registration desk outside of the Mudlarks children's gallery – many of the families make a beeline for our registration desk as soon as they arrive, bypassing the main information desk altogether! Families are given stickers to wear and many of the children demonstrate their familiarity with this routine, as they often arrive either pointing at themselves or at the staff member registering the families, saying "Sticker." Another example of how our routine is embedded within our regular families was demonstrated when we witnessed a child hearing the bell ringing in our children's gallery (signalling that it was time to get ready for the session to begin) and then telling her adult that this meant the activities were about to start and motioning for them to go to the entrance. Over time, this routine makes families feel safe and, in turn, encourages the children to have more confidence to explore, to take the lead and to experience unfamiliar things.

After the bell has rung, we invite the families to suggest a song for the group to sing as they make their way to an activity – this could be in one of our learning spaces or in a gallery. The children almost always ask for "The Wheels on the Bus" and we think this is because they see this song as part of the routine and, for them, this is how the session should always start. We also often see the same children attend but with different carers and having this routine also demonstrates to us the value of this routine for the children as a way to anchor them in the familiar but, at the same time, the children's confidence contributes to new adults feeling safe to attend without any prior knowledge of the session. With regular toddler and baby attendees, we often witness the increase in confidence to try out something new – to take risks, to explore somewhere that they wouldn't have otherwise, or to explore the galleries at all. We have even heard from families who regularly visit the Mudlarks gallery independently that they didn't even realise we had other galleries! One example that brought to life how a sense of the familiar can develop confidence and build a sense of ownership and belonging took place during our Toddler Takeover weekend in May 2017. Two fathers, whose children were regular attendees of Little Mudlarks, offered to help meet, greet and hand out programmes to hundreds of visitors attending our Toddler Takeover weekend. This could have been a daunting and potentially overwhelming experience for them, but it was made possible due to the familiarity they had with the museum's programme, site and its staff.

Once a month in our regular toddler and baby sessions we guide our families, including babies, towards the permanent museum galleries. We do this in different ways. We might deliver a whole session in a gallery, explore a number of different galleries, or create something in a classroom which we later take up to use in a gallery. This type of activity and being in the gallery itself might be a new experience for some families. These excursions from the classroom space aim to demonstrate to families that their child is not "too young" to visit a museum gallery. Anxieties around taking young children into a gallery space have also been a focus for our gallery interventions project, which we discuss later. Visiting a gallery might be surprising or intriguing for some, but frightening for others. For example, our Sailortown gallery is an immersive recreation of Victorian Wapping, which is dark and has atmospheric smells. However, we have discovered that many of the young children, babies included, relish this new type of experience. By using a familiar song, activity or object (we often provide children's torches or plastic candles), we have been able to take families into what we would usually perceive as a scary part of the museum.

Adult involvement

Adult involvement is a priority, not just in Early Years programming at the Museum of London Docklands but in our family programming for over-5s too. Parents and carers attending our Early Years sessions have told us that they enjoy in-gallery sessions the most. From observations and in-depth discussions with regularly visiting families, we have learnt that adults enjoy activities most when they are learning too and/or when they feel that they are actively involved in their child's learning. So, our aim is to ensure that we are creating opportunities for both adult and child to learn together and/or alongside each other. We have found that these joint learning experiences are achieved during open-ended sessions where families are encouraged to explore or create freely, either with familiar materials or in familiar surroundings. A lovely example of this was an activity where families were invited into the exciting world of cardboard boxes, alongside a curated soundtrack and guided by facilitators. The families were provided with familiar resources, such as tape measures and magnifying glasses, and were actively encouraged to explore a world of cardboard boxes. Some families used the resources to look inside, some families stacked the boxes and knocked them over, whilst others got inside them. During this activity, we found that the adults got actively involved in the session with their child(ren) because they were made to feel comfortable to do so and they were familiar with the materials we were using. They were given the permission to play and try something new. One family even described the sessions as "weird" because they had never done anything like this before, but that "weird is good!"

Freedom and choice

One of our guiding principles is to provide choice to families. One of the ways we do this is by following the same themes throughout the month and delivering the sessions by the same four session facilitators on rotation. Each session is given the same name each month: Musical Monday, Messy Monday, etc., so that families always know what to expect and can make a choice to attend based on what they want to do, what they enjoy, or what they feel most comfortable participating in. It is important to note here, though, that these decisions tend to be made by the adult. It might be that the adult is not comfortable with messy sessions at first, but after attending some of our other sessions and becoming more comfortable and familiar with how the sessions work, they might be more likely to give the messy session a go.

Family-friendly galleries

The museum's Mudlarks children's gallery has become part of many families' regular routine. In 2016, 53% of visitors made repeat visits to the gallery and one family visited 36 times during one year! Within the allotted 40-minute time frame, children and adults are free to explore and access whichever activities they like – from water play and block building, to lifting pulleys and loading ships. Some activities are designed for specific ages, but the decision-making is left to the child and adult as to which activities they choose (or choose not) to engage with. How long they engage for is limited in this gallery, due to numbers and health and safety reasons. Once families are comfortable in this space, we find that they start to attend other activities and explore our galleries further – when we speak to new attendees at our weekly sessions, many families tell us they have visited the Mudlarks children's gallery before but not attended any activities. By becoming comfortable in one familiar space first, families seem to then develop the confidence to go outside this space to continue exploring and engaging further with their child(ren). For families with under-5s exploring our galleries, we provide free explorer backpacks and gallery trails which encourage families to move around and freely use our museum space – including magnifying glasses, torches and a set of "can you find it?" cards.

In 2016 the museum began a "family interventions" project – the creation of a series of gallery displays for families placed within the museum's permanent galleries in order to make the museum's collection and stories more accessible to this audience, some of which are specifically aimed at under-5s. Examples include role play areas such as a bakery, grocery shop and tool station, as well as a transport play table and smelling and handling stations. These displays are unobtrusive and some general visitors might not even notice them, but for families they have the element of surprise and discovery and they invite families to play together in the gallery space. A key aspect to their success is the way they have been designed to connect with the everyday interests and activities of families, such as transport and shopping. All of the activities are open-ended, mostly inviting role-play, and have no definitive start or end point. They are also positioned in spaces where families can stay for as little or as long as they like. They provide opportunities for child and adult to play, in their own time, in their own space, creating a safe space and a play routine for them to come back to time and time again.

Benefits and challenges

Encouraging families to visit us again and again also has other positive outcomes for both the programme and the museum more widely: by seeing the museum as part of their everyday lives we hope to inspire young children to become our museum visitors and museum workers of the future. Families who are attending our activities regularly tell us that they are learning and having fun during our sessions and that they wish we could run them more often. Many families have been bringing their children since they were babies and when another baby comes into the family, they bring them too. Building up this kind of network and community of regular families also markets the museum through word of mouth and social media, and becomes a means of sharing their positive (and negative) experiences with their family and friends.

While we are pleased at our success in attracting and encouraging families to become repeat visitors, we also feel that it is important to balance this with the need to make space for new families to join us too. One of the ways that we have addressed this is by only allowing families to book one session at a time, rather than block booking. We feel it is important that we pay attention to new families' needs and create the right climate for them to create new bonds with other families. For example, we have witnessed first-hand at baby sessions how new and repeat families created a friendship group and how going to lunch together in the museum café after attending the sessions became part of their weekly routine.

We have found that our sessions and gallery activities have encouraged children to become more autonomous and have helped encourage their adults to feel confident in letting their children take the lead. The nature of our open-ended and exploratory sessions means that children have the space and time to experiment with different ideas, to make different choices and decisions, supported by the trust and support of their adult(s). But these sessions require skilled facilitators. Facilitators who are able to take a step back and do not need to focus on creating a particular end product or reaching a particular outcome. They must be able to take a step back from delivering and directing and, instead, act as an observer, a demonstrator, a modeller. As well as being able to encourage both the children and adults to be playful and exploratory. These are special and subtle skills and not easy to put into words.

Families also seem to develop a strong sense of ownership and belonging when they visit or take part in activities regularly. We have seen this in the adults in particular, where some of them come back to the museum without their children to adult events – one parent even applied for a job at the museum after attending weekly storytelling sessions and is now a full-time member of staff. In 2016, part of our Mudlarks children's gallery required refurbishment works and many parents and carers expressed that they were upset at the temporary removal of a particularly popular activity as it was their child's favourite. We did ensure that a temporary activity – a pirate ship – was installed in the

Mudlarks gallery to provide an alternative whilst the refurbishment works were carried out, and this demonstrated to us that relationships with our regular visitors have to be respected and nurtured due to their strong connection and sense of ownership over the space.

Final thoughts and implications for practice

Repeated experiences are crucial for young learners but it's still important to consider how we are encouraging new visitors to join us. Consider how you can create a safe environment for both new and regular visitors.

Providing familiar but surprising gallery activities within our museums can encourage families with young children to be more confident in exploring our spaces, using them in different ways and opening up new experiences.

Young children come with adults, so make sure you always consider them and their needs and how repeat visits can support their learning and development too. They might attend adult events once they are comfortable with the Early Years programme and branch out further!

Finally, try to take a step back – be an advisor, an observer, a player! And take the time to see what young children are really doing and what they are showing you.

Reference

Montessori (2017) *Repetition and Child Development in Montessori Education*, Montessori Academy [online]. Available from: https://montessoriacademy.com.au/repetition-child-development-montessori[accessed 7 December 2018].

20

HEALTHY CHILD DROP-IN AND *BABY STAY AND PLAY* AT MANCHESTER ART GALLERY

Katy McCall

This case study focusses on a *Healthy Child Drop-In and Baby Stay and Play* session that runs weekly at Manchester Art Gallery (MAG) and reflects on how the families and practitioners that regularly attend the session respond to the environment we create and connect with the gallery. In particular, it highlights how working regularly with an artist to create an immersive space in the gallery alongside the delivery of health services for families of young children has created an unhurried and convivial space where relationships between families as well as with health practitioners can form and flourish. For over a decade, artists, museums and researchers have been exploring new ways of working with Early Years children, their families and teachers. Much of this work has been inspired by the principles of Reggio Emilio; examining how materials and the environments children encounter can be the third teacher. At Manchester Art Gallery we have begun looking at not only how art can support the crucial development of 0 to 5 year olds, but also how this knowledge can enhance the delivery of public health services for young families.

Manchester Art Gallery sits within Libraries, Galleries and Culture as part of the Neighbourhoods Service, in the Growth and Neighbourhoods Directorate of Manchester City Council. It showcases art and ideas from across the world, inside a centrally located iconic building, close to the other municipal buildings of Manchester Town Hall and Central Library. It's 45,000-strong collection spans six centuries of fine art, design, craft, photography and fashion, and the gallery regularly works with internationally renowned artists to create a programme that is global in its scope and ambition, a key part of the vibrant cultural life of Manchester. The gallery welcomes over 650,000 people each year and makes a positive difference to the city, believing that art and creativity have the power to change lives.

It is important to highlight that the gallery and its art collection belong to the people of Manchester, with the city council as sole trustee. The gallery contributes to achieving the goals set out in the Manchester City Council *Our Manchester Strategy*. This strategy is based on listening to others, recognising people's strengths and working together to do things differently to make Manchester a thriving and liveable city for everyone. The *Healthy Child Drop-In and Baby Stay and Play* at the gallery is a key example of the *Our Manchester Strategy* in action. It reflects the determination of Manchester City Council, even in the face of recent challenging reductions in spending, to work across organisations to pool resources and actively play a part in this new and radical change to ways of working together.

Background to the development of the *Healthy Child* drop-in session at Manchester Art Gallery

I started in post as the Families Learning Manager in 2017 after working as Early Years and Families Curator at Tate Liverpool. Shortly after I started at Manchester Art Gallery, as an organisation we started working in partnership with the Manchester Health Visiting Team and Sure Start. This collaboration came about due to the five-year closure of Manchester Town Hall for refurbishment. St Peters Sure Start was based at the Town Hall and needed a new home and, as the Gallery is next to the Town Hall and part of Manchester City Council, we were approached as an alternative location.

Since previously being involved in another research project, *My Primary School is at the Museum*, my dream had been to locate a Sure Start centre in an art gallery and I saw this as a fantastic opportunity. *My Primary School is at the Museum* tested the hypothesis that there may be beneficial learning, social and cultural outcomes for primary school children and their families when a significant portion of their learning takes place in a museum setting, as well as demonstrating the benefits for museums. I felt there could be similar beneficial outcomes for children and families who had a significant portion of their public health services delivered in a museum setting and was keen to test this out. A full report of the findings from this project can be found on the Kings College website: https://kcl.ac.uk/Cultural/-/Projects/My-Primary-School-is-at-the-Museum.aspx.

We met with partners from Martenscroft Nursery School and Sure Start Children's Centre and the Manchester Health Visiting Team to explore the logistics of relocating a children's centre to the gallery. Supportive relationships were quickly formed, with a shared sense of vision and commitment to working together to improve the outcomes and life chances of children and families in our city. We now run a weekly *Healthy Child Drop-In* and *Sure Start Children's Centre Baby Stay and Play* session at the gallery. The families that come to the drop-in sessions are a diverse group from the Manchester city centre wards and localities and most have not visited the gallery previously. The weekly health drop-in is the first place where parents with well babies access health advice and are signposted to other agencies. Two Health Visitors and a Sure Start Early Years Practitioner are present at the clinic, with both agencies working closely together; welcoming and supporting parents, sharing observations and key data about families to ensure they receive a successful and holistic service.

Artist Naomi Kendrick is a participant at the sessions. Each week Naomi is commissioned to build an immersive environment in our Learning Studio, inspired by the current in-house exhibitions as well as her observations of the babies and parents (Figure 20.1). Using carefully selected materials, Naomi creates a place for families to inhabit, playing with textures, light and space. Prior to the *Healthy Child Drop-In and Baby Stay and Play*, Naomi was the lead artist on a *Baby Art Club* delivered monthly at the gallery. This was similar in terms of her creating an immersive installation, but in the Art Club the families' motivation for coming to the museum was about having a positive and stimulating shared experience for parent and baby in a cultural setting rather than accessing health advice. Although there were huge positives about delivering this monthly session, we decided it was less inclusive of Manchester families, as it was a bookable club on a "first come

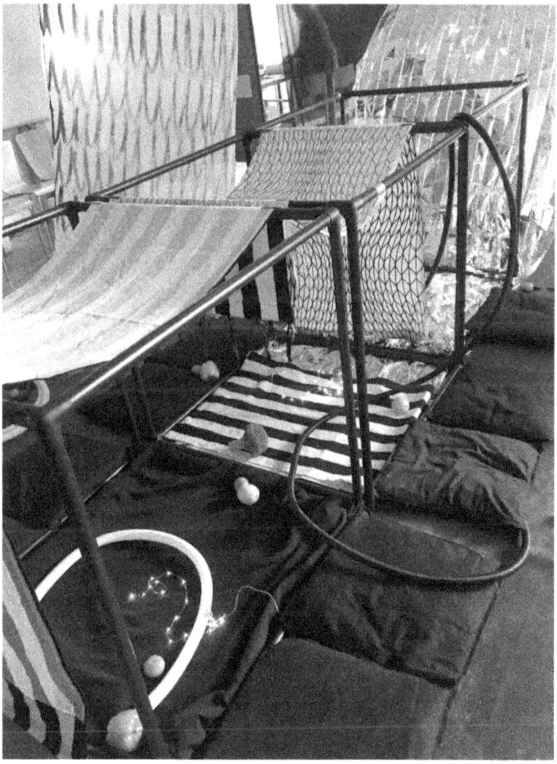

FIGURE 20.1 Immersive environment at the *Healthy Child Drop-In and Baby Stay and Play* at Manchester Art Gallery.
Credit: Andrew Brooks.

first served" basis. Putting the resources and expertise from *Baby Art Club* into the *Healthy Child Drop-In and Baby Stay and Play* has meant we are working in a much more effective and multi-disciplinary way, blending art, health and education expertise to transform a public health service.

Experimenting with materials

Over time, Naomi has observed and attuned herself to what kinds of materials babies respond well to and uses these observations when building the environments for the *Healthy Child Drop-In and Baby Stay and Play.*

> Lights, sound and bold, graphic, black and white patterns seem to be good for tiny babies whose vision is still developing, but appeals to the older babies too. I developed a black and white (with areas of bright colour) installation recently, with the smaller babies in mind. Having observed that in the clinic setting many of the babies are little and can't sit up yet so they actually spend a great deal of time just looking at the ceiling rather than an installation around them, I began to hang more objects and lights and incorporated them on cube frames so that babies could be placed within them and the top of the frame was made stimulating, with a criss-cross of black lines, a bold print and lights.
>
> *(Naomi Kendrick)*

When building installations Naomi considers practical aspects like safety and durability, but mainly her focus is on the "difference of encounter" which leads her to use a range of textures and materials. Food also features in many of Naomi's installations, using fruit, vegetables and spices to encompass smells, textures and taste. During sessions health professionals have welcomed the inclusion of food to handle and play with as being supportive as the babies head towards weaning. As a team, we are now looking at how this can help to support an early intervention initiative led by the Infant Feeding Team that aims to reduce visits to A&E and referrals to paediatric units by offering extra support to families around nutrition and feeding.

Natural materials are used in the installations; earth, sand, chalk, flowers, branches and leaves. Parents can be hesitant about their babies handling some of these substances, often needing a little reassurance that the materials are non-toxic. We are creating a space for families to build their confidence and curiosity about the material world. Naomi also likes to use household objects, brushes, wooden bobbins, hats, sponges, metallic bowls, spoons, plates and mirrors as many of these harness light, reflection, sound and texture. She hopes this usefully highlights to parents that they can encourage babies to explore and handle things at home, beyond their toys and baby equipment. This approach to working has also had an impact on the health and education practitioners who co-deliver the session and together we are beginning to understand more about the richness of ways that babies engage with the material world.

In partnership with Manchester Metropolitan University the gallery has been successful in obtaining funding from the Economic and Social Research Council to fund a doctoral research project to explore the work taking place during the Health and Sure Start sessions. This research will explore how babies and young children's encounters with space, the visual and aural, movements and materials invent new ways for artists, health and educational practitioners to learn from each other about the emerging development of the under 2s. This research will shine a light on the potential of a materially led arts practice, through an exploration of bodily encounters with place and materials, as well as foregrounding the exchange of disciplinary knowledge between health practitioners and artists.

Building relationships and familiarity

From a public health perspective, this collaborative project rests firmly on the principles and policies of *Health 2020: The European Policy for Health and Well-being* (http://euro.who.int/en/health-topics/health-policy/health-2020-the-european-policy-for-health-and-well-being), with its emphasis on inter-sectoral collaboration, integration and co-production approaches to service development. There is an excitement, energy and commitment to the collaboration from all partners at all levels; from management to practitioners. The shared commitment to innovate the health visitor clinic setting through arts input has meant a strong and trusting bond has grown between the families, health visitors, Sure Start workers and the artist. These relationships, wholly supported by senior management, are key to the success of the collaboration.

In one way the immersive environment is the waiting room for families to see their Health Visitor or Sure Start practitioner. Some of the parents that come to the clinic are anxious about either their baby's health or their own health. The environments Naomi creates are social and non-judgemental spaces for parents that promote interactions with their baby as well as with other parents. This space is in contrast to the usual waiting space of health centres (Figure 20.2). Over time we have observed that families positively inhabit this space and we have also noticed emerging patterns to their interactions. New parents tend to "hover" around the edges of the installation with their very tiny weeks-old babies, feeding and observing the session while they wait to be seen by the Health Visitor. After the first few visits they will gravitate into the installation, beginning to interact with the materials, either with encouragement from the artist or Sure Start worker, or following another parent's example. Naomi reflects:

> Some mothers and fathers seem to take it in their stride, others hang back a little, unsure of where to sit and what to do; a little chat about the baby and just pointing out a spare beanbag seems to go a long way. I've noticed the fact that it is well attended with lots of regulars actually helps the new parents to integrate quickly, they observe how other parents interact with the materials with their babies. This group is very social, they welcome

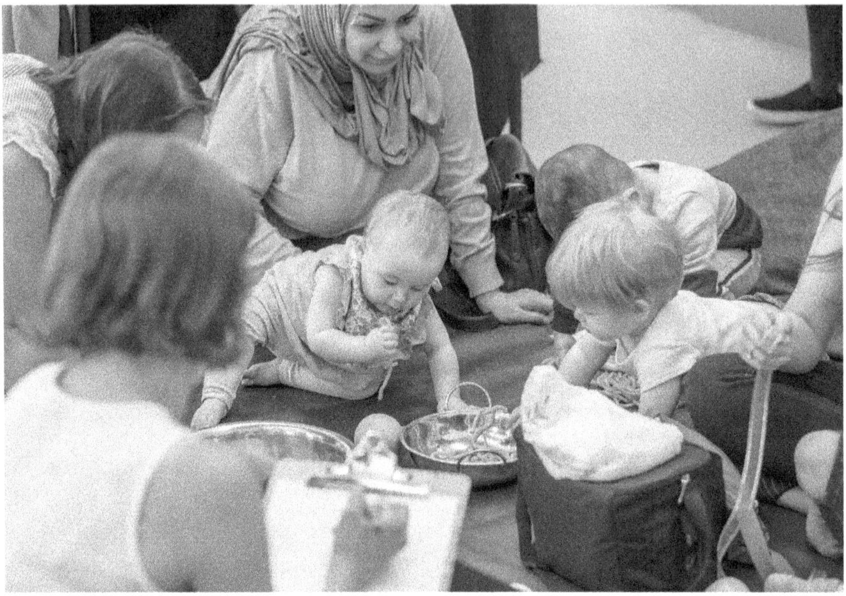

FIGURE 20.2 *Healthy Child Drop-In and Baby Stay and Play* at Manchester Art Gallery. Credit: Andrew Brooks.

> new people, go to the cafe together afterwards, see each other outside of the session. In a way baby clinic reminds me of Making Conversation (the other workshop for vulnerable adults that I do with longer-term regulars); they are both very social sessions, many people are drawn to experiencing with others rather than alone, perhaps particularly when trying something new (having a baby/visiting a gallery!!), the "side effect" of this is that the space itself becomes familiar, friendly, used. And maybe this is as much applicable to babies as it is the parents?

The *Healthy Child Drop-In and Baby Stay and Play* has been running for just over a year now and we have had the privilege of watching some of the first babies that came to the clinic grow and develop alongside their parents. Some of our initial cohort are now leaving as parents return to work and babies go to nursery. New cohorts are being formed and we continue to welcome mums, dads and grandparents into the gallery. Many of the families are beginning to feel connected to the gallery, attending our public sessions for families or visiting our other spaces. On the issue of accessibility, parents have commented that because it is in the town centre it's easy to reach by car, is close to shops and that they now come to the gallery on weekends also. Others have commented on how it beats sitting in a waiting room and makes a health appointment more like a day out, as well as how it has offered a space to chat with other parents.

Future plans

Since starting the baby clinic, other ideas for delivering services differently have emerged. Recently we ran a trial at Clayton Sure Start looking at how we take the positive aspects of the immersive environment to enhance and innovate the delivery of developmental reviews for 2-year-olds. Another collaborative project sees us working with young mothers who are living in a temporary housing unit in Manchester. The mums are a group that the Manchester Health Visiting Team and Sure Start workers struggle to engage with; appointments and important health checks are often missed. We have set up an art and creativity club at the unit which has created a new less formal environment for mothers and their babies to meet with their health visitors.

It is an exciting time to be a Learning Manager at Manchester Art Gallery. Under the new directorship of Alistair Hudson we are beginning to re-imagine the gallery as an institute for the 21st Century, focussed more on "user-ship" than spectatorship. We are encouraged to think of the public gallery spaces as places to be radical, experimental and imaginative, working with integrity to combine art and ethics throughout all of our work. Currently we are developing plans to move the *Healthy Child Drop-In and Baby Stay and Play* into a purpose-built "Children's Centre" gallery space, allowing us to experiment with our art collection as a tool for social purpose and creating a more visible platform for our unique collaboration (Figure 20.3).

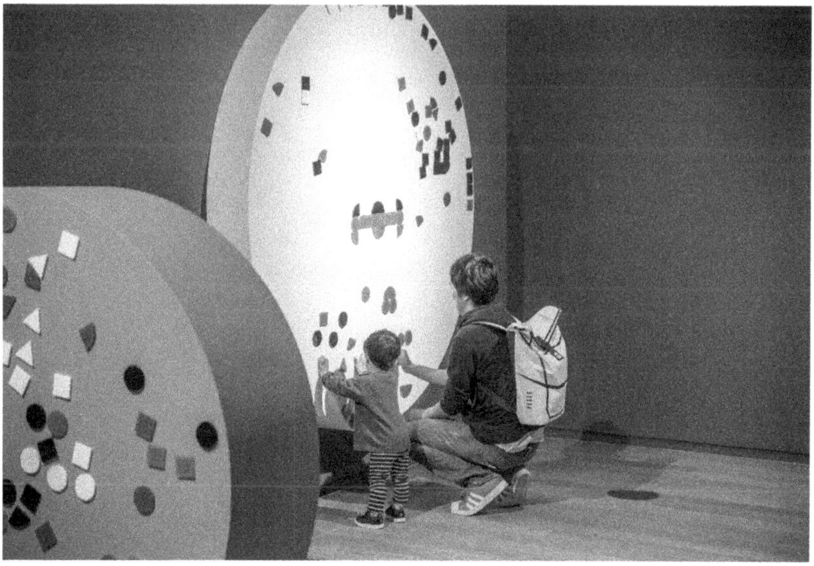

FIGURE 20.3 Children's Gallery (Clore Art Studio) at Manchester Art Gallery. Credit: Andrew Brooks.

Final thoughts and implications for practice

As the collaborative partnership grows over time it becomes more apparent that this creative model of working could be applied across health and education services nationally. There is a growing interest in this work from other arts organisations and from public health commissioners and invitations to forums, advisory boards and focus groups are beginning to take place. As arts practitioners and museum professionals meet and partners begin taking time to listen and learn about each other's roles, we are beginning to build understanding and respect for the different approaches that each agency brings in order to deliver the same goal; *to improve outcomes and life chances for children and families*. By engaging with the priorities of local authority agencies, we have tailored our programme at Manchester Art Gallery to support others rather than running our family gallery offer in isolation.

Through involvement with senior management and strategic leads from all organisations in the NHS and the Local Authority in the project, there has been a growing understanding of our aims and a bubbling momentum around the wider possibilities of these new ways of cross-agency working.

Working with academic partners from the early stages adds a layer of support to the project that has enabled us to step back and think more deeply and clearly about our process. Forging relationships of trust between everyone involved in the project has given us a freedom to test and experiment: all partners are always excited and open about exploring new ways of working. While we are at the early stages of our collaboration and recognise we have more work to influence government policy makers, our project will continue to evolve and adapt as the issues that families face change.

21

COMPLICATING THE NARRATIVE

Preschooler-led museum field trips

Danielle Carter

Introduction

This case study was inspired both by theory and as a result of my own research. Specifically, I drew on museum education theory that foregrounded both the social and the material qualities of engagement with collections. I was also influenced by the Reggio Emilia pedagogy on which the philosophy of the preschool which took part in the study was based. Furthermore, I had found that museums often attempt to attract and educate young children through segregated spaces, exhibitions or programmes that are specifically dedicated to young children and learning through play (Carter, 2018a). I wanted to pilot a project in which children took the lead in responding to the general museum space as well as with museum objects, rather than a focus on the specifically dedicated spaces for young children within the museum. Rather than expecting children to visit predetermined exhibits, this approach allows children to explore the museum at their own pace and in response to their own interests. In this way, the museum space unfolds through a process of collective curiosity. A significant aspect of the project was also an understanding that the engagement with the museum meant more than the actual duration of the visit itself. A vital aspect of the visit was the time spent both before and after the museum encounter: the visit experience was woven into circle-time discussions and art-making both in anticipation of and in response to the museum visits. A guiding principle in the project was not only to follow the object-led movements of children through the museum space, but that, in so doing, the museum experience was always responsive to directions taken by children in and beyond the museum: their interests and their connection-making.

The project

This case study follows eight students (4–5 years of age) from an international, bilingual (English and Swedish), Reggio Emilia-based preschool as they visit four museums in Stockholm, Sweden, over a five-month study period. These child-led museum field trips reveal the complexity and nuance of young children's learning in and through museum visits, as well as exploring the learning experience through museums more broadly. With Falk and Dierking (2000) in mind, I wanted to learn more about how children's preferences and prior knowledge would affect what they learned during their museum visits, and how they would assimilate or further build upon this learning beyond the museum or back in the classroom. I began by embedding myself in the preschool as a participant ethnographic researcher. I played the part of an assistant preschool teacher that facilitated many of the arts activities. The children, however, were also aware of my interest and involvement in the museum field trips.

The Reggio Emilia pedagogy on which the preschool was founded played an important role in the case study research. Because Reggio Emilia focusses on the learning that occurs in daily life and lived experiences of the children, excursions, walks, library and museum visits were common practice at the preschool (although the frequency increased during the study period). The Reggio Emilia pedagogy also focusses on student-determined curricula and excursions, so the idea of choosing museums based on the children's preferences was not unusual to the students. Significantly, Reggio Emilia also focusses on children's various modes of expression. Art-making, discussion of artworks and annotation to accompany artworks are all common practice within Reggio Emilia. This was extremely helpful both for data collection for the study as well as for more general insights into what caught the students' attention and how they understood their experiences.

During the study period we visited four museums (in chronological order): the Stockholm Transport Museum, the Swedish National Museum of Science and Technology, the Swedish Museum of Natural History and the Vasa Museum. To the best of our abilities, we tried to visit museums related to students' interests. Of course, the children were not always aware of what types of museums were available, so we often had to assist them with additional information or suggestions. During a circle time discussion, for example, one of the students suggested that we visit a butterfly museum; unfortunately, no such museum exists in Stockholm, so we instead visited the Swedish Museum of Natural History.

Instead of engaging with children-specific exhibitions, spaces or activities, the idea behind this pilot was that children would lead the way in each museum. Instead of the adults pre-determining the route or the objects encountered, it was the children who determined which specific objects they wanted to see, either by physically leading us or by asking about objects they were interested in. During our first museum visit to the Stockholm Transport Museum, the children were excited but also overwhelmed: they seemed unsure of where to go and there was tension and even a few arguments about taking turns with certain interactive displays. Although I tried to speak with several of the children, asking them about the exhibitions, even the more vocal in the group were relatively quiet. Our next two visits (the Swedish National Museum of Science and Technology and the Swedish Museum of Natural History) were, however, radically different. The children initiated their own directions of movement through the space and were led much more by their curiosity and a sense of inquiry. While I did lead the children to a few exhibits at the Swedish National Museum of Science and Technology (because they were directly relevant to the learning theme at the preschool during the study period), the children were able to confidently draw the group's attention to the objects that captured their interest. The entire group was much more vocal; asking questions and holding discussions at each of the objects that we stopped to inspect. At the Swedish Museum of Natural History, the children were even more robust in determining their shared interests. The children were now far more invested in communicating with one another about what they were interested in, rather than arguing over taking turns for exhibitions.

The children's growing interest in the museum objects was exciting and it could be that their conversations about museum objects during circle time and the post-museum discussion focus on objects they had seen (i.e., "What was your favourite *thing* that you *saw* yesterday?") was also feeding into the conversation in each successive visit. It also seemed that the children talked about more museum objects after each successive museum visit, perhaps demonstrating that, as children became more comfortable with the museum experience as time went on, they were able to engage with a wider range of the exhibits. The children were also encouraged to respond to their visits through drawing. They were most likely to draw about their museum visits following these circle time discussions, whether they were directed to do so or not (there were tables with pens and paper freely available after the discussions).

Before visiting the Stockholm Transport Museum, I asked the children what they would like to see at the museum. Yenifer said that she would like to see "a train that we can drive on," which was promptly repeated by Ursula. Later on, at the museum, the children dedicated most of their time to the tram simulation. The children's personal experiences with public transportation informed their expectations of what they might see at the museum, and their prior understanding of public transport combined with the museum experience to create a more dynamic and nuanced image of how public transport can look (Carter, 2018b: 132–134). For example, in her drawing after the Stockholm Transport Museum visit, Ursula drew a train (inspired by the museum object) but she also included a crown. Just before beginning their drawings, the children dressed up in costumes and Mireia had dressed up as a princess. Mireia and Ursula both included crowns in their post-Stockholm Transport Museum drawings. Furthermore, many of the children included themselves and/or animals in their depictions of trains after the Stockholm Transport Museum visit; perhaps in part also inspired by the old horse-led trams in the museum.

Before visiting the Swedish Museum of Natural History, Mirjam told the class that she had been to this museum already. She told the class that she had seen a "big lion" there. After discussing what "Naturhistoriska"[1] and "natural history" means, the children were asked what they thought they would see at the museum. Adam, Mireia and Yenifer each made some mention of a lion: "a lion … lion bones," "a baby lion" and "the lion," respectively. As the visit to the Swedish Museum of Natural History began, Mirjam remembered that she had also seen a whale in her previous trip to the museum. We stopped to look at, ask questions about and discuss many objects throughout the museum, but the children frequently circled back to their wish to see the whale that Mirjam had mentioned. Mirjam's prior experience guided the children's interests at the museum. Resisting overarching narratives that make sense of a museum collection, the children moved through the museum space under the influence of their prior concern with finding the whale. Together, we eventually found a section of the museum concerning sea life – including a whale – and the children were very excited about finding their target, so much so that this became one of the most-cited museum "objects" during a circle time discussion later in the classroom. Children's connection-making within the museum space – with their prior experiences or other interests – is unpredictable in the moment. Allowing for a child-led movement through the museum space gives children the space to create their own connections – between their prior knowledge, opinions and experiences and the objects and exhibitions within the museum. Although the children cited several aspects of their museum visit during circle time the next day, the whale was overwhelmingly popular among the children, even emerging in Anish's drawing during a period for free draw.

At the Swedish National Museum of Science and Technology, Aleksy asked about a satellite, which we discussed with the whole group. We discussed the shapes on the satellite (rectangles) and its function (floating in space and sometimes taking pictures). For several weeks after this museum visit, some of the qualities of the satellite we saw appeared in children's drawings (Carter, 2018b: 139–140), showing that child-led museum visits and discussions can have lasting effects. Each of the children's drawings after this museum visit reflected the respective child's interests or previous experiences: Mireia – with her well-known fondness for colours – depicted a rainbow in her drawing, while Aleksy drew a Lego Chima[2] man inspired by a robot at the museum and several of the other children created outer-space-oriented drawings, which also related to the preschool's curriculum at the time. The children were often attracted to museum objects that connected with more familiar everyday objects. This reaffirms ways that children's prior knowledge is brought into the museum through their everyday lives and preferences. It also demonstrates how dialogue with their friends also becomes part of their knowledge production and how this also enters and becomes part of the museum collection.

Accepting the idiosyncratic ways that children augment the museum collection and its associated sense-making reframes the museum as a more liminal space. Children are well-placed to demonstrate the potential of the museum to lead us all in unexpected directions and to make unexpected connections. In the words of museum educator Alli Rogers Andreen, museums provide: "one of those wonderful, un-planned opportunities to validate and share the quiet dramas of childhood and life in general" (2018). When children take the lead, young children's museum experiences are not limited to predetermined learning, but the process opens up the entire museum, as it becomes criss-crossed by desire-lines produced through the mingling of the everyday with wonder and curiosity.

Final thoughts and implications for practice

By trusting children within the museum space – trusting their sense of which objects are interesting or important, trusting their sense of timing and pacing, and trusting that they will ask the most relevant questions – children will creatively make meanings as they move through the museum. Child-led museum visits are a means of complicating a unidirectional, behaviouralist, concrete, knowledge-oriented and age-bound institutional narrative. To answer Ripley's challenge "to find new ways to listen" (2018), child-led visits respond to curiosity and produce meandering pathways that navigate the museum in creative and unique ways. Instead of cherry-picking museum objects that fit within the classroom narrative, allowing children to lead museum visits allows for complex learning processes to unfold. By complicating the narrative of pre-school field trips, we acknowledge, accept and embrace the complexity and, possibly, the unknowability or immeasurability of the nuanced learning experience that takes place in the museum space.

- Allowing children to lead visits using their bodies and senses: child-led museum experiences should resist top-down authoritative ideas of controlled behaviour or segregated spaces for children in the museum. Museum trips are part of wider life-long learning and inquiry.
- Children are experts in their own lives (Dockett et al., 2011): their social, personal, cultural and various other contexts, prior knowledge, experiences and expectations all play a role in their learning experience in the museum context.
- Child-led museum experiences work to dismantle the authoritative museum through repeat visits, which boost children's confidence in expressing their own insights, thoughts and intuition (Carter, 2018a: 30).
- Child-led museum visits do not bind children to the museum's or teacher's narrative and learning goals, but allow for a narrative to unfold of the children's own making, based on their own interests, curiosity and social interactions.

Notes

1 This is the Swedish name for the Swedish Museum of Natural History. All of the museums were referred to by their Swedish names to the preschool pupils throughout the study period.

2 Lego Chima is a line of Lego toys that is popular among the children throughout the study period, especially with Adam and Aleksy.

References

Andreen, A. Rogers (2018, 26 June). Playing with authority: reflecting on child-led gallery experiences. *Art Museum Teaching*, https://artmuseumteaching.com/2018/06/26/playing-with-authority, accessed: 28 September 2018.

Carter, D. (2018a). The museum as playground: approaching the museum with a playful attitude. *Acta Academiae Vilnensis*, *84* 15–33, http://leidykla.vda.lt/lt/leidinys/1293521618/edukacija-mene-menui-per-mena.

Carter, D. (2018b). Narrative learning as theory and method. *Studies in Art Education*, *59*(2), 126–144.

Dockett, S., Main, S., and Kelly, L. (2011). Consulting with children: experiences from a museum. *Visitor Studies*, *14*(1), 13–33.

Falk, J. and Dierking, L. (2000). *Learning from Museums: Visitor Experiences and the Making of Meaning*. Walnut Creek, CA: AltaMira Press.

Ripley, A. (2018, 27 June). Complicating the narratives. Solutions Journalism Network. *Medium*. https://thewholestory.solutionsjournalism.org/complicating-the-narratives-b91ea06ddf63, accessed: 17 September 2018.

22

REFLECTING ON CHILDREN'S PLAY AT THE WHITWORTH

Louisa Penfold and Lucy Turner

Play has been identified as a critical education process that supports young children's cognitive, social, emotional and physical development (Hughes, 2013; Schaefer and Drewes, 2014). While art museums have not been traditionally seen as sites for play, this assumption is being challenged as an increasing number of cultural organisations are developing education activities that actively seek to encourage children's experimentation and creative thinking through play-based learning. Art museums are positioned as unique sites for education as a result of their ability to draw on artist's experimental practices to support children's learning. Children's participation in these arts-based play activities present as opportunities to encourage their "imaginative capacity" to encounter the world from new and multiple perspectives (Greene, 2000).

Reflective practice in art museums can support learning teams in considering how learning emerges across small events that unfold when children encounter spaces and materials in galleries. This case study discusses a research partnership that looked at pedagogical documentation, a critically reflective process that seeks to make children's learning visible, and how this could support reflective practice in the Early Years Atelier programme at the Whitworth.

The Atelier at the Whitworth

The Early Years Atelier, or children's art studio, was first created by the Whitworth's Learning and Engagement team in its opening year of 2015. During 2014 the Whitworth building underwent the largest physical transformation in its 125-year history with a £15 million capital project that saw the gallery open up its spaces, inside and outside, making the building more welcoming to the diverse communities that surround it. The redevelopment also featured an expansion of the existing gallery spaces, including the construction of new learning studios for people of all ages.

The Atelier runs every Monday from 10 am to 3 pm and is a free drop-in space for child-led artistic exploration (Figure 22.1). The Atelier is a place where babies, toddlers and preschoolers can get messy, play creatively and follow their own interests. Every week, the Atelier is full of materials for children to choose from, such as paint or clay one week to cardboard or sand the next. It runs alongside numerous other activities for babies, toddlers and preschoolers including sensory play sessions designed especially for babies who are not yet walking and their parents/carers. In addition, there are Forest-School-inspired nature play sessions that take place in the beautiful setting of Whitworth Park. The Atelier is inspired by the philosophy of Reggio Emilia, an educational approach that underpins the Whitworth's learning programme as a whole. The environment plays a key role as part of this pedagogy. There is also an emphasis on natural light, as well as access to the outdoors and space to encourage independent play. The Atelier provides just that; huge folding doors let light flood

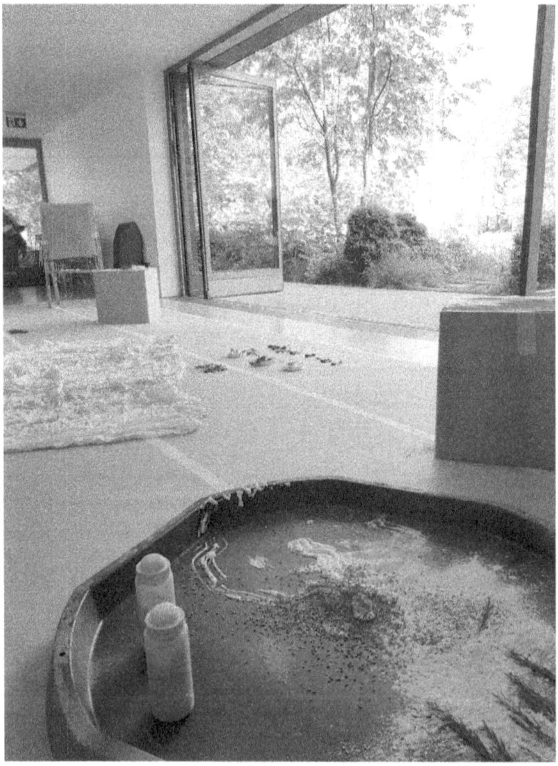

FIGURE 22.1 The Clore Learning Studio space where the Atelier sessions are held. Credit: Lucy Turner for the Whitworth.

into the room and open straight out into a sensory art garden, extending the room and blurring boundaries between the indoors and outdoors.

The Early Years Atelier was designed with the aim of creating a space to engage young visitors with the Whitworth's art collection, its buildings and park, through hands-on play that explores ideas, materials and techniques. The Atelier sessions break down the barriers of a pre-booked offer by opening up the programme and gallery to a more diverse audience, one that better represents the local community. The Atelier also provides an opportunity to develop confidence, creativity and expression in both children and adults. Additionally, the Atelier is also a model of practice that investigates early childhood practice through research-based gallery practice. An Atelierista, or studio assistant, is always on hand to help. Their role is to guide and observe rather than teach. The Atelierista keeps a diary of observations such as notes, photographs, audio recordings and videos documenting the learning that they observe in the space. This information is then uploaded onto a blog as a means to share the learning and development with a wider audience.

Feedback from parents has helped the art museum to learn that the drop-in child-led nature of the Atelier works best for our audiences. This is particularly true for:

- those with two or more children who find it difficult to manage a led workshop and prefer a more relaxed, self-directed option;
- those where English is not their first language and might find a booking system difficult;
- home educator parents and carers who want to take part in social activities with their children;
- dads who more frequently seem to prefer the flexibility of a non-bookable session in comparison with mums;
- parents and carers with babies who have just begun to walk/very active toddlers who are keen to explore and not sit still;
- those who seek opportunities for messy play as they lack the time and space at home.

Ongoing evaluation of the Atelier has also indicated that visitors participating in the programme appreciate the play-based nature of the Atelier and how this can support children's confidence, creativity and self-expression. The drop-in nature of the Atelier has also been acknowledged as important in allowing the activity to be adapted to family's needs and interests.

Researching pedagogical documentation as a way to reflect on practice in the Atelier

In 2016, a collaborative research partnership was formed between the Early Years Atelier team and PhD researcher Louisa Penfold. The partnership aimed to investigate the use of pedagogical documentation as a form of reflective process that supported reflective practice in children's art museum activities.

Pedagogical documentation is a process that strives to make learning visible through iterative cycles of planning, observation, reflection and change (Rinaldi, 2001). Records such as photographs, videos, audio recordings and observation notes are collected and used by groups of people to discuss what is happening from different perspectives. Pedagogical documentation can be understood as a complex and open-ended event that supports educators in continuously reconsidering their assumptions, beliefs and practices towards children in a specific time and place (Olsson, 2009). By visualising children's learning through photos, videos and written field notes, art museum learning staff can then critically reflect on and think deeply about different pedagogical events. Pedagogical documentation can then act as a process that produces early childhood practices, rather than an activity that seeks to simply display the products of learning (Pacini-Ketchabaw et al., 2014).

Reflection on children's learning can also support deep thinking on the power structures and dominant discourses that function as "regimes of truth" in children's education (MacNaughton, 2005). Pedagogical documentation's use in art museums can support the development of early childhood practices that shift from a singular, universal paradigm of "best practice" towards the construction of educational experiences that value uncertainty, contextuality and subjectivity in learning. Connections between children's creative improvisation and adult's response to these learning events can also be made. While this practice has been explored in early childhood settings, its use in art museums in still relatively new.

To investigate pedagogical documentation as a mode of reflective practice in the Atelier, the research project was carried out over a 13-week timeframe and included the development of nine Atelier sessions. During this time, two artists, one Early Years coordinator and the researcher investigated how pedagogical documentation could be used to critically reflect on children's learning events as well as the assumptions that shaped the Atelier's practice. Photographs, videos, artist interviews and meeting transcripts were generated before, during and after each Atelier session to generate results and explore the research focus. The following section gives a descriptive account of how pedagogical documentation was used to reflect on one boy's play event in a paint Atelier session.

Case study: Oliver and "the brother trap"

The "paint" Atelier was presented as a drop-in activity for babies, toddlers and their families. The artist facilitating the session created a large 3-D cardboard "canvas" that children could use to play with paint, as illustrated in Figure 22.2. Additional tools such as rollers, paint brushes and stamps were also laid out in the space as resources that children could use to creatively explore the materials in different ways. The following descriptive account explores one boy's interactions with the paint, cardboard, masking tape and other people in the space.

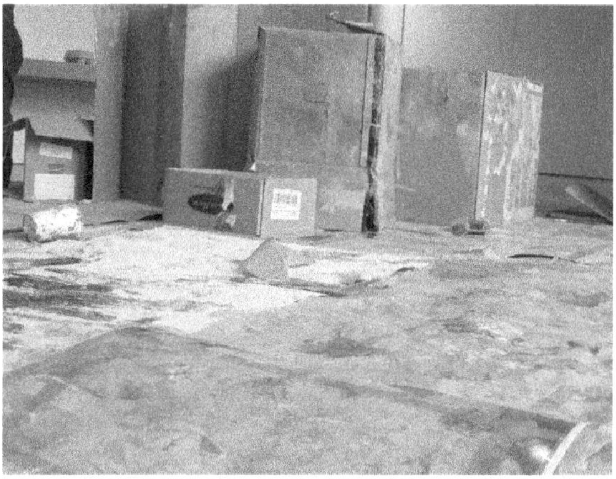

FIGURE 22.2 An image taken of the paint Atelier while it was in session.
Credit: Louisa Penfold.

Oliver (not the child's real name), aged 3.5 years, enters the paint Atelier with his younger brother and mother. On arrival, he discovers a large cardboard box that another family has just finished playing with. The box already has many blue paint marks on it and has lost much of its original form.

Oliver asks his younger brother James (not the child's real name), 18 months, to play with him inside the box. James is disinterested and continues to paint the window with a roller. Oliver begins to make paint marks on the box with a small paint brush. The soggy box falls over. Oliver holds it upright with one hand while continuing to paint with the roller using the other. Oliver then spots an egg carton on the other side of the room. He runs over, collects it and brings it back to his cardboard box. He tries to stick the egg carton to the box using a roll of masking tape. The egg carton does not stick to the wet cardboard as it has become soggy due to the large amount of paint on it.

The artist watches from afar then approaches Oliver to ask if he needs a hand with anything. He replies, "I can't get the door lock to stay on, the sticky tape is not stick enough." She asks him what might be making the cardboard so slippery that the masking tape won't stick onto it. He replies, " ... maybe the slippy paint. I could put some more tape on and stick it where the paint isn't there." Oliver tries sticking the egg carton on again. It sticks. He then paints it with the paint brush (Figure 22.3).

Oliver has now been painting the box for 30 minutes. His mother comments, "he has quite a long attention span. He often finds a project and spends hours working on it. I think it is unusual for his age." She asks Oliver what he is making. He replies, "a trap to catch James, it is a brother trap." After a few more minutes, Oliver picks up the cardboard box and places it on top of his baby brother. James giggles then starts to cry when he

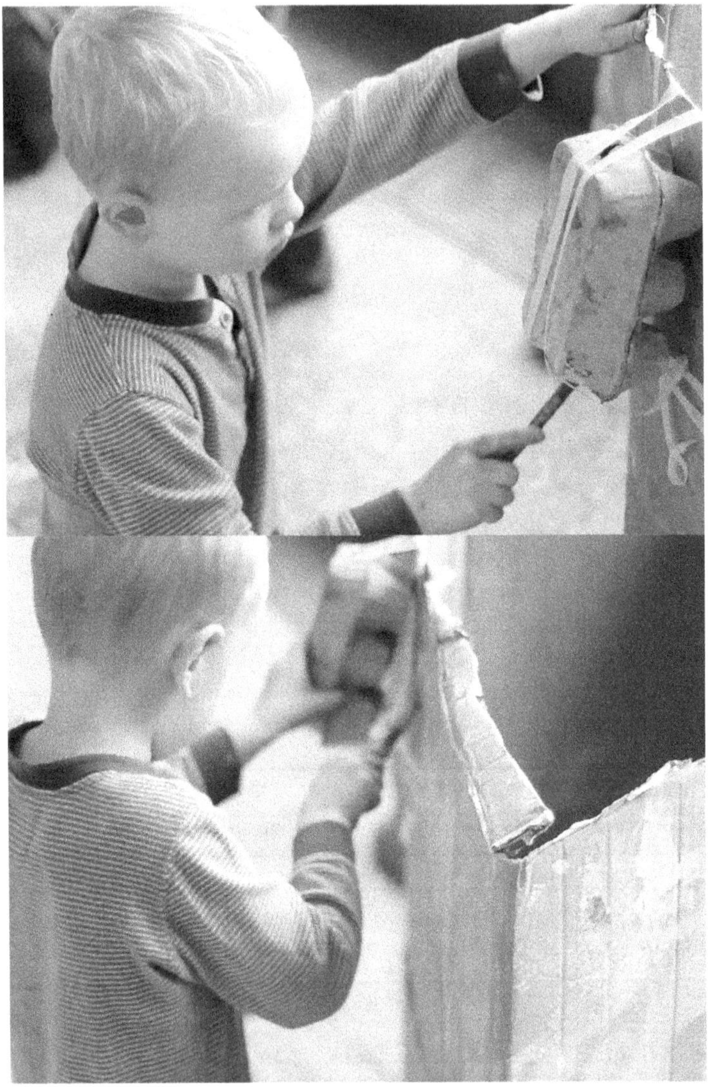

FIGURE 22.3 Oliver's play in the Atelier.
Credit: Louisa Penfold.

realises he cannot get out. Their mother sees what has happened, picks up James and the three leave the Atelier to get some lunch.

The documentation of Oliver's encounter served as a rich starting point for reflecting on play in the Atelier. The event was reflected upon first by the researcher and then shared amongst the Atelier team and visiting parents to discuss and debate what was happening in Oliver's play. The group's reflections included the following: Oliver takes his time to explore the application of the paint to the cardboard box. The physical properties of the materials, including how the paint is absorbed into the cardboard, influence what Oliver can and cannot do in his experimentation. The distorted shape of the cardboard box also seems to invite a unique interaction with Oliver, for example as he applies more paint to the cardboard, the surface becomes soggy and difficult for the masking tape to stick to. These non-human components of the Atelier provide opportunity for interaction for the children and families inside the space, creating complex moments for learning (Figure 22.4). Oliver practises fine motor skills by holding a tool in his hand and by balancing his weight against the box so that it stands up. In this encounter, he explores the material qualities of different resources in the Atelier including paint, cardboard, masking tape and the artist's technical knowledge of how to use these. Through this encounter we see him respond to these material qualities by engaging with concepts such as coverage, balance, consistency, surface tension and measurement.

Oliver combines the materials, tools and techniques in divergent ways through the experimentation. As he does so, different ideas emerge through interactions between himself, the box, the paint and the other people around him: all moving him towards the goal of creating "the brother trap." At the same time, Oliver's play in the Atelier raises questions around the role of artworks in his learning. Does it matter that he isn't viewing the artworks from the collection as he plays with the paint? And what does it mean for a child to engage in a gallery activity? These questions were then used to fuel future lines of enquiry in subsequent Atelier activities, supporting the development of experimentation and improvisation in the learning team's practice.

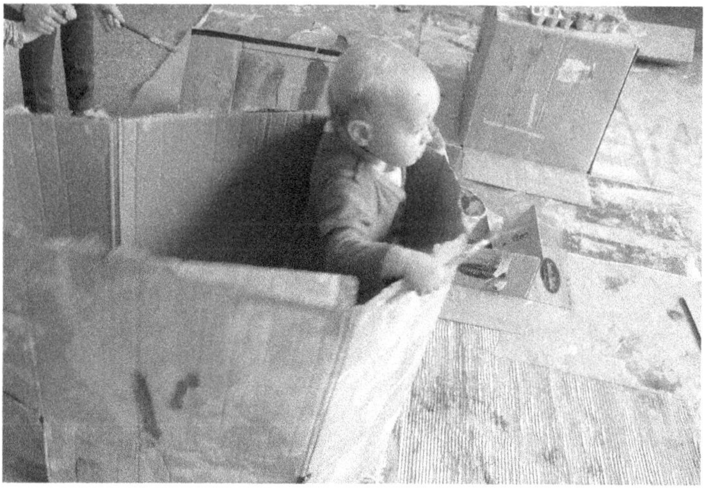

FIGURE 22.4 Oliver's "brother trap" in the paint Atelier.
Credit: Louisa Penfold.

Final thoughts and implications for practice

While reflective practice in art museums can be developed in many ways, pedagogical documentation allows for attention to be drawn to ways that children's learning unfolds during encounters and complex patterns of behaviour in the gallery spaces. The reflection and discussion of Oliver's play that was generated in the Atelier encouraged the team to consider how learning events took place through encounters with paint, cardboard, art tools, peers, adults and the museum space. Oliver's creative improvisation with the Atelier's diverse components allowed him to make dynamic connections between himself, works of art, materials, concepts, other people. This critical reflection on his learning processes then allowed the Atelier team's thinking to become more complex and for that complexity to be made visible and open to interpretation from others.

Outcomes of the research suggest that pedagogical documentation can support a gallery team in exploring the contextuality, contradictions, politics and ethics that shape children's learning and art museum practices in a unique social, cultural, historical and political context. Pedagogical documentation can act as a reflective process that encourages dialogue and debate surrounding children's learning and art museum practices, developing what Murris (2016) articulates as a "community of philosophical enquirers."

References

Greene, M. (2000). *Releasing the Imagination: Essays on Education, The Arts, and Social Change*. San Francisco: Jossey-Bass.

Hughes, B. (2013). *Evolutionary Playwork*, 2nd ed. Abingdon: Routledge.

MacNaughton, G. (2005). *Doing Foucault in Early Childhood Studies: Applying Poststructural Ideas*. Abingdon: Routledge.

Murris, K. (2016). *The Posthuman Child: Educational Transformation Through Philosophy with Picturebooks*. Abingdon: Routledge.

Olsson, L.M. (2009). *Movement and Experimentation in Young Children's Learning: Deleuze and a Virtual Child*. Abingdon: Routledge.

Pacini-Ketchabaw, V., Nxumalo, F., Kocher, L., Elliot, E., & Sanchez, A. (2014). *Journeys: Reconceptualizing Early Childhood Practices through Pedagogical Narration*. Toronto: Toronto University Press.

Rinaldi, C. (2001). *Making Learning Visible: Children as Individual and Group Learners*. Reggio Emilia. Cambridge, MA: Reggio Children & Harvard Project Zero.

Schaefer, C.E., & Drewes, A.A. (2014). *The Therapeutic Powers of Play: 20 Core Agents of Change*, 2nd ed. Hoboken: John Wiley & Sons.

23

ON WHAT GROUNDS

Alex Thorp

This chapter reflects on the project *On What Grounds*, a collaboration between The Portman Early Childhood Centre, designer Bahbak Hashemi-Nezhad and Serpentine Education.

In the outdoor play space of the Portman Early Childhood Centre in North West London thick black iron railings separate the nursery from the surrounding streets. Inside the centre is a small outdoor play area with a sandpit, wooden slide, climbing frame and a bank of dirt for mud play. Beyond the railings is the Church Street neighbourhood, made up of high density social housing with little outdoor space. *On What Grounds* asks what if it were possible to move beyond nursery gates and the limits of formal playgrounds to open up local neighbourhoods as spaces for play.

Through the *Changing Play* programme, Serpentine Education commissions artists to collaborate with children, parents and staff at the Portman, a state-maintained nursery school for 2 to 4 year olds, and develop projects that respond to local issues. It is part of a series of programmes at the Serpentine that takes seriously children and young people's perspectives on the places and spaces they live in.

In late 2016 I approached designer Bahbak Hashemi-Nezhad to discuss a potential project. I was familiar with his practice of developing projects with people that explore issues related to public space, regeneration and play. I also knew that he was knowledgeable about the area, having worked in the neighbourhood for over ten years. Our initial and subsequent conversations touched on ideas of the city as a playground (Ward, 1979), loose parts theory (Nicholson, 1971), adventure playgrounds, wayfaring (Hackett, 2015) and listening to young children (Rinaldi, 2006). Bahbak was invited to spend time at the nursery, to observe and talk to children, parents and staff before developing a proposal. *Changing Play* is framed as a collaborative research process that evolves over 12 weekly sessions, with the opportunity to produce a toolkit to share the project more widely.

Over several months and in conversation with staff at the Portman the project coalesced around a number of questions: what are the physical and imaginative qualities of a play space? How do we create the conditions for play? Where are the spaces for children in the city? How might we reclaim pockets of the city for free play and imagination? We wanted to look at what children actually do when they play, to deepen our understanding of play and think about how we can support these play experiences in the here and now.

Following visits to alternative sites, Bahbak settled on Parson's House – a 21-storey tower block surrounded by wide open spaces, hidden corners, vantage points, contrasting scales and surfaces. The proximity of the site to the Portman Centre combined with the diversity of the spaces and architectural elements within it suggested multiple play possibilities. Bahbak's intention was to observe the children in the space and to gradually and playfully introduce objects with no fixed function, with the hope that these would support children in their interactions with one another in the environment.

The nursery arranged for a group of six children aged 4 and 5 years old and two staff from the Portman to take part. The children had a choice about whether they wanted to take part or stay in nursery. We planned for the visits to take place at the same time each week, to ensure the same children could attend and so that the children could become familiar with the site. Two children with SEND, who did not use speech at the time, were invited to take part. Each session lasted between one and two hours, often ending when the children became tired or cold.

Session one: 2 March

Walking in pairs and threes we set off from the Portman, passing familiar places and people, stopping occasionally as a child points out their house or says hello to a neighbour. It is evident that the route to Parsons House is familiar to the children, who live close by.

As we approach the site the children let go of our hands and run towards the raised platform. We watch as some children scramble up the banks and run onto the expanse, returning briefly to help pull us up. This action serves to shift the power dynamic between children and adults. The children run around the tower to a large open concrete area, chasing one another, arms held wide, screaming, laughing, enjoying the vast open expanse and the feeling of the wind.

The children spend a significant amount of time exploring the boundaries of the space, testing the limits of where they are allowed to go. Frequently they dip out of view, down stairs and around corners as we run after them.

On the lower level is an empty underground car park. A few of the children are fascinated with this dark and cavernous area and the gate which marks the entrance to it. Initially they try to figure out how to open it and, finding it firmly fixed, they try to explore the space from the outside, first by throwing their voices inside, then by sending stones through the bars. Some children begin to ask questions about who lives there, what they do and how it might be possible to enter and exit.

The children move towards a refuse area featuring large bins overflowing with household rubbish, which gives off a pungent smell. The dark area attracts the children and when they draw nearer they are repelled by the smell, but take enjoyment in daring each other to approach this olfactory boundary.

A group of children return to the raised platform, using their whole bodies to slide down the sloping banks, clearly enjoying the physical challenge and repetition of this movement (see Figure 23.1).

Session two: 9 March

We are met by the children at the Portman excitedly asking if we are going to Parson's House. As we walk together to the site we talk about what we might find. When we arrive, it's evident that it has rained heavily overnight as the site is covered in large puddles. The children run to the large open space and into the water, jumping, splashing and finally lying on their backs in puddles stretching out their arms and moving them overhead.

After 20 minutes, Bahbak unfolds a large square of transparent plastic sheeting. He has chosen this object in response to the children's movement in the wind the week before. We watch how the children hold the sheet above their heads,

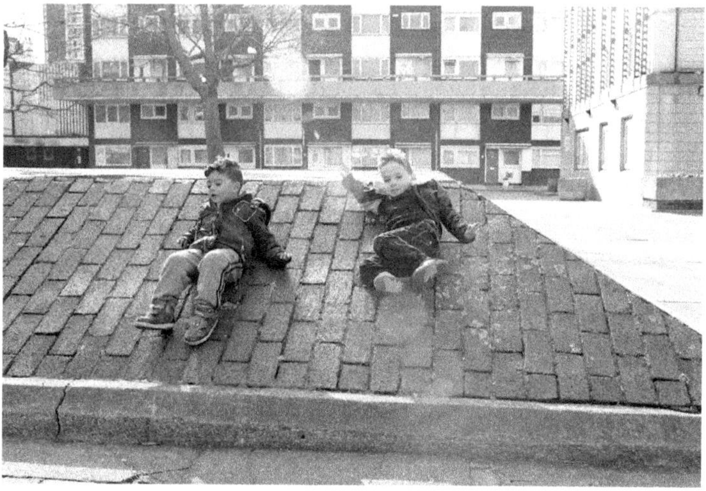

FIGURE 23.1 The children use their bodies to slide down the slope, an action they repeat in the following sessions. Bahbak Hashemi-Nezhad, *On What Grounds*, Serpentine Galleries 2017. Photograph: Bahbak Hashemi-Nezhad.

looking up at the sky through the material. Finally they bring the material onto the ground and into the puddles, where it becomes another surface to be stamped over and splashed on.

A small group of children cluster around a spherical drain on the edges of the open space. M has found a stick and is using it to make circular motions above the grate and is explaining to the other children that she is a witch and is making a spell.

Bahbak introduces some coloured rolls of tape, which the children use on the sloped banks of the platform, taking it in turns to alternate between sliding with their bodies and rolling the tape. Z and N use a thin red washing line to wrap, weave and tangle the concrete bollards separating the pavement from the road. In the process a traffic warden becomes caught up in the string and for a moment he becomes one of the children's play materials.

Session eight: 11 May

Bahbak and I place the materials in the space before the children arrive, to see if it will provoke different play possibilities. We tie ten coloured ropes in and around two mature trees, lay out wooden planks and long cardboard tubes. Within the first few minutes the careful set up has been dismantled by the children.

M and K use the ropes to dangle down or "fish" from an upper vantage point, carefully lowering the line to the car park below and pulling it back when they have a catch.

Bahbak introduces a 50 m-long piece of blue debris mesh. M and A unravel the net, rolling it along the large concrete open space and running the length of the fabric (Figure 23.2). After ten minutes they climb into it, covering one another and wrapping themselves in the web. Finally they lose interest and move away. Bahbak watches and walks over to tie the mesh to two lamp posts, creating a hanging pathway. The children run into the fabric, enjoying the feeling of resistance against their bodies. The intervention makes it possible to sit in the mesh like a hammock and the children invite us to swing them back and forth.

Z holds my hand and leads me to the perimeter of the open space, to a rough uneven surface. She walks along it, enjoying the sense of unsteadiness this brings, as I walk beside her. As she negotiates the irregular walkway she smiles and begins to grow confident, quickening her step.

For the children the repeated visits gave the project a ritual quality. When we arrived at the Centre each week the children excitedly gathered round us and the speaking children would ask if we were going on "the trip." Recurrent visits also enabled children to explore their own interests: A's fascination with the solar system; D's love of trees and flowers; M's interest in witches and sorcery; Z's growing confidence with physical challenges. Our growing familiarity with the children meant we were better able to support them as individuals in their differences over the course of the sessions. Visiting with the same group

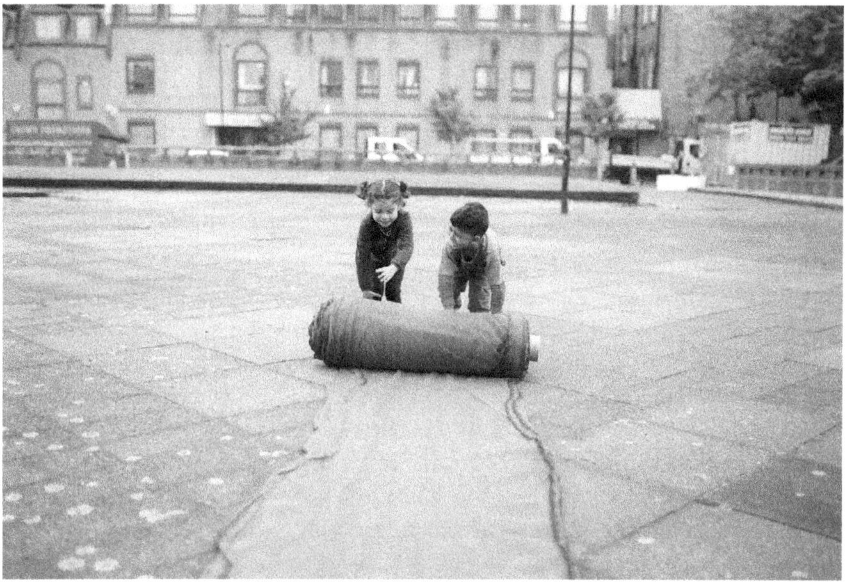

FIGURE 23.2 The children encounter the blue mesh for the first time. Bahbak Hashemi-Nezhad, *On What Grounds*, Serpentine Galleries 2017. Photograph: Bahbak Hashemi-Nezhad.

also allowed space for friendships between the children to develop and deepen, and for them to disagree and resolve conflicts independently.

The spatial arrangement of the site was significant too. Each of the three areas that make up Parson's House has a distinct atmosphere, which the children responded to in different ways. The open concrete space seemed to invite physical exploration; the platform space populated with trees and bushes opened up encounters with nature; the gated car park, variously described as the secret space, the scary space and the cave, generated neverending "multi-modal" narrative possibilities (Kress, 2009). The children were also routinely drawn to liminal spaces. These areas represented the edges of danger or were out of the direct gaze of adults, where they could congregate independently. Although each space had particular characteristics, the children moved freely between them, constantly in motion. Often there were small clusters of children gathered at different areas of the site, with the artist and curators running after them, playfully responding to the children's movements and gestures.

Through the project the site became familiar to the children, but was never static; the interaction between children, adults, objects and space was in constant flux. We found traces of people on the site each week and these unexpected encounters often shaped the session. A supermarket trolley was repurposed to become a vehicle to move and spin around. The crack in the pavement caused by construction work signalled the presence of a monster or meteorite. A dead pigeon opened up a conversation about injury and death that continued long after we returned to the Portman. We also met people; construction workers, parking attendants and residents of Parsons House who became momentarily absorbed into the play. The weather played a major role in determining what would happen; the wind, rain or sunshine dramatically influencing the course of the session. Bahbak's sensitivity in responding to these unexpected elements opened up rather than closed down possibilities (see Figure 23.3).

Over the course of ten sessions it became clear that some objects had more play potential than others. The most popular materials were those that provided opportunities to use the whole body, could be shared with others, were portable and offered different ways of exploring the architectural features. Thick rope was used to wrap around trees or abseil up the bank, longer rope was used to fish from the platform and shorter lengths became Rapunzel's hair. Wooden planks supported the children to take physical risks (see Figure 23.4). We observed how the children worked together to hold down the ends of the board as each person carefully took turns to cross. By contrast, the plastic bread baskets had low play potential in this context. They were rigid and the children found them difficult to move. The children readily moved between scales, one moment running the length of the 50 m blue debris mesh, the next stopping to collect tiny jewels found on the floor to admire and share with friends.

The walk to and from the nursery was a meaningful part of the encounter. Bahbak devised various methods of involving the children in collectively moving the parts to the site. The wooden planks were large enough that four children had

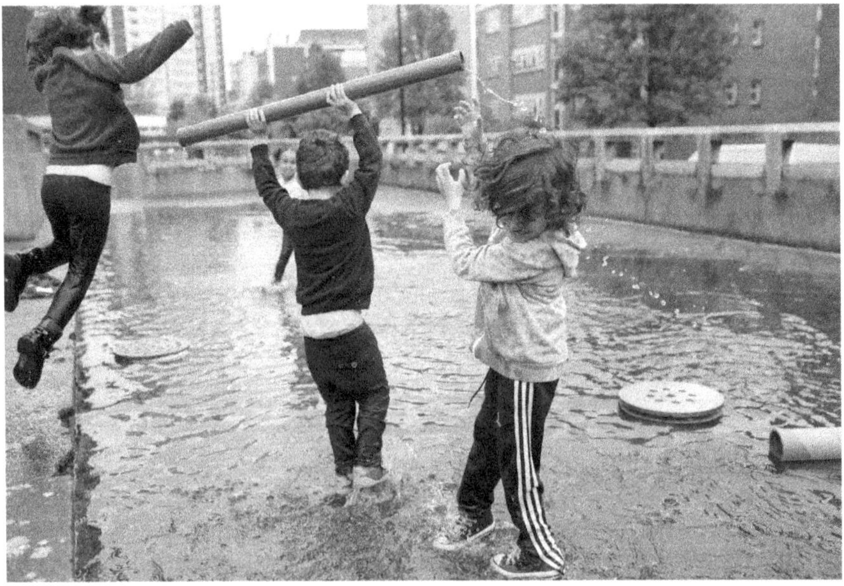

FIGURE 23.3 A rainwater puddle that appears overnight becomes the focus of the session. Bahbak Hashemi-Nezhad, *On What Grounds*, Serpentine Galleries 2017. Photograph: Bahbak Hashemi-Nezhad.

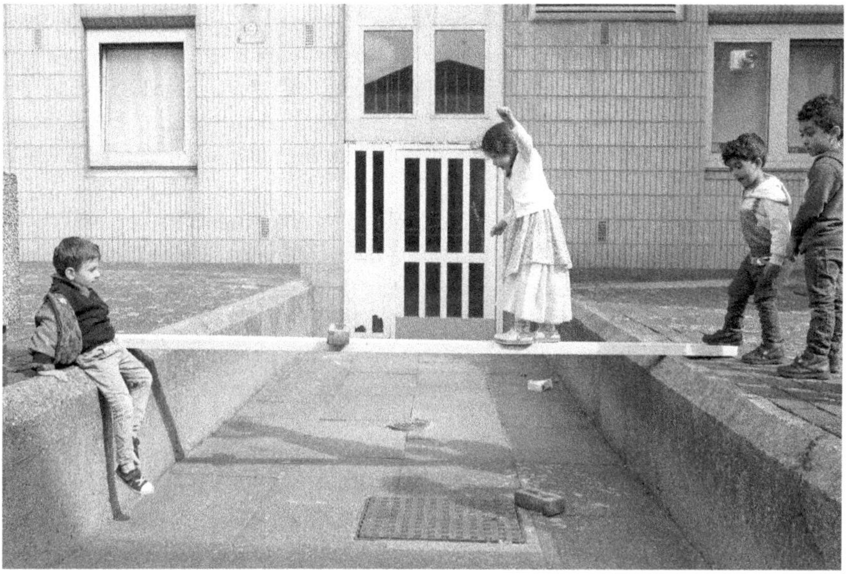

FIGURE 23.4 The wooden planks support the children to take risks in the space. Bahbak Hashemi-Nezhad, *On What Grounds*, Serpentine Galleries 2017. Photograph: Bahbak Hashemi-Nezhad.

to work together to carry them, with support from adults. This labour of actively transporting the objects as a group gave the children ownership over the project. The walk was also a time for the children to make connections to their daily lives and introduce us to people or places important to them. Both children and adults made associations between objects introduced on the site and those found in the neighbourhood. At one point N casually pointed to the blue debris mesh that was being used on building works on the street, calling it the "blue smoke." Bahbak responded by introducing this material in the following session.

Working with unpredictability means working with questions rather than predetermined outcomes. At times we were required to creatively activate or introduce new objects, allow ourselves to become play material or intervene when we felt there was a risk. In this kind of improvised project, reflection processes are essential. After each session the designer, curators and researcher would spend an hour talking about what had taken place and planning for the following session. Bahbak would then source, make or adapt objects, playfully responding to what had emerged the previous week.

Final thoughts and implications for practice

Listening to young children is complex. Our aim was to be in solidarity with their ways of being and thinking about the world and to be sensitive to all of their languages in the most expanded sense (Edwards et al., 1998), including their movements, gestures and interactions with one another. Yet each adult on the project could only provide a partial reading of what had taken place: the constant motion meant we glimpsed only fragments of the action, we each had different relationships with the children and varying degrees of familiarity with Early Years pedagogy.

Photographs of the session were a critical tool in creating more complex, multiple interpretations of play (Clark, 2001). Bahbak documented each session by taking sequences of images and we fell into a weekly rhythm for passing the photographs to the centre. These images were used as the basis for reflective conversations between designer, Early Years workers, children, curators and parents.

Through the project we aimed to shift adults' perceptions about the built environment, to help them to look again and see play potential in everyday spaces. We worked towards this in three ways: by inviting parents to take part in the final session; developing a series of play kits and workshops for local Early Childhood Centres; and producing an animated film to share with a wider online audience – www.serpentinegalleries.org/learn/changing-play/what-grounds. Today we face rapidly dwindling public space, fears of perceived risks such as "stranger danger" and traffic and an increasing focus within education policy on rote learning. In this context it is more important than ever to continue the discussion about childhood, public space and the value of play.

References

Clark, A. (2001) *Listening to Young Children: The Mosaic Approach*. London: National Children's Bureau.

Edwards, C., Gandini, L., and Forman, G. (1998) *The Hundred Languages of Children: Reggio Emilia Approach Advanced Reflections*. Greenwich, CT: Ablex Publishing Corporation.

Hackett, A. (2015) Young children as wayfarers: learning about place by moving through it. *Children & Society* [online] [accessed on 30 November 2018]: http://eprints.whiterose.ac.uk/86870/1/young%20children%20as%20wayfarers.pdf.

Kress, G. (2009) *Multimodality: a Social Semiotic Approach to Contemporary Communication*. London: RoutledgeFalmer.

Nicholson, S. (1971) How NOT to cheat children, the theory of loose parts. *PLACE Landscape Architecture Journal*, *62*, 20–34.

Rinaldi, C. (2006) *In Dialogue with Reggio Emilia: Listening, Researching and Learning: Contextualising, Interpreting and Evaluating Early Childhood Education*, New York: Routledge.

Ward, C. (1979) *The Child In The City*. Harmondsworth: Penguin.

24

COMMENTARY ON PART III

The lived materialities of the museum – a new research agenda

Kate Pahl and Jennifer Rowsell

This Part describes the lived experience of the museum as seen through the eyes of museum educators who, in turn, are describing children's encounters with the museum. These are generous and enabling chapters. They bring to mind the idea of research as lived, through moments, entanglements and engagement with real-ness. In our joint book *Living Literacies* we wrote about the idea that sites and spaces can generate thinking about literacy (Pahl et al., 2019). There is an exciting open-ness in these chapters, to questions of emergence and what "could be." The idea of emergence and being "in the moment" with young people is one that has increasingly been important in literacy research. Ehret (2018) describes this as "thinking-feeling":

> Thinking-feeling moments as pedagogical orientation require being in the moment with youth, and imagining together what youth can do and who they are becoming.
>
> *(p. 56)*

Our work has celebrated this "withness" (Wargo, 2018) and continues to develop in conversation with children and young people in schools and communities. In this book, we propose a research agenda of "lived materialities" to honour the work described here. Museum work has always been strongly artifactual and the wonder of objects shines through this Part (Pahl and Rowsell, 2010). These chapters celebrate the mundane, the everyday, the "ordinary affects" of encounters in museums (Stewart, 2007). The idea of practice as "materially led" shines out from these studies.

When we think about Smith's discussion of familiar spaces and returning to the same space as if no time has passed, this opens up a continuous tread of songs, objects, movements and meaning. This offers an in-the-middleness that has no beginning and no end, but continues along. A withness or in-the-middleness recalls Deleuze and Guattari's (2004) theorising of a rhizome as a continuous stream of movement and transformations. Museum spaces presented in this Part share a similar brand of dynamism, freedom and liberation to them. All of the spaces manifest this degree of in-the-middleness that creativity and spontaneity preserve across time and place.

In our research, we have noticed that this closeness to the everyday realities of life produces accounts that take ideas from the field and transform them, thus producing new knowledge. One of the aspects that is particularly engaging about these chapters is the observational eyes of the museum practitioners. This becomes itself a new kind of research practice, one that provides a lived account of the materialities of the museum:

> The children run around the tower to a large open concrete area, chasing one another, arms held wide, screaming, laughing, enjoying the vast open expanse and the feeling of the wind.
>
> *(Thorp)*

Research as a form of attentiveness, a lived practice, is present in these accounts. Children "screaming" becomes something else, something that tells us about the world.

> Oliver tries sticking the egg carton on again. It sticks. He then paints it with the paint brush.
>
> *(Penfold and Turner)*

The "stickiness" of things becomes a property that can inform our own perspectives and understandings of matter. Emotions are "sticky" and stuff can leak across and between bodies and spaces (Ahmed, 2014). Implicit to this stickiness are the entanglements of bodies, things, and affective and sensorial engagements that provide the kind of richness McCall features in her case study of a *Baby Play and Stay* programme at Manchester Art Gallery. Valuing this process is part of the noticing of the ways in which learning happens, as an unfolding:

> the children moved through the museum space under the influence of their prior concern with finding the whale.
>
> *(Carter)*

Research that is attuned to the unexpected and listens to how children perceive the world has the potential to unsettle the determinisms of developmentalism and instead produces accounts of children that follow what they do and where they go.

> they are both very social sessions, many people are drawn to experiencing with others rather than alone, perhaps particularly when trying something new (having a baby/visiting a gallery!!), the "side effect" of this is that the space itself becomes familiar, friendly, used.
>
> *(McCall)*

Here, the line between the two spaces (having a baby/visiting a gallery) becomes blurred as both are part of a complex web of experiences. Experiences that involve a blending and blurring of time, histories, objects, people and spaces that play a role in creating cultures. Children, young people and adults are simply doing stuff and being in the middle of things – unaware of any learning or thinking that unfolds. The world is experienced through the eyes of the children, the spaces, the parents and the museum educators and this entangled vision brings the gallery work to life. Our joint work in *Living Literacies* celebrates the "stickiness" of literacy, the generative power of sites and spaces and the importance of sociality in literacy research. Such attuned research methods have, in these chapters, enabled fine-grained observations of the materialities of museums and the lived entanglements of children, parents and educators in those spaces.

References

Ahmed, S. (2014) *The Cultural Politics of Emotion*. 2nd ed. New York, NY: Routledge.

Deleuze, G. and Guttari, F. (2004) *A Thousand Plateaus: Capitalism and Schizophrenia*. London: Continuum.

Ehret, C. (2018). Moments of teaching and learning in a children's hospital: affects, textures, and temporalities. *Anthropology & Education Quarterly*, *49*(1), 53–71.

Pahl, K., & Rowsell, J. (2010) *Artifactual Literacies: Every Object Tells a Story*. New York: Teachers College Press.

Pahl, K. and Rowsell, J. with D. Collier, S. Pool, Z. Rasool and T. Trzecak (2019) *Living-Literacies*. Cambridge, MA: MIT Press.

Stewart, K. (2007) *Ordinary Affects*. Durham: Duke University Press.

Wargo, J.M. (2018). Writing with wearables? Young children's intra-active authoring and the sounds of emplaced invention. *Journal of Literacy Research*, *50*(4), 502–523.

INDEX

Lightning Source UK Ltd.
Milton Keynes UK
UKHW021809290822
407867UK00016B/154

9 781138 353008